Animals' Rights—a

Animals' Rights
- a Symposium

EDITED BY

DAVID PATERSON
RICHARD D. RYDER

CENTAUR PRESS LTD.
1979

First Published 1979 by
Centaur Press Ltd, Fontwell, Sussex
and 11–14 Stanhope Mews West, London SW7
ISBN 0 90000090 2

not found

A record of the proceedings of the Symposium held under the auspices of the R.S.P.C.A. at Trinity College, Cambridge, on The Ethical Aspects of Man's Relationships with Animals, 18th and 19th August, 1977.

Printed in Great Britain by Bristol Typesetting Co. Ltd., Barton Manor, St. Philips, Bristol

Contents

THE THREE MAJOR AREAS OF CONCERN

I FARMING:

II WILDLIFE

III EXPERIMENTATION

THE RIGHTS OF ANIMALS

A Declaration Against Speciesism

Inasmuch as we believe that there is ample evidence that many other species are capable of feeling, we condemn totally the infliction of suffering upon our brother animals, and the curtailment of their enjoyment, unless it be necessary for their own individual benefit.

We do not accept that a difference in species alone (any more than a difference in race) can justify wanton exploitation or oppression in the name of science or sport, or for food, commercial profit or other human gain.

We believe in the evolutionary and moral kinship of all animals and we declare our belief that all sentient creatures have rights to life, liberty and the quest for happiness.

We call for the protection of these rights.

This declaration was signed by some one hundred and fifty people at the time of the symposium at Trinity College, Cambridge on August 19th, 1977. The signatories included the following:

Richard Adams, John Alexander-Sinclair, Rev. Jack Austin, Mary Rose Barrington, Brigid Brophy, Bill Brown, R. MacAlastair Brown, John Bryant, Susan Bryant, Dr. Stephen R. L. Clark, Rev. Kevin Daley, Carol Dear, Anne Douglass, Clare Druce, Maureen Duffy, Robert Elliot, Dr. Michael Fox, Ann Cottrell Free, Prof. R. G. Frey, André Gallois, Clifford Goodman, Judith Hampson, Clive Hollands, Susan Hough, Lord Houghton, Robin Howard, Helen Jones, Ronnie Lee, Rev. Andrew Linzey, Jack Lucas, Ian MacPhail, John Melville, Mary Midgley, Chris Murphy, David Paterson, Kerstin Petersson, John Pitt, Ruth Plant, Prof. Tom Regan, Jan Rennison, Richard D. Ryder (Chairman, R.S.P.C.A. Council), Mike Seymour-Rouse, Prof. Peter Singer, Violet Spalding, Dr. Timothy Sprigge, Margery Sutcliffe, M. E. Tait, Angela Walder, Robert Waldie, Phyllis Walker, Barbara Walton, Caroline Wetton, Dave Wetton, Alan Whittaker, Rev. B. Wrighton, Jon Wynne-Tyson, Robert Young.

Foreword

Problems of morality appertaining to man himself have, until comparatively recently, appeared to be so great and so overwhelming in themselves as to exclude the spending of time or thought on extending such considerations to animals. Now, however, a fuller and more logical development of the unity of nature has brought us to a gradual realisation that there are in fact no rational grounds for an absolute division between human beings and other animals. The claim for " animal rights " rests upon the thesis that if the use of such a concept as " rights " is appropriate and possible for humans then it is also appropriate and possible for the rest of sentient creation.

Inspired by this proposition and indeed by the basic need to formulate first principles as a basis for further action, the R.S.P.C.A. acted as host to a mixed group of theologians, philosophers, scientists, lawyers, politicians and ordinary thinking people, at Trinity College, Cambridge, during the summer of 1977. For two days nearly two hundred of us participated in a very active and inspiring Symposium, the main papers for which appear, by popular request and for further reference, in this volume.

Several short papers given by " Discussants " at various stages throughout the proceedings are included with the main text, under the relevant headings, and the sixteen main contributions are given in full. Despite this, no one Symposium could reasonably set out to give the entire philosophical basis for animal welfare together with details of all its problems and areas of concern, so the reader has also been referred elsewhere (see especially Appendix 3 for particular issues).

A full statement of animals' rights must include a consideration of their:

(i) right to life,

(ii) right to be protected from suffering,

(iii) right to live free from interference (save possibly for the benefit of the individual),

(iv) right to live in accordance with their "natural requirements",

as well as considering various areas of concern which involve or seem to impinge upon such rights. For further extensions of thought on these matters, the reader is also referred to other works (Appendix 4).

Lastly, the Animal Welfare Movement, like any other, must not only establish its own first principles and select its own goals; it must also determine their manner of achievement.

The statement and justification of these objectives is the achieved goal of the Symposium.

David Paterson
Richard D. Ryder

Acknowledgments

The Editors would like to thank the Rev. Andrew Linzey for the important part he played in organising the Symposium, and they are also indebted to Mr. John Bryant, Mr. Julian Hopkins, Mr. David Luetchford and Mr. Jon Wynne-Tyson for their invaluable assistance in preparing its publication.

Preface

When I first became aware of the issue of animal rights, I thought the ethical case for a radical change in our attitude to non-human animals was overwhelming, but the idea of rights for animals was too far ahead of its time. That was in 1970. Now there are signs that the idea is catching hold more rapidly than I thought possible. One very significant indication of this change was the Symposium held at Trinity College, Cambridge in 1977 and now published in the book you have in your hands.

A few years ago scarcely anyone took seriously the idea that animals might have rights, or that it could be wrong for us to use them for purposes like eating their flesh, testing hair shampoos on their eyes, wearing their skins, or hunting for sport. The major animal welfare organisations, led by the R.S.P.C.A., appealed to our kindly instincts, never to our sense of justice or respect for rights. Beneath the surface, however, changes were under way. They emerged into the public spotlight when Richard Ryder, one of the initiators and organisers of the Rights of Animals Symposium, became Chairman on the R.S.P.C.A. Council. From that time on, rights for animals was no longer an idea confined to a few philosophers, vegetarians and other "cranks". It became a slogan for the vanguard of the animal welfare movement, and may well be on the verge of becoming an influential political force with widespread support among the voting public.

This book represents several different currents in the thought of those who support the general idea of rights for animals. The papers printed here tackle the issue at many different levels.

Among those taking part in the Symposium were university teachers of philosophy, and their contributions express the heated debate over the moral status of animals which is now taking place in philosophical circles and in academic philosophy journals. Other papers deal with more down-to-earth issues, discussing the abuses animals are subjected to, and the tactics we should adopt to stop these abuses.

Do not expect to find unanimity. The different perspectives in these papers testify to the coming together of diverse groups and individuals from many countries and different professions, all concerned with rights for animals. We cannot predict the future, but it is not impossible that when, a century hence, people ask where the newly victorious animal rights movement got started, historians will point to the meeting held at Trinity College in 1977. If, like me, you were unable to be there, all you can do is kick yourself and be thankful that, with the publication of this volume, you can share in the ideas then presented.

Peter Singer
December, 1978

Section One

HISTORICAL AND SOCIAL PERSPECTIVES

The Struggle Against Speciesism

RICHARD D. RYDER

" The day may come when the rest of the animal creation may acquire those *rights* which never could have been withheld from them but by the hand of tyranny . . . the question is not can they *reason*? Nor, can they *talk*? But, can they *suffer*?"[1]

So wrote JEREMY BENTHAM in 1780.

The philosopher had a cat called Mr. Blackman who eventually came to be called the Reverend Dr. Blackman owing to his thoughtfulness and general solemnity.[2]

It would seem that a case could be made for asserting that respecters of cats have made better champions for the rights of animals than have lovers of the more subservient dog!

Dr. Johnson, who fulminated against vivisectors, personally bought oysters for his cat Hodge,[3] and MICHEL DE MONTAIGNE tells us how he enjoyed playing with his cat:

" We entertain one another with mutuall apish trickes. If I have my houre to begin or to refuse, so hath she hers ".[4]

Montaigne published his *Essays* in 1580 and, with some justification, is regarded as the father of the modern movement towards a more compassionate view of the other species.

However, I feel SIR THOMAS MORE's *Utopia*, published in 1516, deserves more careful reading in this respect. He writes of his Utopians:

" They kill no living beast in sacrifice, nor they thinke not that the merciful clemencye of god had delite in bloude and slaughter, which hath geven liffe to beastes to the intent they should live."[5]

They also despise the "foolyshe pleasures" of hunting and hawking:

> "thou shouldest rather be moved with pitie to see a selye innocent hare murdered of a dogge: the weake of the stronger, the fearefull of the fearce, the innocent of the cruell and unmercyfull."[6]

Both More and Montaigne were, no doubt, influenced by PLUTARCH and PYTHAGORAS—the two great zoophiles[7] of classical antiquity. But I feel one should not overstress the effect of example. Original thought is particularly likely in this field, where philosophy can spring from the spontaneous experience of sympathy for the sufferings of other creatures, and it would be quite misleading to assume that a writer's humanity necessarily depended upon that of his predecessors.

I remember well in my own case that the step from sympathy to philosophy was a personal one. When I promulgated the awkward word *speciesism*[8] to describe mankind's arrogant prejudice against other species, I was not conscious that anyone else had published on the subject of animals' rights at all—indeed, at that time I felt very much alone.

I do not, unfortunately, have space to deal with the history of the idea of Animals' Rights in detail. I intend to concentrate mainly upon the very significant growth of interest in the moral status of animals which is found in England in the eighteenth century.

Before I do so, let me sketch a few points: in the Middle Ages, under the predominant influence of AQUINAS and not ST. FRANCIS, man's dominion is considered as practically absolute.

Although LEONARDO became vegetarian on moral grounds,[9] the Renaissance saw no general improvement for the brute creation. In the sixteenth century there is More and later, PHILIP STUBBES[10] who attacks hunting and bear-baiting as abuses of God's Creation:

> "If any should abuse but the dog of another man, wold not he who owneth the dog think the abuse thereof resulteth to himselfe? And shall we abuse the creatures of God, yea, take pleasure in abusing them, and yet think the contumely don to them redoundeth not to him who made them?"

In the following century there continue to be scattered writings. I would commend to the historian of the subject, FRANCIS QUARLES,[11] a fashionable writer of his day, expostulating in 1641 :

> " The birds of the aire die to sustain thee; the beasts of the field die to nourish thee; the fishes of the sea die to feed thee. Our stomacks are their common sepulcher. Good God! with how many deaths are our poor lives patcht up! How full of death is the life of momentary man!"

Far more important is CHIEF JUSTICE HALE,[12] about 1662, who is the first I know to use the word " justice " in this context. He writes: " I have ever thought that there was a certain degree of justice due from man to the creatures, as from man to man."

Towards the end of the century there is the remarkable Gloucestershire shepherd THOMAS TRYON[13] whose birds and fowls of heaven complain :

> " But tell us, O Man! we pray you tell us what injuries have we commited to forfeit? What Law have we broken, or what Cause given you, whereby you can pretend a Right to invade and violate our part, and natural Rights, and to assault and destroy us, as if we were the Agressors, and no better than Thieves, Robbers and Murtherers, fit to be extirpated out of the Creation?"

This must be one of the first mentions of the rights of animals.

Long before Martin's Act of 1822, the Puritans under Cromwell had temporarily banned bear-baiting and cock-fighting, although their motives are unclear.[14] But a little earlier still, in 1641, their Puritan cousins in New England had legislated against cruelty,[15] and NATHANIEL WARD'S Liberty 92 reads: " No man shall exercise any Tiranny or Crueltie towards any bruite Creature which are usuallie kept for man's use ". But even earlier—and here I am indebted to that distinguished historian Sir George Clark for putting me on the track of this much forgotten piece of legislation—Thomas Wentworth, as part of his " civilising " and " anglicising " reforms in

Ireland, passed a law in 1635 prohibiting the pulling of wool off sheep and the attaching of ploughs to horses' tails; one of the two reasons for this law being given as "the cruelty used to the beasts",[16] which is probably the earliest legal reference to this concept in the English language.

It is, as I have already said, in the following century that the movement rapidy accelerates. LECKY[17] considers that this advance was limited to the Protestant countries and I shall concentrate upon the British manifestations of this movement.

For convenience, one can divide the writers into the religious and secular. For the former group, in order to advance the cause of animals, it seemed to them desirable to discover scriptural support or to prove that animals have immortal souls—a view advanced by many minor theologians and some major ones. JOHN MILTON, ROBERT FLUDD, and the leveller RICHARD OVERTON[18] had been of this opinion; so also were JOSEPH BUTLER[19] in 1736, JOHN HILDROP[20] in 1742 and RICHARD DEAN[21] in 1767.

I have found some of these writers surprisingly readable. They had to oppose the pernicious doctrine of RENÉ DESCARTES[22] (1596–1650), and such followers as MALEBRANCHE, that animals do not have consciousness. How Descartes logically could take this view while at the same time dissecting the brains of animals "in order to ascertain in what memory, imagination, etc., consist", is hard to understand. Animals, he declared, are machines, incapable of thinking or feeling. The cry of the dissected animal is only a mechanical sound like the creaking of a wheel or the squeaking of a hinge.

JOHN HILDROP scathingly retorts:

> "Surely nothing but the Vanity of a Frenchman could ever expect that so absurd a scheme could pass upon a learned world for sound Reason and true Philosophy. For my own part, I could as soon expect to see Gallantries between a couple of amorous Clocks or Watches, or a Battle betwixt two quarrelsome Windmills"[23] (pp.8–9).

On October 18th, 1772, JAMES GRANGER got into trouble with his parishioners in rural Oxfordshire for preaching a sermon entitled " An Apology for the Brute Creation ".[24] He notes in a postcript : " The foregoing discourse gave almost universal disgust to two considerable congregations. The mention of dogs and horses, was censured as a prostitution of the dignity of the pulpit, and considered proof of the Author's growing insanity." His sermon was, however, more kindly reviewed by the literary press.

The sermon is dedicated to Tom Drayman, whom Granger warns that if he breaks any more whips about his horse wishing himself " damned and double damned ", then damnation will certainly follow. A letter to Granger from his publisher three months later records : " this extraordinary accident to the unhappy wretch to whom your Sermon was dedicated looks indeed, like a punishment for his brutality ".[25] An alternative explanation is that many violent delinquents then, as now, are emotionally disturbed and accident-prone, provoking violence against themselves.

The definitive eighteenth-century theological work advocating mercy to animals is DR. HUMPHRY PRIMATT'S[26] *the Duty of Mercy and the Sin of Cruelty to Brute Animals* published in 1776. " Pain is pain ", writes Primatt,

" whether it be inflicted on man, or on beast; and the creature suffers it, whether man or beast, being sensible to the misery of it, whilst it lasts, suffers evil . . . the white man . . . can have no right, by virtue of his colour, to enslave and tyrannize over a black man . . . for the same reason, a man can have no natural right to abuse and torment a beast."

Primatt's is an important work for the additional reason that it was read (and republished) by the REVEREND ARTHUR BROOME who, nearly half a century later in 1824, was to found the society which became the R.S.P.C.A.[27]

Interestingly, Primatt's Old Testament references cited to support his thesis, outnumber those of the New Testament by about five to one. Educational tracts of the R.S.P.C.A., published in the 1860's, show a similar ratio.

A continental divine, CHRISTOPH CHRISTIAN STURM,[28] had taken a humane attitude but also cautioned against the " opposite extreme " of a " ridiculous and extravagant affection " for animals. This was the line taken by the celebrated MRS. TRIMMER[29] in her famous book for children which was first published in 1786 as *Fabulous Histories: Designed for the Instruction of Children, respecting their Treatment of Animals*, later renamed *The History of the Robins*. This work continued to be published up until about 1911 and must have had incalculable effects upon the mentality of the nation.

The whole subject of educative animal books for children is an unexplored field for the social historian. Early ones argue strongly against blood-sports and angling,[30] or take the form of pseudo-autobiographical pleas for kindness from horses, dogs, mice or donkeys.[31] Later in the century such books become rather dainty and altogether less radical.

On the secular and adult side, the eighteenth-century outpourings on this subject are even more numerous than the religious, commencing with a cluster of pithy and witty magazine articles by RICHARD STEELE (*Tatler*, 1709),[32] JOSEPH ADDISON (*Spectator*, 1711),[33] and ALEXANDER POPE (*Guardian*, May 21, 1713),[34] shortly followed by BERNARD DE MANDEVILLE in *The Fable of the Bees*, 1714.[35] These men were all acquainted. VOLTAIRE, who lived in England between 1726 and 1729, was also part of this literary group, and subsequently attacked vivisection on the continent.[36] In the middle of the century, DR. JOHNSON weighed in against the vivisectors[37] as had Addison and Pope before him, and in 1751 DAVID HUME[38] advocated humanity and " gentle usage " to the animals.

In 1776 Johnson remarked that there was " much talk of the misery which we cause the brute creation ",[39] and it was in this last quarter of the century that the movement really began to gather momentum with the writings of BENTHAM,[40] SOAME JENYNS[41] in 1782 (an influential and popular Member of Parliament much quoted in this context by Broome,[42]) JOHN OSWALD[43] in 1791 (a soldier poet carried off by a cannon ball only two years later), GEORGE NICHOLSON[44] who in 1797 produced what is probably the first anthology of writings on this topic, and was a strong advocate of vegetarianism, and THOMAS YOUNG[45] in 1798—appropriately a Fellow of Trinity College,

Cambridge, as was also the Rev. C. Hoyle who prefaced the work with an " Ode to Humanity ". Young uses broadly utilitarian arguments and is strongly anti-bloodsports. Indeed, most of these writers, including Pope, Jenyns, Nicholson, and Bentham, were explicitly critical of hunting, shooting or angling, and although his ambivalence on fox hunting is not typical, perhaps the most influential (besides Bentham) in this secular group of writers was JOHN LAWRENCE.[46] He published prolifically on sporting and agricultural topics, invariably advocating the duty of humanity to animals, and was among the first to emphasise the idea that animals have rights.[47] " Life, intelligence, and feeling, necessarily imply rights ", Lawrence claimed, and he applied this principle in defence of human and animal rights alike. After his death in 1839 in his eighty-sixth year, he became almost entirely forgotten until he was rediscovered by E. W. B. NICHOLSON[48] forty years later. There is an important copy of Lawrence in the Bodleian Library, Oxford, into which Nicholson says he has transcribed annotations made by Lawrence in 1835 to 1837; among these is the note : " Mr. Martin, M.P. for Galway, subsequently took up this cause on my recommendation, and got the animal protection bill with much difficulty thro' Parliament. Mr. M. and myself had many conferences on this subject ".[49] Lawrence's political importance stands largely on this claim.

Lawrence tells us, as do others, that although laws were lacking, the magistrates in his day, especially those in the capital, were tightening up on cruelty cases. The honour of being the first to attempt modern legislation in this field (specifically the prohibition of bull-baiting) goes to SIR WILLIAM PULTENEY, an independent-minded Scottish M.P. and old friend of David Hume, who introduced his Bill in the year 1800. It failed, under attack from the appalling William Windham. So did another in 1802, despite the support of WILBERFORCE.

From here the history of reform is well known and excellently told by E. S. TURNER in *All Heaven in a Rage*.[50] Those two rollicking heroes, LORD ERSKINE and RICHARD MARTIN, finally succeeded in buccaneering a law through Parliament in 1822;

I believe they succeeded partly because they brought wit and undeniable masculinity to the proceedings, by their very personalities refuting any charge of weakness or effeminacy.

The contributions of HOGARTH and sensitive poets such as COWPER, BLAKE, WORDSWORTH, BURNS and BROWNING have been fully documented. To the movement in the eighteenth century, it was JAMES THOMSON[51] who was the outstanding poetic inspiration concerning the caprices of "the steady tyrant man".[52] Artists and authors usually have taken the animals' side: LEWIS CARROLL and RUSKIN, for example, fought the vivisectors of Oxford,[53] as at the turn of this century did GALSWORTHY and BERNARD SHAW.[54]

Although in the mid nineteenth century an aura of stultifying respectability had gripped the movement, there was another burst of commitment towards the end of the Victorian era, inspired by serious writers like HENRY SALT[55] and led by powerful reformers such as FRANCES COBBE, STEPHEN COLERIDGE and LIND AF HAGEBY.[56]

But after 1918—what? With a few glorious exceptions such as the protection of birds and the achievements of C. W. HUME,[57] the movement slowed, the inspiration evaporated, conviction and leadership dwindled.

This is certainly true as regards the philosophy of Animal Rights until, at least, the publication of BRIGID BROPHY's *The Rights of Animals* in 1965.[58] In this century and in this country, animal welfare became a form of decency, but it also became dull. Compassionate people continued the good work, but no longer was there political or intellectual sparkle or even academic acceptability.

Partly, this may have been because animal welfare had gained a middle-class connotation that made it unfashionable among liberal and socialist reformers in an age of new class politics.

Also, in earlier days it had been recognised that children are "naturally" cruel to animals as well as sympathetic, and humanity to animals was therefore considered among some people to be a mark of refinement and maturity; but by the end of the century a reaction had set in. The excessive association of kindness to animals with nursery education, and the rather precious and quite inconsistent approach to animals fostered by the late Victorians, began to make the subject appear childish and sentimental, and not one for serious or manly consideration.

I am tempted to find an additional and more structural cause for the decline: namely, *the effects of wars*. If one looks, for example, at an unbiased list of the serious publications in the animal rights field, a fascinating pattern emerges. Henry Salt's 1894 Bibliography[59] shows two major clusters; one in the last quarter of the eighteenth century preceding the period of the Napoleonic Wars, the other at the end of the last century. The latter, we know, was extended in effect by Salt's own writings, eight of which appeared before the end of the First World War. There is even a lesser cluster between 1824 and 1846, a few years before the Crimean War.

Between these clusters are clear-cut gaps from 1798 to 1824 and 1846 to 1873 following outbreaks of war. I would maintain that from about 1918 till the 1960s represents another such gap, during which serious intellectual debate on animals' rights was at a low ebb.

As far as I can ascertain, legislative reforms show a similar pattern.

I suppose all this is hardly surprising. Indeed, I think a case could be made for other social reforms being affected in this way: Wilberforce, for example, became very distracted by Napoleon, and so of course were all politicians at that time, so that discussion of the obolition of the slave trade was certainly delayed.

It has often been said that Britain has led the way with social reform. Am I being too cynical if I suggest that this partly may have been because Britain also led the world in the introduction and practice of particularly obnoxious forms of exploitation, whether concerning women and children in the factories of the new age of industry, slaves in her colonies, or animals mercilessly hunted, baited and overdriven? Perhaps Britain was a pioneer of reforms because she was also a pioneer of cruelty!

In the case of animals there are several recorded instances

of foreigners visiting this country before the late 18th Century and being shocked by what they saw.[60] Steele said as much in 1709 concerning the Shrove Tuesday cruelty of throwing at cocks: " Some French writers have represented this Diversion of the Common People much to our Disadvantage . . . as they do some other Entertainments *peculiar to our Nation*, I mean those elegant Diversions of Bull-baiting, and Prize fighting, with the like ingenious Recreations of the Bear-Garden ".[61] Pope reiterates this view in the *Guardian* in 1713, James Granger[62] in 1772 sees England as " the Hell of Horses ", and in 1798, Thomas Young thinks " that the English have more of cruelty to animals in their sports in general, than any of their neighbours ".[63]

Furthermore, it seems to me that this country has an unsurpassed record of *exporting* organised animal cruelties: bloodsports and flesh-eating to its old empire, intensive farming and experimentation techniques today. Britain is now one of the chief traders in animal misery: fur, whale oil, livestock and speciesist ideas.

I believe the organised exploitations of the twentieth century bring misery to more animals in Britain today than at any time in our past. Have we progressed in 200 years? If the criterion is the sum of animal suffering, then we have not; indeed the opposite is true.

Yet, in our day, we have the advantage of being post-Darwinian and aware that we are only " naked apes ". We can no longer have the excuse that there is a gulf between us and the brutes which justifies the ideology of exploitation. But, as Singer [64] reminds us, ideologies resist refutation and when their foundations are knocked from under them, " new foundations will be found, or else the ideological position will just hang there, defying the logical equivalent of the laws of gravity ".

I do not put this down to deliberate cruelty: rather to the commercial motive and to custom. " Inveterate custom, which bars all reflection, is the grand source of cruelty towards brute animals ", as Lawrence put it.[65] It is no longer customary to be cruel to animals in the streets. Modern cruelties take place behind the locked doors of laboratories or are concealed in factory farms and cattle ships. Here, in self-contained sub-cultures, it is considered acceptable to mistreat animals in a way which would provoke violent indignation if it were to be done publicly.

The performance of customary cruelty, whether to man or animal, gives little indication of the character of the perpetrator. Ordinary men will do terrible things if they become part of an evil system—witness Auschwitz or My Lai.[66]

On the other hand, individual acts of solitary cruelty or exceptional kindness can both be signs of unusual character, and among those who are idiosyncratically cruel to other animals are some who are severely disturbed and may be just as cruel to humans.[67]

I would think that those who champion the animals' cause fall into two major categories. First, those whose bitter experience of other humans has forced them to turn away from their own species. Second, those whose heightened sense of compassion extends across the board to humans and animals alike. This last group includes most of the great reformers, including Wilberforce, Buxton, Romilly, Erskine, Martin, J. S. Mill, Shaftesbury, Dickin and Cobbe. Mary Wollstonecraft and Mrs. Despard[68] spoke up for animals as well as for women, and Cobbe, Lord Coleridge, Lawson Tait and Gompertz were also feminists. Certainly, a few reformers have been considered un-balanced, but it does not surprise me that neurotics will some-times make good trail-blazers, for they can establish an independence from their culture and sometimes have access to increased levels of drive. To be neurotic is not necessarily to be wrong.

I have little doubt that humans are quite spontaneously interested in other animals: one invariably notices this with infants. I also suspect that the sympathetic[69] impulse is just as universal as the sadistic, and that the two can co-exist. These conditions are not peculiar to reformers. What distinguishes the reformer is the ability to question convention, and motivation powerful enough to do something about it; the latter can take the form of a feeling of outrage, religious conviction, yearning for fame, exceptional compassion often intensified through personal suffering, a sense of mission, or a combination of all or any of these.

Today, animals are by far the most oppressed section of the community : their exploitation is as great an evil as were black slavery, child labour and the degradation of women at the begining of the last century. It is the great moral blind spot of our age. Yet with a moment's thought it can be seen that the moral issues are more obvious, the injustices more vivid, the need for reforms more glaring than are those of a thousand threadbare clichés of conventional politics.

Our own day also sees a resurgence of idealism, arising perhaps out of the moral void of our times. The great conservation movement and the new feeling for animals are parts of this, and there is no doubt that the recent wave of serious books dealing with man's relationship with the other species matches or surpasses that explosion of intellectual concern at the end of the eighteenth century, which bore fruit in the animal welfare legislation of 1822 and after.

In recent years we have also seen a revival of the R.S.P.C.A. itself; an unprecedented spirit of co-operation between organisations in " Animal Welfare Year ", the emergence of direct and militant action by Hunt Saboteurs and the Animal Liberation Front, and now the imprisonment of men and women in the cause.[70] This has been accompanied by the splendid inspiration given to us all by Lord Houghton, the ideological achievement of Professor Heuse, and this very important Conference here at Cambridge.

Will all this give velocity to the struggle against speciesism sufficient to allow it to escape the gravitational pulls of custom and self-interest which have held it down for so long? I hope so mightily.

Animals' rights must become an accepted political issue. The continued deafness of politicians and the indifference of Governments to this subject are generating levels of frustration that are becoming increasingly hard to bear.

Man's Place in Nature

JOHN ASPINALL

I come before you without any qualifications at all—no degrees, no diplomas, no baccalaureates, nothing. All I have, perhaps, are some credentials. I have been described as a fanatic and an amateur, and I willingly admit to being both. A fanatic, in its original derivation, means a man inspired by the gods, and an amateur means somebody who loves what he is doing, and I willingly submit to that. It has also been suggested that I am a neurotic trail-blazer, but I am uncertain of whether I would admit to that description!

" Man's place in Nature " is the subject of this talk; I think we have to consider what place man has arrogated to himself in Nature's pantheon and what is the reality of this place, for obviously these are two different things.

Man has deified himself : he has made his own species ' god '. He believes in this, which is often fatal if one recollects certain great Emperors and rulers who decided, for religio-political reasons, to make themselves gods : like Augustus and perhaps Alexander. The fatal moment arrived when some came to believe that they really were gods—of course Augustus and Alexander never fell for this, but Caligula believed that he was a god. Mankind as a species is now at about the same mental stage as Caligula at his maddest. He fights phony battles, he wins crazy victories. Do you recollect that Caligula insisted on his legions attacking the channel with their short-swords and claimed a triumph of the first order when he returned to Rome for having conquered Neptune? Well, those are the sort of victories that mankind has had. Most of his victories are false victories, because as he

declares himself a triumph he declares his own ruin—as indeed
Caligula had a brief, albeit spectacular, life.

So we have the place that man gives himself, deifying himself.
In this particular sophistry the idea is that he is a god as a species.
All faiths except Buddhism seem to combine to further this belief :
Judaeo-Christianity, Marxism, Islam : a troika for one passenger
only—man. Curiously enough it is the main theme and the one
factor of these three disparate faiths. Buddhism stands back from
this dogma. I think Gautama Buddha was wiser than the three
other prophets. Unfortunately his teachings, possibly because
they gave a place to all living things in his philosophy of ahimsa,
were rejected by man. Only Asoka, 200 years after Buddha's
death, made a brave attempt to implement his teachings. He was
the world's only eco-crat, the greatest ruler, probably, who ever
lived, whose example we could watch today; but he is discarded
and his life is seldom taught in Western schools. I certainly never
heard of Asoka until I had quit my formal education, but he was
a man of colossal vision.

So therefore all of us inwardly believe that we are gods. We
have deified ourselves as a species. I almost believe it myself,
because it has been drummed into me from my earliest years
that man is different from and superior to all other living things.
It is very hard to discard what has been instilled into our race
for over two thousand years. It is very difficult, but some of us
still make stumbling attempts to shed this sophistry.

One can accept, I think, man's mastery, which is a different
thing. I think it is quite possible that evolution intended us to be
at the apex of the faunal scale. I think that we could take our
place—we could have primacy—we could be the first. Whether
evolution intended us to be dictators, to be absolute overlords of
such vast regions of earth and sea is, I think, doubtful. I cannot
believe that evolution is a faultless process. I believe that
evolution has, in the past, blundered. A palaeontologist would
agree, I am sure, that the trilobites and ammonites were probably prolonged disasters because they delayed the evolutionary
process for 50 million years or more. Humboldt, when he was in
the Columbian forests 150 years ago, wrote that the aim of the

natural process was that the optimum variety and volume of living things should subsist in a given area without resultant environmental deterioration and depletion of natural resources. That is evolution's aim—that, in a forest like the Columbian rain forests, an area of immense generosity, a great variety and volume of different organisms can live in symbiosis. A system in which man can keep his primacy as indeed he did in Humboldt's time, when the Amerindians were still number-one in the faunal scale.

In contrast, at the North Pole, comparatively few species can live in a given square mile because of the inclemency of the conditions.

Humboldt saw this too as he, even in those days, witnessed the forests being hacked down and the extraordinary complexity which had taken 40 million years to evolve being swept away and replaced by a monoculture of rubber trees and coffee plants, where once was Arcady, even Paradise. All this has been described as progress and *is* described as progress even today. To me, it is a regress. Most of the story of the planet, since domestication of the barley plant 14,000 years ago, has been the march of regress. I think that man's dictatorship has been retrogressive in the terms of Humboldt's philosophy. I think that man has been the greatest curse which this planet has ever known : his sins are so great that they are probably irremediable. I am the extreme pessimist and I can offer you nothing except misery for yourselves.

We seem not to be able to learn anything from Nature's fully-evolved overlords—as the tiger is in his natural wilderness. My own ancestors were in India for 150 years and I have read the early memoirs of my family who were most of them hunters and shikaris. When they went into stronghold tiger country (the tiger being here indeed the overlord and beneficial predator) they noted the fertility, the variety and the volume of life there. Here you have a natural ruler, for these great mammals are superior to us in what matters. We have, I am sure, greater guile, ingenuity, intellectuality, intelligence and cunning. I would say that most of these abilities are in fact dark sanctuaries of incapacity, because what we *fail* to have is wisdom and judgement without which all else is worthless. Everything that we have done is meaningless unless we have wisdom, and the best of all wisdom is not wisdom arrived at through academic toil—indeed that is a poor way to wisdom—it is behavioural wisdom. Wisdom is in what one does and what one does not do—that is wisdom, and on this basis the great mammals are wiser than we.

Seneca said that no amount of intelligence can add up to wisdom. Konrad Lorenz said the other day that if our species disappears from the face of the earth, which he thinks it will quite shortly, it will be from a surfeit of knowledge that it cannot apply, let alone digest : I side with Konrad Lorenz completely. What is knowledge? The most over-rated nonsense that ever existed. Remember what Goethe said of knowledge : that the only thing more dangerous than knowledge was more knowledge still. Think of all the excitement when they split the atom—is there a man today who does not regret the splitting of the atom about which we knew nothing, and about which wise men could foretell the consequences? Yet, now they want to split the gene in America! Millions of dollars have been put aside for this attempt to split the gene. They attack the gene; they manufacture strange viruses, rare strains, with which they bombard the gene. One of these strains is believed to have escaped and dozens of people died for no known cause. Yet this is described as knowledge for the sake of knowledge! In an American university half the professors walked out on these experiments and said that they did not believe that the human being had enough grandeur, had enough wisdom to handle the sort of knowledge that might come. I look at it also another way—what insanity is this, that we, miserable parvenus, pinchbeck upstarts that we are as a species, whose catastrophic overlordship has lasted a mere 15,000 years, even seek to handle such knowledge? How can we say what these knowledge-seekers are saying, that evolution got it wrong when she evolved the gene after 400 million years of field work and so let us investigate it and improve it? When we seek to split the atom to gain the secrets of energy, we are saying that nature got it wrong, that she stupidly locked energy up in the atom, so let us

split it open. This is the overweening god-like hubris that is in
most of our heads : we really believe that we *are* gods : we have
sanctified ourselves.

I remember I was once in Calcutta and I visited a death-
house a mile long, in which the Indians were ' horizontalised '.
They were so ill they could not sit up, let alone stand, and they
were being fed a pabulum of squash and lentils with spices—some
300 or 400 calories a day. There must have been thousands in
this house. It was so long it was unbelievable. Here I found a
group of young Americans from WHO and one or two English-
men from OXFAM, very well-educated—mostly from Harvard
or Yale—really delightful young men in their twenties : eager,
compassionate, keen, they showed me this terrible thing—humans
dying in rows, being fed on just enough nutrients to maintain
life and no more. Living/dying vegetables. They pointed out
their problems, they showed me everything, and they said :
" What do you think of the work we are doing, Mr. Aspinall?"
And I said : " You are wasting your time." They said : " What
do you mean, we are wasting our time?" I said : " Why do you
keep these people? My answer to you all is to let them die." They
said : " We cannot let them die, they are human beings." Then
the spokesman for this group said : " The trouble is, there are
360 million sacred cows in India " (they are very good at
statistics, the Americans) " and each cow represents 2.7 human
consumption units. There are 55 million buffaloes in India and
each buffalo represents 3.4 human consumption units. And there
are 11 million camels and 94 million sheep, etc. . . . so therefore
the subcontinent has to support not only 670 million humans but
the equivalent of another 1,000 million in the form of animals,
most of whom are sacred." They said : " it is the fault of their
stupid religion, their crazy religion has gone and sanctified the
cow." I answered that I was aware of this and agreed that it was
a distortion of history that one animal should be isolated and
sanctified. But I also turned on them and said : " But have not
you made a bigger error yourselves? My friends, come closer to
me." So they came closer and I said : " You have made an error
so vast, and so much greater than did these poor human beings—

you have sanctified yourselves. You have literally deified and sanctified your own species, of which there are 4 billion on the earth, a blunder so far-reaching that one is breathless at the thought of it." " Oh, my God," they said, " Mr. Aspinall, you think we are not sacred? The sanctity of human life is the only thing that keeps us going." I said : " The sanctity of human life is the most dangerous sophistry ever propagated by philosophy and it is all too well rooted. Because if it means anything it means the in-sanctity of species which are *not* human."

Now, perhaps sanctity is not a word a naturalist or an evolutionist would use about organisms. If I came towards you, with my well-known love of wild beasts, and said : " I believe in the sanctity of rhinoceroses," you would think that I was crazy and I would indeed be mad if I put forward this suggestion. Yet any politician can get to his feet, or any priest, and talk of the sanctity of human life, and everyone claps. Now such a remark is equally inane; it is meaningless, you see, and yet it is *believed* by everybody—this is the greatest of the problems which faces us all.

Mankind has caused such terrible destruction. He has denatured himself—he has half-domesticated himself. He is obviously unfit for the imperium which he has grasped from the world and I am filled with nothing but foreboding for the future. I must say that I am among that group of people who, to borrow an expression from Teddy Goldsmith, would regard a demo-catastrophe as an eco-bonanza. In other words, I would be very happy to see $3\frac{1}{2}$ billion humans wiped from the face of the earth within the next 150 or 200 years and I am quite prepared to go myself with this majority. Most of you sitting here are redundant in every possible sense of the word. Even though you may be the vanguard of the youth politik of the " rights of animals ", you are as redundant and as unnecessary as are most other human beings, when you come to it.

I would just remind you of Professors Revie's famous article in the *Scientific American*, in which he described the increase of man's population from one million years ago, when he estimated the world population of human beings at 100,000 (which is a third of the population of Nottingham) to a time after the discovery of fire, when the figures started to soar to today's four billion. If that is not redundancy, if that is not a burden of unnecessary bio-mass, then I don't know what is!

Let us all look forward to the day when the catastrophe strikes us down! With what resounding applause would the rest of nature greet *our* demise!

This speech was spontaneous

Section Two

RELIGIOUS AND THEOLOGICAL
PERSPECTIVES

Buddhist Attitudes Towards Animal Life

JACK AUSTIN

Many services are begun with an act of contrition. This approach is the right one, since none of us is one hundred per cent kind to himself, to his family, friends, those disliked, nor to animals. We are all able to be kind when people or animals fit in with our own wishes, but find it hard to be so when we are crossed by another will, whether human or other animal.

I say " other animal " because we are all animals, and the distinction between human beings and other animals is, to us Buddhists, one of degree rather than of kind. But like human beings, all animals persist in having wills, ideas and whims of their own. The " bad dog " who is burying his bone in our flower bed is, from his stand-point, just doing his own thing.

We need to take a wider perspective than that of our usual self-interest if we are to get things right. In the overall pattern of nature, each being has its place, and this includes our place. At present, we are demanding much more than our rightful place in the scheme of things, with the result that the whole of the world's ecology is thrown out of gear. We behave as though only our own immediate needs mattered, whereas the satisfaction of these needs must be seen in relation to the lives of other people and other beings.

The first precept taken by Buddhists of all denominations is simply : " I undertake the pledge not to kill." This non-killing refers to all living things, and when we infringe it we are urged not to make plausible excuses, but to admit the breach of our promise. Ahimsa, or non-harming, is central to Buddhist thinking, and colours all Buddhist practices. As the R.S.P.C.A.'s booklet puts it so well: "the welfare of people and animals is inextricably interwoven."

It is true that we need to eat in order to live and that this eating will inevitably destroy at least vegetable life, and may involve the sacrifice of animal life in much of the world and at many periods of history. As realists we must accept this, but we need not extend it. We can in fact *reduce* it significantly by altering the pattern of our own habits.

Not all Buddhists are vegetarians, certainly not at all times. Some are as a regular routine, amongst them Zen monks, who may not eat other than vegetarian meals: they keep the precept literally and faithfully. Others have token vegetarian days when they do not eat meat or fish. Many of those following the Buddha are not yet ready to carry their ahimsa to its logical conclusion in this way, but all pay homage to the ideal, and few would kill other than in necessity, even where they fall into the easier way of eating what has been killed already.

Vegetarianism is not the whole of the matter, though. To cause an animal to live in miserable or cruel conditions is worse than killing it for food after it has had a carefree and happy life of its own. It is the intention to cause suffering which is evil, and the infliction of pain, for any reason, which must be avoided by the deeply religious person. So battery farming which inflicts an unnatural and unhappy, when not downright cruel, regime on animals is a greater evil than eating meat itself, for it prolongs suffering for much or even all of the creature's life. This, like any kind of hunting for "pleasure", is entirely outside the scope of permitted activities for one who would call himself a follower of the Compassionate One, the Buddha.

The Buddha allowed his monks to eat meat under certain conditions. They must neither authorise, nor ask for, nor encourage, nor witness the killing of an animal for their food. By a logical extension of this attitude, he preferred not to have animals killed for him and his followers. By another equally logical extension of his edicts in the matter, actual cruelty of any kind was entirely ruled out. This cuts out not only hunting, but painful experiments on animals for such trivialities as cosmetics, "scientific knowledge", and all other such activities. Most of the experiments carried out seem to be for utterly silly projects, and should be stopped immediately they are detected, by pressure of public opinion and by any legal means which are available.

We are not monks, and the rules applicable to monastic living are not for us. Those who are seculars, living in this world with all its pressures and obligations, cannot apply the Zen monk's rules. But the same spirit should animate us, and the aim must remain—no deliberate killing. It is, in any case, better to have a high ideal, even if not always realised, than to lower that ideal to something easily achieved. An ideal needs to be just beyond our grasp, or we cease to strive to reach it, and that very striving is necessary for our spiritual development.

Under certain stresses, and in peculiar situations, we may well kill people, let alone animals. The theoretical, absolutist position is untenable in our everyday lives, and it is always unwise to deride those who do not share our beliefs. Far better to try, gently, to encourage them to accept the more noble goal, even though neither we nor they will often achieve it. In the same way, it is better to reduce the amount of killing of animals by gradually lessening the amount of meat consumed, and this involves our eating less ourselves if it is not feasible to eliminate it entirely, owing to many factors which make up our complicated lives. The spirit of compassion will inspire us, even when we have to make difficult decisions; we are not answerable to extremists who demand total commitment to any rule under all circumstances, but to our own consciences.

As a vivid, if simplified, example of the need to kill sometimes, it has been known for a mass murderer to be felled by the police as he was machine-gunning a crowd of people in a confined space. Who would reprove the police officer who killed this murderer and saved the lives of many further victims? In some parts of the world and in many different circumstances, the only available source of food may be animal or fish. In old Tibet, for example, even the compassionate Buddhists had to eat yak meat for lack of anything else. If the only alternative is to starve to death, would you expect anybody—would you yourself be prepared—to starve to a slow death rather than eat meat?

In our relative world, nothing can be absolute; we may well be in the position of such a policeman or such a starving man, and would have to break the precept not to kill. Meantime, none of us is perfect, and those who would demand perfection from others must look carefully to themselves. Sometimes, also, the seemingly imperfect will conceal something greater. Here is a short story of a Zen follower.

Ban-Zan was walking through a market, and he overheard a conversation between a butcher and his customer. " Give me the best piece of meat you have," demanded the customer. To this the butcher replied " Everything in my shop is the best. You cannot find anything here that is not the best." At this Ban-Zan became enlightened. So a vegetarian received just the jolt he needed to get him out of conceptual thinking into enlightened recognition by a chance encounter with a butcher.

We are not in a position to wave a finger of admonition at those who do not share our beliefs, since we do not know the whole story, in anybody's life, and we are less than perfect ourselves. Since all humanity, as well as all forms of life in which humanity is included, have a relationship, we are ourselves responsible for the state of things which we deplore. How many people of evil lives have been driven to them by " good " people whose lack of understanding, lack of love, helped to cause this? We are responsible, in some degree, for every murder, and for every animal slaughtered for meat or in the pursuit of " pleasure ". Let us have the humility to recognise this. It may be painful, but it is more constructive than any amount of mere condemnation.

Unhappily, not all those engaged in propaganda for animal welfare, or vegetarianism, are kindly people. Some, frankly, are insufferable bores. I am sure this does not apply to those here present, but we must remember that it is not unknown, and may be responsible for putting many people off our cause. Not all meat eaters are cruel people. Far from it. Many are kindly souls. We may think them mistaken, and if we do then we must try, very gently, to convince them that it would be a good idea to be kind to animals by not eating them.

On the other hand, it is common for those whose standards of kindliness are low, to defend their positions by sneering at others who take a more merciful stand. This is done, of course, to justify the lower standard rather than to deplore the lack of achievement by those with higher ones. To comment that so-and-so does not live up to his or her professed ideals neither invalidates those ideals nor condones any lapses from them. It merely shows that we are all humanly fallible. But in a general way, those of us who preach should at least try to live up to our professed convictions. We shall not always do so.

The Buddhist doctrine of ahimsa stems from the idea that life is interrelated, and that to harm another creature is to harm all creatures, including the one committing an act of violence. Of the two main attributes of the Buddha, Wisdom and Compassion, it is the Compassion which is most easily seen, because Wisdom is often misunderstood by the unwise. But Wisdom is the ability to see things as they actually are, and not as they may appear at a superficial glance. For this reason we must beware of superficial judgments.

It is the inner attitude that counts, since from this stems everything else. As the first verse of the *Dhammapada* puts it : " All that we are is in the result of what we have thought : it is founded on our thoughts, it is made up of our thoughts." For this reason, amongst others, if we ever have to kill, let us never do so with any pleasure or satisfaction, nor with any facile justification for doing so. How anybody can take pleasure in seeing any creature torn to death is so far beyond me that I find it hard to understand at all, but we should not judge where we do not understand.

It will often be necessary to kill something that lives, even if only in self-defence or to save crops for human consumption. We have to recognise inescapable facts, and any attempt to impose by force an unrealistic viewpoint will only harm our cause. We may think, as I personally do, that to kill for food in this age is as up-to-date as putting leeches to a sick man would be in a modern doctor's practice. Hunting, in the ritualistic manner of fox-hunting, is as anachronistic as the stoning to death for adultery now being reintroduced into some Islamic countries. Both are barbarous and misconceived, no matter what biblical or other justification may be adduced for them.

There is the beautiful story of the Buddha and the swan. A hunter shot down a swan, which the Buddha rescued and restored to health. The hunter came to demand the swan, which he said was his since he had shot it. The Buddha replied that the swan was his, since he had saved its life, which is a far more meritorious act than the destructive and cruel one of attempting to kill.

Cruelty, like all evil, is essentially a lack of its positive counterpart, compassion. Love of our fellow beings, including animals, precludes all deliberate cruelty, though, being human ourselves, and being imperfect people, we shall sometimes act cruelly and often act thoughtlessly. Not by deploring blood sports shall we save animals so much as by trying to convince people that it is better to be humane. It is by our own lives and examples that we shall best propagate this ideal. As we show in our lives this love that inspires us, it will impress others far more than anything we say.

Activity is good, if inspired by love, but sometimes the less obvious approach is more effective than the blunt confrontation. A story, again from Zen Buddhism, illustrates this.

There was a monk who had handed over the family estates to a nephew, who then proceeded to spend his money on a prostitute. Relatives asked the monk to remonstrate with the profligate, since the property was being dissipated. And you know how worried families always are when their inheritances are affected, even if a young man's misbehaviour fails to stir them!

So Ryo-Kwan went to see the young nephew, and was warmly greeted, being asked to stay the night. All night long, Ryo-Kwan sat in meditation, and as he was leaving next morning he asked the young man to tie up his sandals, saying that as he was getting old, his hands shook. The nephew obliged willingly, and then the monk commented: "Thank you. As a man becomes older, he gets feebler day by day. Take good care of yourself."

He left without another word, never mentioning the matter of the courtesan or the relatives' complaints. But from that time on the dissipations ceased, and the young man managed the estates properly.

In the life of the Buddha himself, animals played a big part. His first sermon was in a deer park at Benares, where he preached the famous indictment of extremism. He pointed out that a life of mere pleasures was a pagan practice, unworthy, unprofitable, whilst one of self-mortification as undertaken by ascetics is painful, and also unprofitable in the spiritual life. Hence the need for moderation, for a Middle Path between extremes. The symbol of this sermon is that of the Wheel of the Law, or Wheel of the Dharma, which he set rolling then, flanked by two deer adorned with ceremonial scarves, symbols of respect.

When Gautama sat under a hot sun, a legend has it that a large snake reared its hood over his head to shade him from the glare, and there are representations of this in Buddhist art. Similarly, the Buddha often has snails covering his bare scalp in art as well as in tradition. Many similar stories testify to the close relationship which existed between the Enlightened One and animals, and he was himself compared to the Lion which was the king of beasts. A common term for a good talk on the Dharma is to compare it to the lion's roar, which dispels other and less wise comments. The title of a popular modern Buddhist periodical is just this one—*The Lion's Roar*.

When the Buddha passed into Parinirvana in his 80th year, he was surrounded by all the animals of the jungle, who mourned the passing of one who loved them, and this picture, the Nirvana Picture, is often displayed on the day of our celebration of the event—the 15th of February.

In view of all this, it is not surprising that Buddhists place emphasis on the sanctity of all life, animal life included, and try to avoid its destruction, let alone its painful exploitation. It is not out of mere sentiment that we do this, but out of a deep conviction that we are ourselves but a fleeting manifestation of life in our present form. We do not believe that only human beings have " souls " and that other sentient beings are devoid of this intrinsic element which is supposed to distinguish us from them. We do not, indeed, believe that any of us has a permanent, separate soul which could justify our living at the expense of others, either physically or spiritually.

It is sometimes alleged that the United Nations does nothing, and is useless. In fact it is useful in many ways, and has done a great deal, through its various agencies, to help people in many parts of the world. Not only does it mitigate international strife, even when it cannot prevent it due to lack of adequate support by the big powers, but it also encourages and supports efforts to produce more food, and so on. But the important thing is this— what else is there to do the work? And would not increased support make the work more effective still?

Similarly, the R.S.P.C.A. has been criticised for its short-comings, and we are aware of some of these. No human organisation can ever, in the nature of this world, be perfect. We have to do the best we can with imperfect tools. Nothing is ever achieved by sitting back and belittling the efforts of others to do the things which manifestly need doing.

In those far-off days of 1824 an Anglican priest started the Society which we have today, and we have every reason, whatever our religious affiliations, to be grateful to him and to other such ministers. I hope that my own co-religionists will prove as active in the attempts made to prevent exploitation of animals, and will not content themselves with mere pious platitudes, which do not of themselves achieve much.

Knowledge gained at the expense of others is contaminated, and when these others are defenceless creatures, it involves what we term " bad karma ", which will recoil on the perpetrators and their passive supporters. The Buddha often avoided discussions about theoretical knowledge, with the comment that it did not lead to better behaviour and did not conduce towards enlightenment. Wisdom and Compassion need to go hand in hand to be profitable in the real, the spiritual sense.

Let me conclude in the words of a famous exponent of Buddhism in modern times, the late Dr. Daisetz Suzuki, who wrote *The Way of Compassion*: " I believe a kind of chain exists between flowers, animals, people and Buddhas. This chain is called the chain of love —or compassion. Where this chain is perceived and appreciated, there is human serenity and peace."

May we *all* find that serenity and peace.

Animals and Moral Theology

ANDREW LINZEY

In approaching such a wide subject, I intend to divide what I want to say into three sections. First I shall begin by giving a very brief outline of the formative ideas concerning the status of animals from within the Christian tradition; secondly, I shall assess what appear to me as the respective strengths and weaknesses of these insights; finally, I shall draw some tentative conclusions, hopefully relevant to our purposes today.

A. 1. Viewed from the perspective of theology, the world is Creation. It is not a biological accident or a self-activated process of evolution, but a gift from God. " Creation is grace : a statement at which we should like best to pause in fear and gratitude," writes Karl Barth. " God does not grudge the existence of reality distinct from Himself : He does not grudge it in its own reality nature and freedom."[71] This claim about the origin of the world and its natural order has a primary place in Christian doctrine. God is absolutely prior to all that is, and nothing exists without his creative will. It follows that both man and animals inhabit the universe as creatures who are not just created once and for all, but are continually dependent upon God for their life, sustenance and well-being. All that we can see, the richness, diversity and complexity of the natural world with all its fullness of beauty, exists, in theistic terms, because of the creative design of God.

2. Understood from this starting point animals are seen as non-moral beings. While both man and animals share the same ontological characteristics as creatures, men are made in the " image of God ", divinely endowed as spiritual and moral beings

uniquely capable of moral consciousness, rational discernment of just ends, and able to act altruistically in response to them. Animals, on the other hand, are viewed as incapable of rationality or conscious thought, and therefore are devoid of moral status as we understand it.

3. This fundamental separation of man from the world of animals has in particular been reinforced by the Biblical writers in their concept of man's " dominion " where humans are seen as divinely destined to control or subdue animal life.[72] Theological reflections upon man's superiority over animals, particularly with regard to their intelligence and rationality, led some of the earlier Christian thinkers, such as St. Thomas Aquinas, to regard animals as incapable of possessing an immortal soul—a tradition, incidentally, which still widely characterises Catholic theology to this present day. It is exactly because it has been supposed that rationality is the prerogative of humans that René Descartes, for example, was able to claim that animals possessed no mind, and logically as mere *automata* had no seat of sentiency. Some modern theological writers have been quite categorical in denying that animals feel pain. " It may be doubted whether there is any real pain," writes Charles Raven, " without a frontal cortex, a fore-plan of mind, and a love which can put itself in the place of another; and these are the attributes of humanity."[73]

4. The concept of man's dominion over animals has in consequence led to the formulation of another idea which has widely influenced secular moral judgments, namely that animals hold an instrumental value to human beings. One Roman Catholic theologian, Karl Horrman, argues in this way :

" It is evident to natural reason that among the things which exist, the less perfect are there for the sake of the more perfect, that plant life should serve for the maintenance of animals and both serve man."[74]

Other theologians, such as John Hick, tentatively conclude that

" the sub-human animals exist because they represent possible forms of being, and therefore of goodness, and because their existence is accordingly necessary to the fullness of the created world."[75]

5. It is not surprising therefore that animals have been traditionally regarded as beyond the scope of moral rights and duties. The harsh judgment of the Jesuit Joseph Rickaby that

> " Brute beasts, not having understanding and therefore not being persons, cannot have any rights . . . We have no duties of charity, nor duties of any kind, to the lower animals, as neither to sticks and stones "[76]

is, whatever modern liberal Catholics may argue, the substantial verdict of the Catholic tradition. Pope Pius IX, for example, refused permission for the opening of an animal protection office in Rome on the grounds that men owed duties to his fellow men, but none to the lower animals. The Christian tradition has firmly held that in order to possess rights one must be a human person, for rights and obligations flow from our capacity to be moral agents and to act and reason rationally. While most Christians now recognise some obligation not to cause animals to suffer needlessly, the Catholic Dictionary on " lower animals " in 1897 puts animals totally beyond the scope of proper treatment. It argues :

> " They (animals) have no rights. The brutes are made for man, who has the same right over them which he has over plants and stones. He may kill them for his food; and if it is lawful to destroy them for food, and this without strict necessity, it must also be lawful to put them to death, or to inflict pain upon them, for any good or reasonable end, such as the promotion of man's knowledge, health, etc., or even for the purpose of recreation."

B. I want now to turn to assessing some of the strengths and weaknesses of these (mainly negative) influences.

1. Let us begin by agreeing that humans are supremely moral beings. Alone and unique in the universe we do appear to be the only species capable of those capacities for morality and rationality, no matter how infrequently we may use them. This observation is supported by recent Biblical exegesis of Genesis where it is suggested that the concept of man's dominion over animals, far from meaning the human tyranny the Christian tradition has

often supposed it to be, actually finds its meaning within the theology of Kingship and the exercise of responsible authority under God.[77] We are, according to the Biblical writers, responsible to God for our treatment of the natural world. We hold it in stewardship and like all stewardship it involves accountability. We need to hold in tension therefore our understanding of ourselves as superior with the Biblical insight that we are morally accountable.

2. While we may still regard humans as the supreme example of rationality, we will find it increasingly hard to deny some, albeit rudimentary, rational capacity to lower animals and an even greater capacity to the higher mammals. Recent work on the intelligence of whales and dolphins, simply to take one example, insists: " The literature that exists on the relationship between the brain's appearance and intelligence is not particularly sophisticated. Human beings have simply assumed that they were the most intelligent and have then looked for the morphological support for that assumption. But the assumption itself may be wrong."[78] The authors go on to argue that if we define intelligence in human terms, such as for example the ability to pass intelligence tests, then it is not surprising that only human candidates are successful. This observation also applies to our understanding of sentiency. If we, with Raven as cited earlier, define pain in such a way as to make it an exclusively human experience, we simply pre-condition the result. What we have yet to grasp sufficiently fully, and without theological blinkers, is the simple truth that animals do feel pain and arguably more so in certain circumstances. Our concern here is simply that animals feel pain rather obviously *as animals* and I can see no reason why we should not assume that their experience of suffering is as important to them as ours is to us.

3. Are animals incapable of having immortal souls, and moreover what meaning does this distinction have in relation to the non-human world? In so far as it reinforces the great emphasis in the Christian tradition laid upon man's status as a spiritually discerning being, it will present us with little difficulty. But if it is meant, as clearly the argument of Aquinas suggests, that

such a delineation is based upon the complete irrationality of
animals, then it is difficult to see how we could maintain such a
judgment with conviction. Indeed our modern understanding of
rationality in animals would appear to make them prime candidates for immortal souls. But more fundamentally, whatever
spiritual status we ascribe to animals, we must be quite clear
that this status is not in itself a morally relevant criterion for
justifying abuse. Foetuses and young children may well have
diminished spirituality but nevertheless possess rights. As C. S.
Lewis observed, the lack of soulfulness on the part of animals
makes the infliction of suffering (and although Lewis fails to grasp
this, also the infliction of death) not more but less morally justi-
fiable.[79]

4. Of all the ideas emanating from within the Christian tradition, the claim that animals were made for human use or benefit
appears singularly misplaced. Indeed, John Burnaby is surely
right in seeing in this idea an early perversion of Christian
doctrine.[80] Latterly a group of Anglican Theologians have argued
that " Although it cannot be denied that man is very much at
the centre of biblical teaching on creation, this teaching does not
hold that nature has been created simply for man's sake " and
goes on to argue that to imagine so " is a mark of folly ".[81] But
these later denials of man's absolute place in creation would, to
say the least, appear more convincing if the welfare of animal
kind figured a little more prominently in their ethical conclusions. It is to my mind extraordinary that a group of theologians
can on one hand hold that it is foolish to suppose that animals
possess a purely instrumental value to human beings and insist
that they have " intrinsic value " independent of ourselves, while
on the other refuse to comment on the morality of cruelty and
in particular the hunting of them.[82]

5. Accepting the above observations, it is surely more difficult
to dispense with the issue of animals' rights, as have previous
theologians. If animals are not sentient of course it would be
illogical to ascribe to them a right to be protected from suffering.
If animals are totally devoid of rationality then any question of
a right to protection from mental stress does not arise. Again if

animals possess a purely instrumental value to human beings then a conflict of rights is logically impossible—for each and every time we should (as we invariably do) subordinate their interests to our own. But it is, as we have seen, exactly these assumptions which are questionable.

C. Allow me then to turn to the third stage of my analysis, and draw together some tentative conclusions.

1. Theological perspectives change and the development of Christian insights into their full maturity is the work of generations. Part of the job of a theologian must be that of discernment, that is discerning that which is received in tradition and testing anew its validity and worth. Theology like any other discipline is ever absorbing new data, holding in tension the new and the old. We need ever to be aware of the dictum of Erasmus that " In identifying new learning with heresy we make orthodoxy synonymous with ignorance." This process of raising new areas of work and the task of discernment has not been sufficiently continuous— especially, we should add, in the area of man's treatment of animals. The Christian tradition has rested in well worn grooves and has simply failed to question its own assumptions. The lack of modern specifically Christian analysis of this subject is staggering when one considers its scope and social implications.

2. Our task then is to begin this process of theological discernment in a far more thorough and systematic way. If we reject or refashion our heritage as I have suggested then I believe we come inescapably to the idea that animals should be objects of our moral concern.

We also need to reject the idea that there is an absolute distinction between man and animals and to take seriously the evidence of the natural sciences concerning the similarity of animal life.

3. In particular we need to confront the question of rights more directly. We have to ask what theological ground we have for denying the rights of animals, if we accept that such terminology is legitimate in relation to our fellow humans.[83] For, once we have accepted that animals have not only an instrumental

value, but also an intrinsic one, then I believe we have to come
to terms with—and ultimately embrace—the concept that on a
theistic world view, creation has rights which can be derived
from the God-given autonomy and nature of each species. In
stating that humans do not have absolute rights we already come
close to envisaging the possibility of animal rights. Moreover, a
recognition of the value of creation seems to me to be inherent in
the Christian doctrine of creation as fundamentally good. How
specifically we define these rights and what criteria we adopt for
their recognition and possible conflict with other rights, are
questions beyond the scope of this present paper, although I have
sought to give some small account of these possibilities elsewhere;[84] but I want to insist that such a recognition of rights,
while not logically entailed in our acceptance of the value of
other life forms, can at least be deduced from it.

4. Such a notion of animal rights is I believe essential if we
are to counteract in principle and practice the immense anthropo-
centricity of Christian thinking. Anthropomorphism of course
may not in itself be wrong, indeed in many ways it is not, I
judge, a mistake to understand our relationship with animals
in terms of our own human emotions. As Konrad Lorenz
aptly writes : " The similarity (between animals and man) is not
only functional but historical, and it would be an actual fallacy
not to humanise."[85] Neither is anthropomorphism wrong if it
highly places man's considerable moral abilities. But anthropo-
centricity has the clear danger of minimising or at worst relegat-
ing the worth of other species and of glorifying the human brain
above all other. The concept of animal rights sets limits to the
claim that human life and well-being must always take primary
consideration in our evaluation of moral duties.

5. I wonder if it will occur to you, as it does most profoundly
to me, that the human species is only one of thousands if not
millions of species existing on this planet and that there exist
other species containing in themselves the fullness of God's created
life within their own particular modes and nature of being. As
Hans Hass writes :

" It is an old tradition that the earth and all that lives on it was made for man, thus entitling us to do what we will with the rest of nature. But modern research suggests quite the contrary. The planet earth and all the life that flourishes on it were quite clearly not created for man's use or pleasure. Rather we are only one part of a process of development which had its beginning with the first organic structure of three billion years ago ".[86]

Whatever we may assert about the moral superiority and intelligence of man, it appears to me most unacceptable that we should therefore claim for ourselves a relationship with animals which fails to do justice to our own moral senses. Victor Hugo recognised this discrepancy when he wrote of the need for man to become " civilised towards nature ".[87] But it is surely extraordinary that despite our present pre-occupation with man's misuse of the environment and the ethical issues involved in that sphere, we should have failed to give serious attention to the similar issues raised by man's treatment of other, often higher similar, animals. And if we believe our capacity as moral beings is a gift from God freely bestowed upon us as an inherent part of our being made in the image of God, then we need to regard our moral responsibility towards animals with a degree of seriousness and urgency which hitherto has eluded us. In this connection the recent statement by the Archbishop of Canterbury in accepting the Presidency of the R.S.P.C.A. that " Animals, as part of God's creation, have rights which must be respected. It behoves us always to be sensitive to their needs and the reality of their pain ",[88] is a timely indication of the change of attitudes required of us all.

6. Let us be realistic, however, and accept that Western culture is inextricably bound up with man's exploitation of millions of animals as food, as research tools, for entertainment, and for clothing, and for enjoyment and company. The sheer scope and complexity of our exploitation is, I contend, an indication of how far we have accepted the dictum that animals exist for man's use and pleasure. It is sheer folly to suppose that we can completely extricate ourselves from this complexity of exploitation

with minimal disturbance to Western society as we now know it. Nevertheless, having begun the slow and often tedious task of challenging traditional assumptions, new fields of sensitivity have already begun to emerge, and it is this task of hastening the moral evolution of the consciousness of our fellow humans that we must undertake. The Christian tradition with its vast influence on Western culture has a unique role to play in showing its ability to change perspectives and challenge even its own most cherished assumptions.

Animals and Moral Theology (2)

ERIC TURNBULL

In the many problems that challenge human conduct today we need guidance, guidance which gives a grounding that is authoritative and yet not authoritarian, for the principles being applied. Such guidance must be based on a radical treatment which displays the roots of the problem at issue, seeking a course between rigid legalism on the one hand and woolly-thinking individualism on the other.

In the past this has rarely been the approach of moral theologians to animal rights. One illustration may help. A few years ago a former Regius Professor of Moral Theology at Oxford defended the practice of fox hunting " because of the high place in the hierarchy of being accorded to man." Whereas, if one accepts the early chapters of Genesis on their face value it appears that the Creator, possibly in a moment of absent-mindedness, gave man a position of superiority on earth, it does not follow *ipso facto* that man has a blank cheque to do what-ever he likes with creation ! Genesis is neither trying to describe an hierarchical structure resulting from a completed creative act nor attempting to give us a lesson in biology. The impact of textual research and biological discovery alone should drive us away from such an uncritical position.

Genesis provides us with two sets of facts. First about God; that his activity in creation continues as long as creation lasts : that he is not bound or limited by creation but rather works in it, and through it uses the universe to tell us about himself. The second set of facts is about man : that he is a creature intended to have communion with the Creator and, given a distinctive role in God's creative purpose, a stewardship. The verses in Genesis about man's dominion have so often been wrested out of context. *Before* we confess our belief in man, Genesis says first affirm our trust in God : *this alone is the context of man's dominion,* which rests on our ability to participate in the continuous act of creation.

These two sets of facts at the beginning of the Old Testament are but the first strokes of the brush in our search for moral guidelines to motivate man in his relationship with his fellow creatures.

From this start we turn to the prophets. Hosea, who was clearly familiar with the Genesis narrative, is the first to envisage the outcome of God's plan for the whole of redeemed nature. " I will make a covenant on behalf of Israel with the wild beasts, the birds of the air and the things that creep on the earth " (2 : 15)—a passage which concludes with the promise that a time will come when war will be no more. Hosea hands on the torch to the first Isaiah who in the familiar passage (11 : 6-9) describes the golden age when there is complete mutual trust between all God's creatures.

When we look at the Gospels in the New Testament a benevolent attitude is assumed—e.g., the story of the Good Shepherd. We can hardly expect detailed moral directives from the narrative because this was not the way of Christ. To quote briefly from Bishop Gore's book *Jesus of Nazareth* :

" Our Lord's refusal to give plain answers to plain questions —his constant habit of dealing with one question by asking another—was, we should gather, part of a general refusal to teach explicitly and dogmatically, lest he should thereby stunt a man's capacity for finding his own answers to his own questions by the light given within him."

Gore suggests that Jesus recognised a society where there was an hierarchy of orders, although he was so deeply opposed to the exploitation of the weak and the helpless.

There is of course one incident in the Gospel narrative that some find embarrassing—the destruction of the herd of pigs at

Gadara. However, the precise determination of what happened in this incident simply cannot be established. It is possible to rationalise the story, as some do, by suggesting that the pigs were terrified by the noise and gestures of the demented man, and that it was the crowd who later concluded that the demons entered the pigs. New Testament scholars are agreed that (a) it is by no means certain that the incident of the pigs is part of the original story, or (b) that Jesus did not necessarily share the Jewish prejudice about unclean animals.

It is in St. Paul, especially in Romans 8 : 19ff, that we find positive guidance for our attitude and behaviour to fellow creatures. There is no systematic code : Christians must still do their own homework in working out the implications of those insights which he gives us. Paul says that the whole natural order is to be rescued from the sufferings with which it is surrounded. He is thinking as one commentator puts it "of the sufferings, overwhelming, inexplicable useless sufferings with which it is surrounded; of the exploitation and sufferings of animals, the weak devoured by the strong, the ruthless destruction of plant life, of natural catastrophes of all kinds." St. Paul pictures in that passage the whole creation groaning together, waiting eagerly for their rescuer, Christ.

Now how much of this is poetic licence? It is easy to say everything will come out all right in the end, but is there any evidence to support such a claim? Yes, for Paul is really dealing with the consequences of the Incarnation whereby we believe God became one with creation and the consequences of the life and death of Christ. Here are *FACTS*, facts which can focus hope on our anguish as we consider some of those subjects on the programme of this Symposium. For the apostle the last word does not lie with suffering, evil and waste. Paul regards the situation as full of hope because he sees life on earth neither as something to run away from with dreams of pie-in-the-sky nor yet as a slough of pessimism; the apostle tells his fellow Christians that they themselves have a vital role in redeeming creation and this is part of their stewardship. Christ through his death and resurrection has restored to us and to our fellow creatures the hope of fulfilment " to enter upon the liberty and splendour of the sons of God."

Nothing less than Paul's vision should guide our thinking on animal rights, and this is why I say that in the past animal rights have been poorly served by moral theologians. Of course, we are dealing with different species, but it has been scientifically established in the words of Professor Thorpe " that most of the differences seem to be of degree rather than kind ". (" Man's place in Nature," *Theology*, Feb. 1969). What is one to reply, armed with Paul's vision, to those scholars who claim that moral theology is only concerned with what is distinctively human and deny rights to animals because they are not free self-conscious beings capable of voluntary action and moral choice? It would seem that any animal's pleasure in life is in the exercise of inherited behaviour patterns. Where these are denied them animals are in danger of a deprivation that is equivalent to mental or physical cruelty. When in a large number of domestic animals and mammals we observe signs of a clear developing personality, an independent intelligence capable of elements of reasoning, we are perhaps only beginning to explore the depths of an animal's inherent behaviour patterns. Is not this the first stirring of the redemption of creation itself—a feature of traditional prophecy throughout the Judaic-Christian tradition?

There is still a gap between animal powers and those of a normal human being. As Christians we believe that God moves and inspires our wills. Animal symbolism, so prominent in Christianity and not unknown in Judaism, sees the drama and mystery of the divine embodied in the activity of animals. One feels compelled to ask if our fellow creatures have a share in our God-given free will?

My belief is that we should see animals from a theological perspective. Such an approach is not unlike that of the modern scientist who believes that there is a pattern to be discovered. If there were no order or pattern it would be impossible to establish any general principles; it would be impossible to discover any laws of nature. When we observe animals living and working in close contact with their fellow creatures, men, we plainly see that trust, mutual respect and affection can positively banish frontiers between species; we know then that this is unquestionably something more than " an automatic response to an outside stimulus " (Waddams).

Animal Rights and Nature Liberation*

M. W. FOX

THE STAGES OF HUMAN DEVELOPMENT

I. Steward and Co-creator:

The history of man's changing relationship with animals and nature as a whole reflects, with great clarity, the development of man's consciousness—his attitudes, and the way in which he perceives others in terms of his values, needs, and personal priorities. An overview of this is needed, not only for people to grasp the concept that the way in which we regard and treat animals is a reflection of our own development (and collectively, of the evolution of our culture). It may also, and more importantly, provide a framework wherein one may discover one's own place in life.

Biotic or Symbiotic Stage

At the most primal " pre-ego " stage of development as between a young infant and his mother or a tribe of " primitive " people and nature, the relationship is one of symbiosis. At this stage of development, the infant's consciousness is such that it does not see itself as being separate from the mother : oneness is of dependency. Later, the child grows apart and develops its own sense of self—the ego. In an analogous way, early man was himself part of nature, at one with the seasons, the terrain, the elements, and all other living creatures. He was wholly dependent upon " mother " nature, an integral and harmonious part of the ecosystem.

*This paper represents an abstract of material being prepared for a book entitled *Towards the New Eden: Animal Rights and Human Liberation.* Viking, New York, 1979. Ed.

This state of being and awareness is still reflected today in the philosophy and naturalistic religions of many cultures, particularly among the American Indians and more " primitive " hunting societies. Animistic beliefs characterise this state of consciousness. The reason why there has been a recent surge of interest in such a mode of consciousness (as witness the revival of Amerindian philosophy, folk tales, mythology, etc.) is not a retrograde shift in the ecology movement. Its relevance will become clear when the later stages of development of consciousness and of man's relationship with nature are discussed.

Egoic or Dominionistic Stage

As a child aged 2-3 years of age begins to develop its own individuality and regard its mother now as an entity separate from its own ego, the mother is still seen in terms of satisfying the child's needs. The perceptions and thoughts of the child in relation to its mother are still dependency-related, but the child is now the centre of its own world.

Thus, with ego-individuation, a person becomes the centre of his or her own world and the world around is regarded only in terms of satisfying/gratifying that person's wants and needs. It is at this stage that man becomes separate from " mother " nature, for better or for worse. Historically it has been for the worse, since to regard others—including people, animals, trees, rivers and natural resources—solely in terms of satisfying (or frustrating) one's own needs, has been the cause of wars, slavery, extinction of species, and the blind exploitation and destruction of nature, which is regarded solely as a resource.

The expression of this stage of human consciousness occurred in incredible synchrony in many civilisations throughout the world some 10,000 years ago when man first began to domesticate plants and animals. With one's own domesticated plants and animals, land rights and the concept of property and ownership came into being: man was no longer an inseparable part of the world; he began to claim larger parts of it for himself. Religions emerged with personified gods, and man was " given " (actually he gave himself) dominion over all the earth and over every creature, since only he was made in the image of god. Religion thus reflects accurately the stage of consciousness which in turn affected man's relationship with nature. He assumed unconditional dominion over all as the superior species with a " god " (self) given right to do as he chose, within a moral framework which concerned itself only with how man should treat other men. Eventually the interests of society and a consensus-morality controlled all : the work ethic and motives of production and profit, status, power and control (personal and national), gained absolute value. The individual ego became a collective ego (of state or nation), and with no concern for nature outside of personal interests the biosphere was incorporated into this collective ego—an egosphere, if you wish.

Constraints upon the treatment of animals and the use or abuse of nature and her " resources " were later developed from a basically egocentric view. This should not be unexpected since the world-view has shifted in this egoic stage of consciousness from the zoocentric mode of the symbiotic stage, to a wholly anthropocentric mode.

First Transitional Stage: Humanitarian and Conservationist
With the further development of the ego, however, there comes a stage where, through anthropomorphic projections, *empathy* towards animals is born. Just as one can see others in terms of satisfying one's own needs, one also perceives others in terms of how one would feel or react if one were in their place. In relationships between people, empathy can be extremely supporting, creating an ambience of care and compassion. It can also disrupt relationships, as when someone projects how they think or expect I will react or feel. It is even more likely to be off-the-mark with an animal, which cannot explain how it feels.

Because of this, and perhaps facilitated by the earlier Descartian view of animals, science at the turn of this century took a radical swing away from the inaccuracies of anthropomorphism, of interpreting the behaviour of animals in human terms.

Rational objectivity evolved, a necessary step in the evolution of human consciousness, separating human ego-projections from the perceived subject/object. We can thank science for this important contribution, but this objective detachment especially from experimental animals, evoked the wrath and concern of the diametrically opposed (in consciousness) and more subjective and empathetic humanitarians. Both sides represent opposite poles in their worldview, yet both are essential and complementary to a wholly integrated consciousness and worldview. Neither side— scientist or humanitarian—can ever resolve its differences until they both see the animal before them in its own right, independent of them themselves. (To use it as a research " tool " or to protect it from pain and suffering both represent personal value-judgments.)

There are a few other modes of thought and action in relation to this egoic stage of awareness that I must air. In the Victorian era, with its anthropomorphism and emergence of the humane movement, there was a strong interest in natural history. The naturalist, nature-poet, artist and mystic, combined in various degrees the objective curiosity of the scientist and a more subjec-tive, aesthetic and empathetic rapport with the natural world. This was no doubt accentuated by the polarising influence of industrialisation. The *naturalistic* mode of consciousness con-trasted a growing *utilitarian* regard for animals, especially farm and draught animals, based upon the already well established dominionistic view. Darwin's work on evolution was conveniently interpreted in support of dominionism and utilitarianism—man being the most highly evolved and therefore being the superior overlord. Also the struggle for existence, competition and " survival of the fittest " in nature somehow justified the competi-tive individualism of growing private industry—most highly developed in modern western multinational corporate empire " states ".

Some fields of science, involving animals, grew from the naturalistic views: thus ethology (the study of animal behaviour) and ecology today complement to some extent the new age of awareness. Animals and natural systems were studied for their own sake and not destroyed in the process. Other fields, notably " basic " and biomedical research, were derived from the dominionistic-utilitarian view, animals being regarded as useful tools, a means to an end for the interest of humans only (be it for health or scientific curiosity). Increasingly, for some, a conflict of interest arose between their values and the vested interests of a utilitarian and materialistic society. Seeing further, beyond immediate needs and short-term goals, the *conservation* movement developed, loosening mankind from his egocentric world view : egosphere must gradually be replaced by eco-consciousness, the more objective world view upon which our survival depends. Survival is an important consideration here, since it alone, as a primary concern, will not necessarily advance human consciousness. While eco-crises may force us to change our ways and be more conservative and frugal in our use of natural resources and contamination of the biosphere, the survival need may not bring with it a new set of ethics. We may, for example, conserve a river system because our own economy and/or health depends upon it, but this is still an egocentric, self-serving world view. Through this process, however, we may begin to see the river system as a part of ourselves, as is every rock, leaf and living creature on earth, and come to value it in its own right. This is the most important and critical transition stage in man's world view and in his relationship with nature.

Second Transition: Natural rights (liberationalist)

This stage is not exemplified, as some would have it, by the more militant humanitarians or radical preservationist or survivalist " whole earth " types. Nor is it evident in the arcadian, return-to-nature cult. This stage, as I see it, is in the objective, rational, transpersonal natural rights movement. The rights of natural objects—trees, rivers, mountains, ecosystems and animals, both wild and domesticated, are being thought about and gradually gaining recognition. This is a natural stage in the development of human consciousness following that of the human rights movement : slavery, racism, sexism and speciesism are all interrelated. Ego-consciousness is becoming eco-conscious, a state transitional and necessary to earthmind (see below), and this is now being implemented by a very different group of people. They are objective, but subjectively concerned and committed, i.e. rationally and emotionally well balanced; their expertise ranges from law and philosophy to ethology, veterinary medicine and clinical psychology, as well as many other diverse callings.

On a strengthening philosophical and legal basis, the natural rights movement represents the new direction that many humanitarians and conservationists are now taking. Mankind, in freeing other non-human beings from his ego-sphere, by according them rights, liberates himself from his own self-limiting mind-trap as well.

Transpersonal or Co-creative Stage: Earthmind

From the natural rights of living and non-living entities we return to the ancient philosophy of Zen Buddhism—the essence of the " thing in itself ".

A nature-ethic breaks down the humanocentric walls of our egosphere and in our salvation is the restoration of the biosphere and consequently man's actualisation and re-integration with earth as *earthmind*. This is the final stage for mankind. Man assumes the role of co-creator, working in harmony with the natural forces around him. It is a stage of integration and synthesis, of consummate stewardship where man's interests are not in opposition with the rest of creation. Rather man's needs complement those of creation, since through him creation is expressed. It is as though nature is gaining its ultimate expression through man as consciousness completes the evolutionary cycle :[89] the organic ascending to the psychic or conscious realm, the created (man) becoming at one with creation (as co-creator).

Here it may seem we are returning to the first part of this paper, namely to the symbiotic stage of man's relationship with nature. But this is not so. When man becomes fully conscious of the symbiosis (and does not exploit it selfishly and so become a parasite) his role and relationship changes. He becomes, at the same time, fully conscious of himself, and since he and nature are now one, the relationship is one of co-creator or stewardship. This apparent return to a simpler, unitive stage of relationship is the natural reflective pattern of evolution and development of

C

human consciousness, i.e. from being aware of the unity and totality of all to being fully aware.

In the formulation of a bio-spiritual ethic the objective evolutionary and ecological facts derived from science and the more subjective, intuitive and empathetic views of philosophy and religion are complementary and mutually supportive. The objective and the subjective modes are integrated; at this new level of integration human consciousness will enter a new cosmic cycle at a much higher vibration of co-creative harmony.[90]

The global crises and concerns that affect us today are to a large degree directing us along this developmental path.

In conclusion, what is needed is what is on hand, a new ethic to foster and direct man's relationship with nature and with all living creatures, human and non-human alike. Similarly C. D. Stone states that " what is needed is a mythos that can fit our growing body or knowledge of geophysics, biology, and cosmos. In this vein, I do not think it too remote that we may come to regard the earth as some have suggested, as one organism, of which mankind is a functional part—the mind perhaps." *Earthmind*.

II. Critique of the Animal Rights Movement

Richard Ryder, in his book *Victims of Science*,[91] was the first to coin the concept of " speciesism ". When applied, as by Singer in his plea for the humane or ethically responsible treatment of sentient beings, it tends to backfire as speciesism to those who have as much empathy for rocks and trees as for wolves and whales! Singer deals with only half the problem when he pleads for humane treatment of sentient beings only: non-sentient creations should be treated with no less responsible concern. While the humane imperative is relevant to our treatment of sentient beings, the ecological imperative of responsible stewardship concerns our treatment of, and relationship with, all forms of creation, both sentient and non-sentient. It is from this imperative that the ethics of *humane stewardship* can be best developed to guide and constrain humanity towards a co-creative harmony with nature. But, as I say, the animal rights issue is an important transition in our efforts to change consensus values and attitudes.

In urging a total dietary reform to vegetarianism, Singer[92] weakens his case by alienating a large segment of the establishment. They are drawn into arguing the pros and cons of vegetarianism and can lose sight of the original purpose of Singer's suggestions. In a flesh-eating culture such as ours this is to be expected. To encourage people to be conscientious omnivores/consumers would be more attractive and realistic. If the farm animals were raised well, might he then eat " happy " meat and eggs, providing the raising of such products were not ecologically and economically contraindicated? This (together with his " speciesistic " ill-definable cut-off at the level of non-sentience) weakens his position : worse, it detracts from the effectiveness of his arguments in promulgating social change. An appeal to " conscientious omnivorism " and responsible consumerism in general would be more realistic and a less radical and a more attractive option for many. While the pendulum of social change and of consciousness-raising may be activated by radical idealism, such extremism will evoke proportionate and often more powerful reactions to counter it. Singer's suggestion to eat less or no meat as a consumer boycott in protest at the way in which farm animals are kept (especially veal calves) is the kind of responsible consumerism that is needed today. So far as animal protection laws are concerned, however, farm animals have almost no rights or consideration. Laws must be created, consumers informed and provided with viable options to facilitate social change conducive to the well-being of *all* life. The fulcrum of social change ultimately rests in education, and the sciences of ecology and ethology have great potential in providing a world-view of responsible and compassionate understanding, where the place of humanity in the cosmos may be seen in its proper perspective.

Singer provides a valuable transitional point for the much needed radical mutation of human consciousness from egocentricity and anthropocentrism to eco-centricity. What is indicated is a non-discriminatory reverence for all life or all creation embracing within our scope of moral concern both sentient and non-sentient creation alike. This brings in the ecological dimension of humane stewardship and of mankind's ultimate role as co-creator, since the human mind is potentially the consummate expression of nature through consciousness : one earth, one mind, wherein human thoughts and actions are guided not by legal constraint but by an inner sense of reverence for all life and responsive compassion : eco-ethics, if you wish.

The issues of animal rights and the rights of non-sentient creations (lakes, forests, etc.) as ably discussed by Ryder, Stone and Singer, are relevant to the times, but they are issues that are themselves simply a product of the times. They are thus transitional and not ultimate goals; stepping stones for the gradual transmutation of society and consciousness, which is being accelerated positively by the self-inflicted crises of finite resources, environmental pollution and eco-catastrophes. The latter crises and the implementation of rights to non-human and non-sentient beings heralds an epoch of increasing litigation, monitoring, regulation and control. This is perhaps the future of the Aquarian age. An inner sense of ethical responsibility and moral concern has become increasingly divorced from science, technology and politics over the last few hundred years and the organisation and values of society are at variance with the basic and spiritual needs of the individual. This schism necessitates an external or legal framework to direct and constrain unethical, immoral and inhumane practices. The issue of animal rights is a part of this, and until such times as these positive external constraints become incorporated as an internalised set of ethical principles, human thought and action will have to be guided and constrained externally.

For those who do not see the relevance of animal rights to the crises of civilisation and to the future of man and earth, such legal constraints are necessary. It is unfortunate that many scientists, economists, politicians and others do not see this connection, since it represents one of the greatest blind spots of our civilisation, and, if not rectified, will aggravate the ecocidal forces of this tragic and terrifying age.

By virtue of our scientific and technological development, we are bound by necessity now to develop both conceptually and operationally a religious orientation towards the world : founded upon a biospiritual ethic, embracing a reverence for all life : Earthmind.

Aldo Leopold wrote this ethical commandment : " A thing is right when it tends to preserve the integrity, stability and beauty of the biotic community."

All political and socioeconomic systems—liberal, socialistic and conservative exploit nature with a technology that is discordant with the natural order. There is nothing wrong with technology; what is wrong is the values which underlie our use of it. The human spirit and potential will only be free when we have earned our freedom by becoming at one with earth—one earth, one mind and one body. This will not be a static equilibrium, but rather a steady state which would be the firm foundation from which humanity can harmonise co-creatively with the energies of life, of the universe.

III. Toward a Theology of Nature/Earth

God may be conceptualised as a person, the creator, and Nature as the material manifestation of His creation. This is the creationist's view. The (or at least *this*) one evolutionary viewpoint is less personal in that God is not conceptualised as a person, but as a process (of evolution/creation). Nature is thus the material manifestation of evolution.

Fundamentally there is a conceptual difference between these two views, but in the face of the ultimate reality of nature, both gnostic and agnostic, atheist and pantheist, are one in the same reality of relatedness and experience. Truth lies in our awakening to that which is manifest in the leaf, the river and the singing bird : awakening to the manifest reality of life and apprehending our relationship in life with all life.

Before such awakening and self-reflection, we remain severed from life, soul-torn from the continuum (by ego-centredness or self-preoccupation). Being severed from life is death. One appropriate Christian definition of inner death is " to be separated from God ". Salvation and " eternal life " come when one surrenders (i.e. gives up ego-centredness) to God. One then becomes God-centred.

This Christian view of inner death as being man's separation from God is based upon a strictly personalised view of God. In the transcendant non-personal view (where God is a process and not a person), this Christian definition becomes significant in relation to the crises of the modern world. Separation from nature is death. Theology and ecology converge in man's relationship with creation and nature : God is not dead (nor is nature). But man is, when separated from God/nature, because he is separated from life.

Such separation and alienation also occur when man regards nature " objectively " solely as a mechanism, as a scientifically measurable and quantifiable system. This mechanistic world view is perhaps the most dehumanising consequence of scientific investigation and technological application. (Nature is seen as a " resource ", the ocean as a non-living " system "; a sick person is a patient : all living entities become reduced to the level of mechanical processes and systems.)

As God is dead, so nature is dead in such a world view, nature being no more than a non-living material resource. This " denaturisation " of nature is mirrored in the repressive socio-economic and political forces which " dehumanise " and " deanimalise " humans and animals alike. Such a mechanistic Cartesian view of reality has sown the seeds of our own destruction.[93] The only feasible solution is to complement the positive gains of the " logos " of science and technology with a new " mythos " and reverence for all life. Both logos (the objective, rational scientific left hemisphere of our brains) and mythos (the subjective, intuitive, empathetic and mystical right cerebral hemisphere) must be harmonised. The right hemisphere has been repressed for too long in our materialistic pursuits of progress and happiness. The one-sided view of the world which prevails today can only lead to further misery, illusory progress and ultimate self-destruction.

A balance between these two hemispheres and between these two conceptual realities is needed for mankind to think and relate harmoniously with the natural world as it really is. Both logos and mythos must be integrated and constrained within an ecologically and humanely sound framework of ethical values, as distinct from those humanocentric needs and values of materialistic growth, progress, profit and power, and those quasi-spiritual excesses of mysticism, occultism and other world-negating escapist beliefs and practices.

According to Christian doctrine, in order to live again (or more correctly, to be born again and have eternal life), one must love God. Love as a state of " being in harmony " can be achieved through prayer, ritual and belief. But since God is nature, one must also love all of creation on earth and live in harmony with nature. Historically it would seem that much religious ritual and belief has separated mankind from this relationship between the " above " and the " below ". Since nature is the physical manifestation of God (or of the evolutionary process), mankind must love both : one cannot be loved to the exclusion of the other. Love as a faith without responsible action, has no place in the natural physical world. Love as action is manifest as responsible compassion for all creation, and harmony with it.

Thus, to attain " heaven on earth " and everlasting life, are not unrealistic illusions of religious faith. In a very practical earth-sense, they can be accomplished and will be, as we learn to have dominion over ourselves. From the wisdom gained from our mistakes, the world-wise already know that our only future is to be in harmony with nature. This religious promise of human fulfilment is the ecological imperative of survival. Both indirectly imply man's role of stewardship, working in harmony with nature, and with the forces of creation contained within the limitations of natural order. To love God in this way, is, practically speaking, an ecological imperative, since our future depends on it.

Historically a humanity that is drawn close to God becomes more and more removed from nature. A theology of nature/earth places humanity in balance as interlocutor, for God, man and nature are one and inseparable.

A theology of earth, a belief system based upon the laws of nature, can give us the key to dominion over ourselves; it constrains our actions so as to promote harmony in our relationships with all life : not just with human life. We slowly learn that all life is a divine celebration and an expression of eternity. We also begin to sense what it is to be immortal, to have everlasting life : that sense of eternity within the soul is part of the continuum of life, of evolution.

The earth is our church within which we respect all life equally. Heaven is on earth and we can rejoice in the leaf, the river and the singing bird. . . .

Section Three

PHILOSOPHICAL PERSPECTIVES

The Darwinist's Dilemma

BRIGID BROPHY

Long, long ago, in 1965, the *Sunday Times* invited me to write a full-page article on a subject of my own choice. I did so and I gave the article a title, " The Rights of Animals ", which I now see, with pleasure, has been attached to this symposium.

For my part, I picked the title by deliberate analogy with—or, more precisely and more pointedly, by deliberate extrapolation from—the title of Thomas Paine's book (of 1791 and 1792) *The Rights of Man.*

In other words, yes, I was deliberately associating the case for non-human animals with that clutch of egalitarian or libertarian ideas which have sporadically, though quite often with impressively actual political results, come to the rescue of other oppressed classes, such as slaves or homosexuals or women. I implied that the high barrier we have put up between the human species and all the rest of the animal species, the barrier to which Richard Ryder presently gave the very useful name of " speciesism ", was essentially a class barrier, unjustifiable by reason and kept in place by the superstition and self-interest of those who were on the privileged side of it.

To the impulse towards egalitarianism and social justice I ascribe no historical or political coherency, and still less any historical inevitability. If there *is* anything so coherent as a movement, it has made such huge detours that you could often think it was moving backwards.

All the same, I think one can detect some coherency and even a sort of inevitability in some such progression in at least some people's private histories, the histories of their thoughts.

So far as I can tell, the original class distinction (original, that is, in each individual's experience) is the tremendous gulf between Me and All the Rest of You; any difference I see between You and You is tiny compared with the enormous difference between Me and All Other, a difference I experience in the fact that if I bump you on the head, whether You are in this case animate or a lump of stone, I merely observe the result, whereas if I get bumped on the head the universe, my universe, is totally occupied by an actual, vivid and very unpleasant sensation.

Presently, however, there arises in most of us (perhaps not in psychopaths) a faculty of imagination (I can only label, not describe it), which informs Me that to you, You are a Me. It is this faculty, with its ability to inhabit the other side of the barrier, that knocks the class barrier down. It can never rid me of my egocentric vision. But it persuades me that if I want to make a just appraisal of reality (and I do want to; it's not a virtue; I can't help it) then I must perform a series of intellectual adjustments to discount the distorting effect of the particular point of view from which I am obliged to observe reality.

My pain in the head remains more vivid to me than your pain in the head, but if I adjust for this I have to perceive that your hitting me and my hitting you are acts in exactly the same class; I can't deplore the one without deploring the other; I have weighed them in a balance as accurate as I can make it, found them equally bad, and have thereby set irreversibly out towards social justice.

To my mind, therefore, there was both a logical and a psychological inevitability in basing the claim for the other animals' rights on social justice. I thought there was enough motive force to carry the claim in the fact that we do, for whatever reason, want to appreciate the real world correctly. That is a force that has led people, from time to time, to make considerable and often uncomfortable intellectual adjustments in order to correct for distortions in their own vision. Some humans used to assume that the planet from which we observe the universe must be the centre of the universe—a slight to the sun, which was no doubt well able to bear it, and the source of a distortion in our knowledge of reality which we have now, not without reluctance, corrected for.

I thought that readers of the *Sunday Times*, most of whom I expected to be living in an ex-empire, would have some historical awareness, probably reaching into their own personal intellectual histories, of a long, if spasmodic, series of similar intellectual adjustments which corrected not mere slights to things well able to bear them but actual oppressions of people not able to : I mean the series of corrections to our own vision whereby bit by bit we have withdrawn from the conviction that the centre of the civilised universe is necessarily a white, male, heterosexual Christian with a classical (i.e. western) education and that the people on the periphery, if that is the centre you look from, are the coolie class, to be exploited and kept in their places.

I invoked *The Rights of Man* because it is classically associated with two Revolutions, the French and the American, which were the occasions of quite convulsive adjustment to our vision to correct for the distortions introduced by the class barriers of feudalism and empire.

I invoked *rights*, because rights are a matter of respect and justice, which are constant and can be required of you by force of argument; they are not matters of love, which is capricious and quite involuntary. We are all indebted to Dr. Stephen Clark for translating the term " animal lover " into " zoophile ". The full smeary implications of " animal lover " are clear if you compare " nigger lover ", a term that used to be flung at pink people who respected black rights. But even Dr. Clark has been able only to re-clothe us in the decencies of a learned language. I wish there had been a readily-understood Greek suffix that would imply that I respect animals instead of that I'm fond of them. As it happens, I *am* fond of most individuals of most animal species I meet, though since I lead a sedentary urban life it's fairly easy for me to avoid meeting the ones I'm likely not to like. But I trust that my refusal to harm them wantonly is independent of whether I like them or not, just as I trust that your refusal to do the same to me, even if you were sure of getting away with it, is independent of whether you like me—and, indeed, of whether you think you would like the flavour of me roasted.

To me, then, it all looked—and indeed it still looks—straightforward. Once my imagination has embarked me (and it has, and I can't go back on it) on a course of thoughts making for social justice, it inevitably carries me crashing through the class barriers, including speciesism, which may be the last barrier to fall or at least one of the last. What the movement against speciesism asks, in the light of the theory of Evolution, is that the present high barrier between the human and the other animal species should be displaced and re-erected between the animal kingdom and the vegetable kingdom (though evolutionists will expect there to be a no-man's-land at the border). A millennium from now, there may well be a symposium on the rights of plants. Humans may be working out techniques whereby we could, for instance, derive our food exclusively from fruits, which display as it were a biological acquiescence about falling off into the hands of grasping animals like ourselves. Plants are individuals, they are sensitive, and they certainly demonstrate an instinctual will to live—that is, they assert in instinctual terms a right to live. But their sensibility and individuality are not carried on by means of a central nervous system, and at the moment that is a place where our knowledge stops and seems to be an intellectually respectable place for our imaginations (at least in practice) to stop.

When I make a central (or at least some sort of organised) nervous system the sticking point, I am not of course making pain the sole delimiting factor of an animal's rights, including a human animal's rights. I do not for an instant admit your right to kill me provided you do it by creeping up on me and contriving not to give me pain or fear. I think what I think is that, providing it isn't threatening our life, we have no right to extinguish an individuality that has been formed by negotiating the world by the agency of a nervous system.

I should add, by the way, that if I have become permanently incapable of pursuing my individuality by the usual agencies you will do me (or what remains of me) a kindness if you extinguish me. Euthanasia is the sole instance in which we behave better to the other animals than to our own species.

In all this straightforwardness, as it seems to me, there is a small hiccup. I have called it, in my title for this afternoon, "The Darwinist's Dilemma", but that may be too grand a name : it may be merely a Darwinist's conundrum.

The conundrum goes like this. If we abolish the barrier between humans and the other animal species, what we institute is a sort of egalitarianism between all the species of the animal kingdom. The term " higher animals ", which used to be applied not, where it would have been quite sensible, to giraffes but to the primates and some of the other large mammals, turns out to be another distortion induced by our anthropocentric point of view : by " higher " we just meant " more like us ". Even if we can show that some animals have a more complex physiological organisation than others, we haven't, I think, hit on any really justified sense for " lower " and " higher ", especially since we increasingly find out that some of the apparently simpler animals may be extremely complex in the organisation of their ecological relationships or, as in the case of some of the insects, their social relationships.

We are left recognising that some species are, of course, closer kin to us than others. We may be able to tell that some are better adapted than others to their particular environmental niche. (How much longer *we* shall be able to go on claiming to be well adapted to ours seems in doubt.) By and large we no longer see a hierarchy of animal species but only different types and different degrees of specialisation, including specialisation in flexibility. When I spoke just now of " the animal kingdom ", I was being old fashioned. I should have said " the Animal Federal Republic ".

I used to be confident that I was, by virtue of my species, at least more intelligent than, say, a pigeon. But (especially since I began giving peanuts regularly to a group of pigeons outside my kitchen window) I have realised that, from an intelligence test that had been set by a pigeon, I should emerge as a simpleton. True, I might want to disparage the very idea of an intelligence test, which I do not think would cross a pigeon's mind. I can argue that that shows a higher organisation of intellectual curiosity in me than in pigeons. Even so it is, of course, higher only in terms of my logic, which I have by cultural transmission from Aristotle, not in terms of pigeon logic. I contemplate my visiting pigeons and I see that, at least if I've given them enough peanuts, they show not a sign of being driven by the puritan work ethic; they sit on their branch completely, so far as I can detect, unanxious about whether they are frittering away their lives; and I am obliged to concede that, if intelligence includes wisdom (and heaven help us all if it doesn't), I may well be infinitely less intelligent than even the stupidest pigeon.

However, when I feed the pigeons, I shut my cat out of the room. This is a small infringement of his rights, imposed on him by me by main force. I think it justified, in the interest of the pigeons' rights, because if I didn't he would surely have one of my plump, peanut-fed pigeons for his lunch.

If I lunched on a pigeon, I should think myself immoral. If you do so, I must in honesty say I think you immoral. But I don't think my cat immoral. I think him amoral. The whole dimension of morality doesn't apply to him, or scarcely applies to him.

Here then is the conundrum. Am I setting up my species as morally superior to the cat species? Am I condescending to my cat? Have I torn down the old class barrier only to rebuild it in moral terms?

If I have, I don't think, incidentally, that I have done ill. The old concept of human superiority used to say " We have a more highly organised technical intelligence than any other animals and this justifies us in inflicting on any animal any atrocity our techniques can devise in pursuit of our superior intellectual curiosity or even in pursuit of mere intellectual relaxation." If I now consider myself morally superior to my cat, this at least obliges me to offer him a much gentler message, and it is : " precisely because I am morally superior to you, I shall not treat either you or a pigeon as unkindly as you treat pigeons."

When one is talking about domesticated cats and semi-domesticated pigeons, this is, as I said, merely a conundrum. When one talks about untouched jungle, perhaps the answer is simple : the jungle is the amoral world of the other animals, and our only moral obligation to it is to keep out. This in itself implies that we have already moved in on enough of the earth's surface to serve our own needs; and in fact there isn't much untouched jungle left. We have interfered, often importing havoc, and we now sometimes feel a responsibility to redress some of the damage we have done. At this point, writ large, the conundrum becomes a genuine moral problem which asks "Are we humans justified in intervening to save, for example, tigers from the extinction that now threatens them as a species, given that the preservation of one individual tiger necessarily means the premature extinction of a large number of harmless, vegetarian, ruminant individuals whom the tiger will inevitably prey on?"

Apart from this dilemma, to which I do not know the solution, the matter this symposium is discussing still looks straightforward to me. However, I must now say that there are people to whom, I believe, it looks perhaps equally straightforward but quite, quite different. Where I proceed, like a hurdler, over one class barrier after another towards, I think, social justice, they leap at once to an intense love for all living things and an intense personal relationship to some god or other numinous entity. Instead of devising moral scales, they consult holy writ. Often they believe this delivers them from the subjectivism and proneness to error of making one's own judgments, though of course it doesn't, since they have to take it on themselves to judge which writ *is* the holy one. If there are any rational, secularist zoophiles or opponents of speciesism within earshot today, I want to be overheard saying this: we are engaged in the revolutionary enterprise of demolishing a class barrier; many of the normal mechanisms for changing things are denied us, but two are not, namely forming a popular front and raising the political consciousness of the citizens (which in this case means raising consciousness of the fact that animals are individuals and have rights); and in our struggle there are real lives to be saved.

According to Malvolio, it was the opinion of Pythagoras that the soul of our grandam might inhabit a wild fowl. I think and shall continue to say that I think that that opinion is a delusion. But if that is your reason for not shooting wild fowl, that is at least one palpable wild fowl saved, you and I are allies, and we have won a victory. It is important that those of us who think they know better should not cut themselves off from those who do well.

Among those who do well my first obeisance must be to Lady Dowding. Lady Dowding is the person who has provided practical alternatives to conniving at atrocities. She has brought into being an organisation for providing alternative cosmetics and alternative clothes. She has brought into being a fund for financing non-atrocity experimentation, thereby providing an alternative to the huge quantities of private and state capital that exert such a pull towards the perpetuation of atrocities. She is not the only but the main engine that drives the National Anti-Vivisection Society about its patient work of identifying and harnessing zoophiles among the people who possess actual political power and influence, and its patient and horrifying task of monitoring the atrocities of humans and their hypocrisies, like the recent hypocrisy of Amnesty, which pursued its campaign against torture by applying, albeit under anaesthetic, the mechanisms of torture to pigs.

Some of Lady Dowding's beliefs are, in my eyes, airy fairy. She probably thinks mine, though she is too nice to make a point of it, crassly materialist. But I do not want to leave it unremarked that in the material, practical, down-to-earth, workaday world Lady Dowding has done a hundred times more actual good than I have achieved with what you might call my airy fairy materialism.

I want also, for the same reason, to praise some people of a very different type, the freedom fighters of the animal movement. Here I must adduce a novel by Maureen Duffy called, after Chekov, *I Want to Go to Moscow*. I do so without shame, despite the fact that Maureen Duffy is a friend and colleague of mine; I would like in any case to commend to you a fine work of the imagination that is also a very exciting quasi-thriller; but its particular relevance is that, having been published in 1973, it proved to have anticipated, in the way art tends to do, several events that later really happened.

This it achieved not through clairvoyance but because it

follows out, in artistic terms, the logic of a problem that vexes many minds, including mine, namely whether it is good to break bad laws. Socrates went to his death in obedience to the laws, on the argument that, in a democracy, you are free to try to persuade your fellow citizens to change the laws, and if you fail to persuade them then you must obey the laws as they are, even if it costs you your life. However, Socrates was dicing only with his own life. The moral question bites even harder when it is other lives that are in question. If you can say that some orders are so bad that a soldier can't be excused for executing them on the grounds that he was only obeying orders, then it may be that there are some laws so bad that one has a positive moral obligation to break them. Obviously I am thinking of the laws imposed on Occupied Europe during the 1939–45 war that obliged gentiles to turn in escaped Jews to the authorities; or the North American laws during the last century that said you must return a runaway slave to the man who considered the slave his property; or the present law of this land that says you must not steal a dog from (or if you do steal, you must give back to) the man who considers the dog his property and proposes to experiment on him.

For my own law-abiding conduct I can produce several rationalisations, some of which may even be true, to the effect that I have other responsibilities as well or that perhaps I can be more useful from behind my façade of being a respectable person. But I suspect that the crucial reason why I am not in prison at this moment is that I am a coward. The argument I take most seriously is that, if one breaks a bad law, one has given tacit moral approval to other people who may break good laws (which they of course will see as bad); and perhaps one is giving not only tacit moral approval but actual incitement, a thing one should be very very careful about doing if the beings one is trying to protect are hostages or are so vulnerable that they can easily become victims in the hands of the people one may be provoking. Even, however, if one is finally convinced by that argument, it behoves a coward like me to remember constantly that the pro-animal movement has its front line, as well as its think-tanks and secretariats and supply lines, and that at the front line animal lives are saved and human freedoms are, very bravely, risked.

One must always beware of drawing statistical conclusions from too small a sample. What I want to say next (and last) may well be subject to a distortion in my vision resulting from the accidents of my personal point of observation. When I became a vegetarian I don't think I had knowingly ever met a fellow vegetarian. My husband was a carnivore and our daughter was brought up a carnivore : not because I lack the conviction to try to convert others to my convictions but because I am scrupulous about exerting emotional blackmail on the people, who number very few, over whom I have the power to do so. Now my daughter is a vegetarian, not through my influence, and my husband is a vegetarian, partly through the influence of our now grown-up daughter, who had few scruples about exerting emotional blackmail; and I have several vegetarian friends among my fellow writers (Maureen Duffy, David Fletcher, Shena Mackay, Patricia Highsmith, Colin Spencer), all of whom I met not through the pro-animal movement but in what appears to be a statistically neutral way, namely through the exercise of our common profession of literature. It may not be genuinely neutral, of course, because literature tends to attract imaginative people. Yet even when I have made a few corrections of that kind, it still appears to me that, since, for example, 1965, when I wrote an article on the rights of animals (which I didn't by the way, call " The Rights of Non-Human Animals " because to me there is a necessary continuity between the rights of all animals, as animals, including human animals in with the others), we have begun to assemble the wavery outline of a popular front composed of rationalists, spiritualists and freedom fighters, and we are in a position to offer ourselves and each other a very small amount of encouragement, perhaps in the words, again from Chekov in translation, that Maureen Duffy made the epigraph of one section of *I Want to Go to Moscow* : ". . . later on, others like you will come, perhaps six of them, then twelve, and so on, until at last your sort will be in a majority."

Exploring the Idea of
Animal Rights[94]

TOM REGAN

Not all of the people involved in the humane movement are always free of the human tendency to exaggerate, to oversimplify, to substitute catchy slogans for hard thought. This can be embarrassing. Doubtless we have all had the experience of wishing that one of our allies in the movement would shut up, since all that's coming over is nonsense, which is painful to endure. What is even more embarrassing and painful is when we realise that we're the ones from whence the nonsense is issuing! Worse, this sort of performance can be counterproductive. Careless thought and blundering logic will intensify the prevailing disposition not to take what we say and stand for seriously. Our ineptitude can contribute to increasing the very things we are intent upon diminishing.

We must realise that some people will find in our speaking of a subject such as the rights of animals all the evidence they need to convict us of absurdity. Only people can have rights and animals aren't people. So, the more we speak, in a serious way, of animal rights, the more they will see us as supposing that animals are people; and since it is absurd to suppose that animals are people, it's equally absurd to think that animals have rights. That, for many, is the end of it.

Let us be honest with ourselves. There is little chance of altering the mental set of those wedded to thinking in this way. If they are content simply to spout their slogans ("Only people have rights!") as a substitute for hard thinking, we will fail to change their minds by spouting ours or by asking them to look beneath the words to the ideas themselves.

But give us inquisitive minds and then we can try to make our case, mindful that, in their presence, the burdens of logic, of fact, of intellectual and moral honesty must dutifully be borne, and this in a good spirit. For their minds *can* be changed if only we can find the intellectual wherewithal to change them. *This* is our challenge. In what follows I try to meet this challenge so far as I am presently able.

I shall start with our belief that we have duties to animals. Reflection that starts with this generally held belief can direct us to the less generally accepted view that we have as much reason to believe that they have certain rights as we have to believe that certain humans have them.

I doubt very much that anyone thinks that how animals are treated is a matter of complete moral indifference. I think all would agree, for example, that it is wrong to be needlessly cruel to an animal. Philosophically, the interesting question is not whether we think this, but why.

I call the view I am about to examine " the Kantian account ", not because Kant is the only one who holds the position,[95] but because Kant's statement of it is a particularly clear one. He holds that our duties with respect to animals are based on considerations of our duties to human beings. Apart from its effects upon how humans treat other humans, there is, Kant implies, nothing wrong with being cruel to an animal. What makes this and kindred actions wrong is that such behaviour spills over into how we treat one another. " He who is cruel to animals," Kant writes,[96] " becomes hard also in his dealings with men," whereas " tender feelings towards dumb creatures develop humane feelings towards mankind."[97] Despite well known exceptions (some Nazis practised great kindness to animals) Kant's general psychological point may be right : people who are sensitive to the needs of animals may tend to be more sensitive to the needs of humans, and those who are insensitive to the former may tend to be insensitive to the latter. The point is certainly arguable, and some celebrated anti-vivisectionists—George Bernard Shaw, for example—would seem to rest their unqualified opposition to the use of animals in research on a position like

Kant's in all relevant aspects. "We must," Shaw writes,[98] "apply the test of character, and ask ourselves not merely, "What will happen if I do this particular (experiment)?" but "What sort of man shall I be if I do it?" In Shaw's view, as in Kant's, the willingness to be cruel to animals bespeaks a lack of humaneness on the part of the agent (though Shaw and Kant may, and probably do, differ as to whether it is necessarily cruel to use animals in painful experiments). Whether it is true or not that a lack of humaneness towards animals leads inevitably, or tends to lead, to a lack of humaneness in one's dealings with humans, however, we need to ask whether the Kantian account provides us with an adequate explanation of why we think it is wrong to cause animals to suffer needlessly.

I do not think it does. If we see a man administering a savage beating to a dog, we think it is wrong, and if we intercede we intercede on the dog's behalf, not on behalf of humanity. As W. D. Ross observes,[99] "if we think we ought to behave in a certain way to animals, it is out of consideration primarily for *their* feelings that we think we ought to behave so; we do not think of them merely as a practising-ground for virtue."

Suppose we adopt Kant's terminology. Then we can say that, in rejecting his account of our negative duty not to cause animals to suffer non-trivial pain, we are rejecting the idea that this duty is an indirect one; and we can also say that, when we affirm our belief that it is wrong to do this to an animal because of how the animal is treated, we are subscribing to the view that our duty here is a direct negative duty.

Acceptance of the view that at least some of our duties to animals are direct ones has important implications for the inquiry into whether animals have rights. On the one hand it can help us to see why some arguments against the position that animals have rights are defective; on the other, it can help us see an important reason for believing that they do have certain rights.

Animals, it has been alleged,[100] at least when it comes to the question of their possibly possessing rights, are in the same general category as such things as precious paintings and great works of architecture. People generally are agreed that we do have duties with regard to these and, in particular, that we have a duty to preserve them, to keep them intact and as close to their original state as possible. The basis of this duty resides, some think, in the effects that preserving or failing to preserve them will have for present and future generations of human beings. Thus, the duty we have regarding these paintings and structures is an indirect one, in Kant's sense of the term; and since our duty in this regard is not to the paintings or structures themselves, it is patently fallacious, it is averred, to reason that they (the paintings and structures), have, of themselves, a right to be preserved. If there is a right that is correlative with this duty, it is the present and future generations of human beings who have it, not the paintings and structures.

Suppose we grant this argument.[101] We can then still see why a facsimile of it cannot be applied in the case of animals, since we accept the view that at least some of our duties to animals *are* direct.

The whole question of a connection between duties and rights, in particular of when we can infer that a particular individual has a right against us from the fact that we have a duty to the sort of being that he is, and vice versa—this question of correlativity is an important albeit an obscure one. That there are duties which have correlative rights seems to be clear enough. Correlated with my duty not to kill people, for example, is your right against me not to kill you. What is unclear is whether my duty *implies* your right, or vice versa. If it does, one would think that we would be able to specify some general principle by reference to which we could determine when duties *do* imply correlative rights and when they do not—and vice versa. For not all duties, not even all direct ones it seems, can plausibly be thought to have this implication. Theoretically, our problem is to say what this principle is.

Now, perhaps there is such a principle. Perhaps, indeed, someone already has discovered what it is. Here I must confess my own ignorance: I simply do not know what this principle is. What I plan to do is point out that, at least in the case of some of our direct duties to one another, *we think* there are correlative rights; for example, *we think* that

(a) I have a direct duty not to kill people, and that

(b) you have a right against me not to kill you.

For our purposes it is enough that we think what we think.

Now one thing we think is that we have a direct negative duty not to cause one another non-trivial pain, pain that is intense, perhaps prolonged or incapacitating. And we also think, whether it is implied by this duty or not, that we have a correlative right —the negative right, as such rights sometimes are called—not to be made to suffer non-trivial pain by our fellow man. Earlier, however, we agreed that our duty not to cause animals non-trivial pain is a direct duty, a duty which we have *to them*. And the question I want to pose is this : If we think our duty to animals not to cause them non-trivial pain is, like our corresponding duty to humans, a direct duty; and if we think that, correlative with this duty of ours to human beings, humans have the *right* not to be caused non-trivial pain; then how can we rationally not think that, correlative with our duty not to cause animals non-trivial pain, there is the right of animals not to be caused non-trivial pain? As you might suspect, I do not see how we can rationally avoid thinking this. But since I am intentionally foregoing talk about duties " implying " rights, I cannot rest my belief here on this.

What I shall argue, therefore, is that, in the absence of any relevant difference, we must agree that animals do have the right in question : they have the right not to be made to suffer non-trivial pain since we believe (as I think we do) that all humans who might have this right do, in fact, have it.

Not all philosophers would agree. Even among those who, unlike Kant but like us, think that we have a direct duty not to cause animals non-trivial pain, there are some who think it is rationally possible to deny that animals have a correlative right whilst still affirming that humans do. A variety of reasons have been offered in support of this position, though obviously not all of them can be considered here.

Ross, for instance, would have us believe that we do have a

direct duty to animals not to cause them non-trivial pain but that they do not have a correlative right. At least they " probably " do not. He writes:[102]

> On the whole, since we mean by a right something that can be justly claimed, we should probably say that animals have not rights, not because the claim to humane treatment would not be just if it were made, but because they cannot make it.

Here Ross seems to commit himself to a general proposition to the effect that beings who cannot make the claim not to be treated in a certain way do not have the right not to be treated in this way. The case of animals must be understood as being a special application of this principle: " Since they cannot make such claims, they ' have not rights '."

How adequate is this basis for denying rights to animals? Certainly there are many *human* beings who, because of various mental or emotional incapacities, are themselves unable to understand what their rights are or to claim them. Now given their incapacity to claim them, they would, on Ross' account, not (or " probably " would not) *have* rights. Yet this surely is a concession which we would not wish to make. A small baby or a mentally defective adult lacks the ability to claim the right not to be made to suffer non-trivial pain, but we do not suppose that they therefore do not have this right at all! If, however, this is so, then the ability to make claims cannot be supposed to be a necessary condition of having rights, which implies that, contrary to Ross, the inability of animals to make claims cannot be an adequate basis from which to infer that they do not or even that they " probably do not " have rights.

A similar result emerges if we examine another of Ross' ideas. This is the view, which is by no means unique to him,[103] that it is only moral agents, beings who have the capacity to distinguish right from wrong and who are therefore fit objects of moral praise or blame, who can have rights. But, again, there are many human beings—for example, those who are severely mentally defective and those who are severely psychologically disorientated —who do not qualify as " moral agents " in Ross' sense. As such, these human beings would not be supposed to have any rights. Yet one of our tasks in thinking about rights is surely to make it clear how it is possible for such beings to have the rights which we think they have; not to devise theories which imply that they lack them. Ross is correct in thinking that only moral agents can have *duties*, including the duty to respect the rights of others. This is why we cannot meaningfully speak of an infant or an animal as having duties to us, or as having respected or failed to respect our rights. But Ross is not correct, if the preceding is sound, in supposing that only moral agents can have *rights*.

Our misgivings with Ross' views point to a kind of deficiency to be found in many others. By setting conditions for inclusion in the class of beings who have rights as high as he does—by requiring, for example, that one be a " moral agent "—Ross may well succeed in excluding animals without denying that we have direct duties to them, *but* he does so at the price of excluding many human beings as well.

The demand that we pay this price is similarly implied by many other theories about what sorts of beings do or can have rights—for example, that, in order to possess rights, a being must be rational, or be able to speak, or have a concept of its " self ". In the case of these and kindred theories we *may*[104] be able to exclude animals from the class of beings who possess rights : but we would also exclude many human beings from this class, and that is what makes all such efforts to exclude animals the unsatisfactory theories that they are.

An alternative to this type of approach to the question of right-possession, and one that attempts to account for how even infants and severely mentally-enfeebled humans have basic moral rights while denying that any non-human animals do, is one that holds that *all and only* those beings which belong to a species whose normal, mature members typically have certain capacities— namely rationality and autonomy—can and do have rights. Since normal, mature members of any terrestrial species other than homo sapiens happen typically not to have these capacities, it follows that no non-human animals satisfy the requirements for right-possession.[105]

There are various problems any theory of this type must encounter,[106] but only one will be mentioned here. We begin by noting that we can imagine that a minority, and these the exceptional, not the normal members of some extraterrestrial species happen to be both rational and autonomous. These beings, however, fail to have basic moral rights, given the theory just characterised, not because *they* lack some capacity or other, but because they happen not to belong to a species whose normal, mature members typically have the capacities which these individuals happen to have. Such theories seem to me to be little more than a prejudice masquerading as a principle, one not unlike, in some if not in all respects, racism and sexism, the very embodiment of the "speciesism" that both Richard Ryder[107] and Peter Singer[108] have tried to unmask for what it is. What is typically true of the normal adult members of one's species seems to be as irrelevant to the question of what beings can or do possess rights as what colour one's skin is or what sex one happens to be.

But if both speciesist and Ross-type theories fail, how might some other type of theory succeed? What is wanted is clear enough : namely, a condition or set of conditions that can be met by *all* those human beings to whom we wish to ascribe the right in question. Our problem is to say what this condition is or what such conditions are. I would suggest that it is the capacity to experience pain, and not requirements to do with rationality or moral agency, that provides a logically necessary and sufficient condition for a being's possessing the right not to be made to suffer non-trivial pain. This enables us to ascribe this right to infants, severely mentally defectives, schizophrenics and the like, provided only that they have the capacity to experience non-trivial pain. Now since we do think that these beings do have this capacity; and since we also think that they have the right in question; and since there does not appear to be any other relevant consideration that could be thought to underlie possession of this right; it seems that a human's capacity to experience non-trivial pain *is* a necessary and sufficient condition for his or her possessing the right not to be caused such pain.

By adopting this principle we commit ourselves to the view

that, in the absence of any relevant difference between humans and animals, we have as much reason to believe that those animals who can feel non-trivial pain do possess the right in question as we have for believing this in the case of human beings. True, there may be some entities which are classified as " animals " who lack the capacity to feel non-trivial pain, and these entities will differ from human beings in a morally relevant way, one that permits us to deny that they have the right in question whilst affirming that we do. It is also true that there will be many cases where it will not be possible to say with confidence either that the members of a particular species of animal do or that they do not have this capacity. But that there are literally thousands of species of animals whose members *do* have this capacity is a datum of experience, and one which moral and other varieties of philosophy must endeavour to explicate rather than obliterate. Thus it is that, if the basis for ascribing the right in question to humans is the one I have set forth, then, in the absence of any relevant difference, we must ascribe this same right to those many thousands of non-humans who satisfy it.

But even if it is true that we have as much reason to ascribe the right in question to these animals as we have for ascribing it to humans, it still remains to be asked what there is about non-trivial pain that leads us to think of a *right* not to be made to experience it.

My answer to this question, sketchy though it is,[109] is as follows. While we allow that being made to suffer some pain, even some that is non-trivial, may in certain cases contribute to our good or well being, we recognise the fact that this normally is not so, that normally the experience of non-trivial pain has a negative effect on our well-being. Our belief that we have the right not to be made to suffer non-trivial pain needs to be seen within the wider context of our belief that we have a right to pursue our well-being, our happiness. Our right not to be made to experience non-trivial pain, in other words, appears to be a derivative right, a right that, together with other, non-evaluative premises, can be derived from premises wherein we assert the more fundamental right to pursue our own good.

All of which is to say that if animals also have the derivative right in question, we should expect them to have the more fundamental one as well—the right to pursue *their* good. Clearly, too, we can make sense of their possessing it. Through their behaviour animals provide us with innumerable instances of goal-directed behaviour as well as instances where, on analogy with human behaviour, they behave in ways which exhibit preferences. The good or well-being of an animal is to be understood in terms of the integrated satisfaction of its desires, wants, needs and the like, and hence both the idea that they can pursue their good and the idea that they have a good to pursue can be made intelligible. With this we see that we can give the same kind of account as to how it is that animals possess the right not to be made to experience non-trivial pain as we can in the case of a human being's possession of it : in both cases the right is derivative, and in both the right can be derived from the more basic right of a being to pursue its own good.

This, then, is one thing we are helped to see by the attempt to place our right not to be made to suffer non-trivial pain in a wider context. But a second point which should be made is this : that there may be *other* rights than just this one that can be derived from the more basic right of a creature who can pursue its own good to do so. Indeed, I think there *are* other rights which can be derived in this way. Our right not to be grossly restricted in our ability to move about as we wish seems to be of this kind. Ordinarily to be so confined that I am unable to move my body as I will prevents me from pursuing my good. Thus, my right to freedom of movement, as this right might be called, is derivable in the same way as is my right not to be made to suffer non-trivial pain. But if what underlies my belief that I have the right to move about as I will is (a) my belief that I have the right to pursue my good and (b) the fact that being grossly restricted in my freedom of movement ordinarily prevents me from so pursuing it, then, in the absence of any relevant difference, I do not see how I can avoid attributing this same right to other beings who have a right to pursue their good *and* whose pursuit of their good is adversely affected by being grossly restricted in their ability to move about as they will. Thus, for example, I do not see how I cannot ascribe this right to animals—for they are in the same position, relative to the possession of this right, as are you and I.

There are other rights which are derivable from the right to pursue one's good in addition to the right of freedom of movement and to be spared unnecessary pain. Even our right to life seems to me to be among these, though I know this may be controversial. But at least in my own case I believe that were I to become so physically or mentally impaired as to lose all realistic chance of ever being able to pursue my good—if, for example, I were to become a " vegetable "—then I for one would want it known that I no longer thought that I had a right to go on living. I believe, in other words, that whatever claim I have upon others to permit me to go on living is derivable from the more basic claim I have upon them to permit me to pursue my own good.

There is also a host of other ideas that need further attention. I cannot address myself to all of them. But there are three I would like to spend a moment with, not with an eye to advancing my argument but with a view to clarifying it. After I have done this I shall try to explain why thinking of animals as having certain rights is important, not only theoretically but practically.

Firstly, I trust it is clear that I have not endeavoured to *prove* either that humans or animals have any rights. My argument, as I indicated earlier, assumes that we think that humans have certain rights and then proceeds to ask what reasons we can have for thinking so. I have examined what these reasons are and have tried to indicate why I think we have as much reason to ascribe certain rights to animals as we have for ascribing them to humans. Nowhere, however, have I endeavoured to prove that humans or animals *do* possess these rights.

Secondly, I hope it is clear that I do not suppose that I have given a general theory either about what rights are *or* about what sorts of beings can have them. In particular, I hope it is clear that I have not advanced the view that the *only* beings which can have rights are those beings which are sentient.

Personally, I do not detect anything contradictory in the idea that beings which, by their very nature, are non-sentient, beings such as trees and flowers at least appear to be, may nonetheless have rights. Perhaps they do not, but that they do not is not something that can be established by claiming that the idea that they do is " inconceivable " or " meaningless ". I have addressed myself to this matter in more detail elsewhere.[110] Here I mention it only to clarify what I have tried to argue so far.

Thirdly, it will not have gone unnoticed that my arguments for ascribing the rights I have mentioned to animals always carry the rider, " in the absence of any relevant difference ". This is a troublesome idea, and I wish I could take more time than is available to discuss it. Here I shall say just two things : first, that of course there are many differences that exist between humans and those animals which are sentient. But, second, I personally cannot think of any difference which could plausibly be thought to permit us to ascribe the rights I have mentioned to all those human beings to whom we wish to ascribe them, and to rule out our ascribing them to some non-human animals. The ability to reason, to know the difference between right and wrong, to have a concept of one's self, these will not do the job. For quite apart from the fact that there may be some non-humans who would satisfy these requirements, it seems clear that not all those humans to whom we wish to ascribe the rights in question do. And if not all these humans do, then none of these requirements can establish morally relevant differences between all humans and all animals.

Now, there are not a few other important issues that arise in the present context, issues which, in a larger undertaking, could receive the attention they deserve. I hope it is understood why I cannot give them this attention here. Instead, let me go on to explain, as I said I would, why our thinking of animals as having rights is important, and why thinkers so noteworthy and important for the humane movement as Henry Salt and John Galsworthy, both of whom relegate the question of whether animals have rights to the status of a merely " academic " matter,[111] and, more recently, Peter Singer who says that all that needs to be said about our moral relationship to animals can be said without thinking of animals as having rights[112]—permit me to say why I think these eminently able thinkers have misperceived the actual situation.

To justify attributing rights to animals is important because it provides us with the necessary basis for extending the range of our duties to animals. This can be best understood by first considering cases that involve the maltreatment of human beings who are themselves incapable of claiming their rights—for example, humans who are severely mentally incompetent. Suppose we imagine that such beings are made to serve as subjects in extremely painful research, research which does not benefit them personally, and research the results of which, by any objective reckoning, promise to be quite trivial. Then I think we would say not only that the persons doing the research were failing to fulfil their duty to these human beings, but that we, who are not involved in the research, have a duty to do all that we can to see that it is brought to an end. And if we were asked why we thought this, I believe we would cite the fact that the humans have a right not to be made to suffer non-trivial pain *and* that this right of theirs is being unjustifiably overridden in this case.

Perhaps someone will say, like Singer, that it is not essential to invoke the idea of rights, even in the human case. It is enough if research causes more evil, in the form of pain, than the good it promises. But that this would not do justice to what we think is clear if we think about the following type of case. Suppose the research just as painful, only now suppose it promises to bring about a slightly greater amount of good for others than the evil of the subjects' pain. Still we would think the research wrong, and still we would think we had a duty to do all that we could to end it. Yet here it cannot be supposed that our basis is the utilitarian one that the research causes more evil than it promises good. It doesn't. What it does is violate, in a way that we think is unjustifiable, the rights of the human subjects in question. The introduction of the idea that these beings have certain rights does not appear to be superfluous; on the contrary it seems to play an essential role in setting forth the reasons we

D

would give in support of our belief that *sometimes we have a duty actively to ensure that some human beings fulfil their duties to others.*

The same is true in the case of animals. The idea that they have certain rights can be seen to be a vital element, and not an academic diversion, in presenting the case that we sometimes have a duty to ensure that other human beings fulfil their duties to them. If we are obliged, for the reasons I have given, to think that animals have rights, then we shall also be obliged for reasons of consistency not to permit their rights to be overridden for frivolous or trivial reasons. *Thus we have a prima facie duty actively to ensure that others fulfil their duties to them.* That, it seems to me (granting that compassion is the heart), is the backbone of the humane movement. It's where we can and should build our case when we intervene to halt the widespread practices whose practitioners routinely abuse animals.

But isn't this just the same as extolling everyone to be kind to animals? I think not. A failure to be kind to an animal may be wrong, but kind treatment is not one of the things animals can plausibly be thought to have a right to. In a word, our duty to be kind to animals or to humans, if we have it, does not carry a correlative right.

If, then, animals do have rights or if, at the very least, we are required to think that they do, it follows that we cannot suppose our duties to them to be summed up under the general slogan "Be kind to animals". In addition to our duty to be kind, assuming that we have it, there are all those other duties that attend ascribing rights to animals. And these are duties the performance of which, unlike the performance of a kind act, can be justly demanded of us, if not by the animals themselves, then by those who speak for them.

The Animal Welfare Movement and the Foundations of Ethics

T. L. S. SPRIGGE

This gathering, I take it, is composed of people who regard much of current human treatment of animals of other species, such as takes place even in a country like this which is popularly supposed to be a country of " animal lovers ", as morally wrong and wickedly cruel. It is not just that we think that a lot of wicked cruelty goes on, but that it goes on quite legally and, in many cases, without any widespread moral condemnation. Thus we are supporters of a minority moral position, and what I want to talk about is the bearing of one of the major disputes among moral philosophers on the question of how holders of a minority moral position should view their attempts to convert others to their point of view. The dispute in moral philosophy to which I refer may be crudely described as concerning the question of whether moral judgements are objective or subjective.

How far our position is a minority one will differ from person to person here. If we are against factory farms, we are morally condemning widespread and perfectly legal practices involving perhaps the majority of the human community. If we are vegetarians, we hold a position which is very much a minority one. If we are pretty radical anti-vivisectionists, we also hold what seems to be a minority position, involving as it does a radical criticism of the law and the establishment of this country.

Now if we are going to think out our position seriously, as people who hold and wish to propagate moral beliefs which diverge from those dominant in our society, we are bound to come up against the philosophical problem of the objectivity or subjectivity of moral judgements. Are some actions morally good or morally bad in the same objective way as some objects are round and others flat, or is moral goodness and badness, like the pleasantness of a drink, a matter of personal taste?

Most of us would think that flat earthers are just wrong— not wrong in a moral sense, but in the sense that they are mistaken as to how things *are*, independently of anyone's thoughts or wishes. If, on the other hand, I think gin and tonic a better drink than whisky and soda, I hardly think that one who holds the opposite view is mistaken in any serious sense. Which is the case with morality? If a society is divided as to whether capital punishment for murder is right or wrong, is one side or other mistaken in an objective sense as the flat earthers are, or is it more like a conflict between gin and whisky drinkers?

To make a more useful comparison, suppose a small country can support a national opera or a national ballet but not both. There will be a dispute as to which should be supported, and the matter will get sorted out somehow, but if the decision was reached in an appropriately democratic manner, we would hardly be able to claim it as wrong, in some objective sense, even if the decision went against our personal predilections. Is morality like that, something which leads to disputes which have to be settled somehow, but such that neither side is objectively right or wrong? Or is there an objective right or wrong about it, which may differ from what most people think at a given time? Decision on this point may make a great difference to how we seek to forward a minority moral position, such, for example, as anti-vivisectionism. If the issue here boils down to a matter of different people's ultimately irrational preferences, some for cosmetics and knowledge, others for a feeling of being at peace with other species, then the room for argument may be very limited. One may have to decide either that it is simply one's bad luck that one's tastes are in a minority and try to put up with what others do, or take the opposite line and say that since there can be no real rational proof on either side we must try to win the day for our own outlook by force, subterfuge, wile or windy rhetoric. If, however, we believe that morality has some kind of objectivity, we will see more point in trying to change people's minds by reasoning, trusting that if both sides are honest in argument, there can eventually be agreement among all except the essentially criminal, as to what is morally best and in the attainment of unity in pursuing it.

What exactly is the minority moral position for which members of a gathering such as this are likely to be propagandists? It will certainly differ slightly from person to person. There is, however, one rather minimal principle to which I trust that all here would assent, namely that the suffering or frustration of an animal of another species is an evil of the same general sort as is the suffering or frustration of a human being, and that we humans have the same general sort of moral obligation to refrain from causing, and to try actively to prevent, such evil when it concerns animals as when it concerns human beings.

In defining their precise moral position no one will find this principle takes them more than a little way. It tells us, for example, that burning a live calf's or pig's skin is an evil of the same general sort as burning a live human's skin, but it leaves open the question of how they compare in degree of evil. Nonetheless, it is sufficiently definite a principle to provide a basis for showing that an immense amount of current practice should be abandoned. It bids us, for example, set the moral issue of the use of animals in experiments and in the testing of drugs in the same general context as the use of involuntary human " guinea pigs " for the same purposes: justification regarded to be of an utterly inappropriate sort in the latter case would have to be regarded in the same way in the former. The principle, though it leaves much open, is thus a real challenge to current morality.

Is there, then, any rational way of resolving the disagreement between those who accept our principle, and those who hold that there is an absolute difference in moral kind between hurting or frustrating an animal and doing the same to a human, or is this disagreement just a matter of divergent subjective feeling?

Philosophical discussion of the nature of moral judgement has, for some time past, usually been against the background of a principle sometimes described as Hume's principle since David Hume, the 18th-century Scottish philosopher, gave a striking

formulation of it. According to this principle, it is impossible to
move by any logically valid inference from any description of
any observable or empirically ascertainable fact to any statement
as to what is morally right or wrong, good or bad. If this principle is correct then, to take a particular example, no description
of the distribution of wealth in a country suffices of itself to show
whether any form of redistribution is morally desirable. Moreover,
not even a well-supported judgement of the precise effects of a
particular sort of redistribution, covering such matters as the
reduction of malnutrition, the effects on the country's political
stability, and the consequences of a radically altered incentive
situation for the development of the economy, would logically
imply that some form of redistribution was good or bad, for all
these count as matters of fact. Matter of fact in this context
does not mean something known to be true with certainty, but
something which concerns what *is* happening or *would* happen
if we did certain things in contrast to the *desirability* of its
happening or not. The point is that however much one may win
agreement as to one's view of the nature and likely effects of a
given activity, one cannot use this to prove that one who rejects
one's own moral evaluation of the activity is in the wrong.

Take now the case of various forms of factory farming. We
may think that the debeaking of hens and keeping them in
confined conditions which frustrate their natural behaviour
patterns is wrong. Others think that this is not wrong, perhaps
because they think the availability of cheap chicken a good, and
the lives of the hens, except as a form of food preparation, an
irrelevance. If Hume's principle is correct, no scientific investigation could ever supply any rational way of settling the issue.
Learning more about the facts may change a particular person's
feelings on the matter, but if it does not, we have an ultimate
divergence in moral viewpoint which cannot be resolved in any
rational way, unless indeed there is some quite other form of
rationality from that which is directed at establishing matters
of fact and working out their implications.

It is difficult to get round Hume's essential insight that there
is some kind of basic logical gap between establishing matters of

fact and establishing any kind of moral judgement. (Some philo-sophers claim to reject Hume's principle but the more impressive attempts to deal with the question of the objectivity or otherwise of moral judgements operate on the assumption that Hume has made an essentially correct point.) I want to discuss, briefly, the two main points of view which have been developed against this background. They may be called intuitionism, and attitudin-ism or emotivism. I shall end up with my own suggestion on the matter.

The intuitionist says that Hume is certainly right in seeing a fundamental divide between ordinary empirical matters of fact, including all facts about the consequences of our actions, and matters of moral value and obligation. Nonetheless, moral values and obligations are themselves facts of a special sort concerning which there can be right and wrong, true and false opinions. These facts of value and obligation may be called non-natural facts, and they are known, not by observation, experiment or reasoning, but by rational intuition. One cannot, in any ordinary sense, *prove* that it is wrong to cause innocent suffering—at least under any but very special circumstances—but our rational intuition tells us that this truth is self-evident. One can, therefore, resolve moral issues by reason. One first establishes the relevant empirical or natural fact as well as one may by observation, experiment and reasoning. One then applies moral principles to the situation which are self-evident to a well ordered intellect. If there is still disagreement, that shows either that one party is refusing really to use their mind on the matter because they fear an awkward upshot for themselves, or that their intellects are disordered.

The real trouble about intuitionism is that it gives no adequate account of the relation between moral judgement and the emotional and conative side of our nature. If values and obliga-tions are simply matters of a peculiar sort of non-natural fact revealed to rational intuition why should not the vivisectionist reply to his critics like this—" Perhaps you are right in saying that some of my activities have the peculiar non-natural quality you call wrongness, and I even seem to detect something of the

sort in them myself. All the same, I am personally more concerned to promote scientific knowledge, and perhaps even my
own career, than to avoid actions with this non-natural quality.
Thus, while acknowledging that you may be right about the
quality, I don't see why I should be much concerned about it."
In short, intuitionism doesn't make it clear what sort of connection there is between seeing that an action is wrong and deciding
to refrain from it.

Let me turn then to our second theory of moral judgement,
attitudinism. According to this a moral judgement is not really the
expression of a belief which could be true or false. Rather it
expresses a wish on the part of the people who accept it that
people should or should not behave in certain ways together with
an emotion of distaste towards those who act otherwise, an
emotion which people will not like having directed at themselves. Thus those who call abortion wrong express their wish that
it should not take place, and their distaste for those engaged in it,
a distaste which it is hoped will influence their behaviour. Of
course it may also suggest that there are insufficiently recognised
facts which might change their opponents' attitudes if attended
to. Yet the attitudinist accepts Hume's principle, on the ground
that there is no matter of fact the learning of which is bound to
give someone the wishes and feelings expressed by a particular
moral judgement.

The trouble about attitudinism is that it is, after all, a form of
subjectivism, and that if, after considering all the facts, people
do continue to have fundamentally different wishes and emotions,
there is no sense in which either side is really right or wrong.
Most moral reformers would prefer to feel on stronger ground
than this. In the last resort, neither intuitionism nor attitudinism
can give those who hold a minority moral position justification for
holding that they are in possession of a truth which others would
be rationally bound to acknowledge if they gave the matter
adequate thought.

I want now to suggest a view of moral judgement which incor-
porates the truth in attitudinism, but which is less unsatisfactorily
subjectivist. According to this view, a moral judgement is, as

attitudinism suggests, the expression of an emotion and a wish. When I call an action wrong, I am not really stating any kind of fact, but exhibiting my own dislike of it and wish that it should be hindered. Because of this, Hume's principle is, up to a point, correct. There can be no direct logical step from thinking the facts are a certain way to regarding an action as wrong (since there is a difference in kind between saying how things are, or under certain circumstances would be, and expressing a wish as to how people should act). But where I differ from the attitudinist is in holding that the wishes which are fundamental to ethics stand in a special relation to certain facts, inasmuch as it is logically impossible really to acknowledge the existence of these facts and not to have those wishes.

The facts in question are those which concern the feelings and wishes of other centres of consciousness. One cannot really believe that an emotion exists outside one's own consciousness without participating in that emotion and making it to some extent one's own. This is because believing that something exists or occurs involves treating an image or representation of it as present in one's mind as though it were the real thing. To take a simple example, if I believe that there is a scorpion in my bed my image of it there will give me as effective a wish to get out of the bed as if I had actually seen the scorpion there. Similarly, I can't in any serious sense believe that something I am doing is hurting you without my image of that hurt acting on me as the hurt itself would do if I myself experienced it, encouraging me to desist. I may do it, nonetheless, for the sake of preventing some greater evil, but then that applies also to suffering I directly experience myself.

The principle I am suggesting may be denied on various grounds, but I think that exceptions to it all turn on the fact that in many cases where a person is said to know that he is making another suffer, and this does not encourage him to desist, either this so-called knowledge has a merely verbal character and has not really sunk in, or in one way or another he has an essentially distorted conception of the character of the suffering he is causing, viewing it simply as a merely physiological or behavioural fact rather than as a mode of consciousness, or, as in the case of sadism, wrongly imagining it as shot through with a kind of exciting quality which in the other individual it normally entirely lacks. Properly formulated, I am convinced of the truth of the principle that a genuine grasp of the fact that another feels an emotion necessarily involves taking account of it, in deciding what to do, in the same kind of way as one would if one directly felt it oneself.

It follows from this that one is always acting in a kind of ignorance when one treats one's own interests as having an importance which the interests of others do not have, since one is refusing to recognise that the feelings of others are realities in just the way that one's own are.

The application of this to the case of our obligation to treat facts about animal suffering and frustration as having the same kind of moral significance as facts about human suffering and frustration should be obvious. It is irrational in the same way as is any other form of selfishness. It must rest either on the explicit view that there is a radical difference in kind between animal suffering and frustration and human, which flies in the face of all appropriate evidence, or on a refusal to let the theoretically acknowledged facts sink in and have any real influence on conduct. In either case we have ignorance and irrationality.

What I am urging, then, is that the case against factory farming, and most current experimentation on animals, is one in which there is scope for a rational debate in which I am sure the defender of these practices would be the loser. If the facts of animal suffering and frustration are not explicitly denied, but simply not allowed to sink in so as to influence conduct, then the animals' supporter is using an essentially rational method if he does what he can to make them sink in, by forcing the details of what actually happens in upon people's consciousness. He is only working on people's emotions in the sense that he is making them aware of facts about the feelings of animals which cannot really be grasped without a subsequent wish to rectify the situation.

If the view outlined here is correct, namely that people cannot really grasp the nature of the suffering which their behaviour creates without wishing to refrain from it, you may ask how do experimenters, factory farmers, cattle transporters, etc., carry on? The answer is, in one way or another, I believe, that they do not *really* grasp what they are doing. At some level it may be right to say " Forgive them, for they know not what they do ". But the immediate task is to make people realise sufficiently what they, or others on their behalf, are doing, so that it will be done no more.

I must make it clear that my suggestion is not that reform can rest solely upon argument with individual vivisectionists, factory farmers, etc. We must get their activities prohibited by law. However, in working for such prohibition we need not present ourselves as simply trying to make our personal subjective feelings dictate the behaviour of others. The restraints we are seeking to impose are ones which can only be opposed by a failure in empathy towards non-human animals which constitutes an irrational blindness to the fact of the basic sameness of suffering in whatever species of animal it occurs; an irrationality incompatible with clear thought about the issue.

How to Calculate the Greater Good

STEPHEN R. L. CLARK

Those moralists who deny that non-human beings have rights generally mean that there is no moral reason to consider the feelings or wishes of those creatures. I myself agree with the early Cartesians, that if a creature has feelings then we ought not to torment and kill him or her.[113] Their absurdity in concluding that it would therefore be inhumane to think that animals had feelings does not discredit their initial insight. I am happy then to agree that animals have rights, and I shall not argue the point further.

But moralists opposed to animal rights may have a slightly different point in mind. Certainly, they may say, we should not multiply animal suffering unduly, nor wantonly diminish animal delights. In that sense, animals have rights. But this admission is compatible with a strictly utilitarian treatment of non-human creatures which we are generally unwilling to extend to the human. Those who believe in human rights believe that human creatures have a right to a say in what is done to them and to their world. Perhaps the sophisticated social engineer can see, and correctly see, that a certain policy will bring long-term advantage, yet he has no right to implement that policy if it conflicts with the standing rights of the human creatures affected. Perhaps I ought, for example, to give most of my goods to the poor, for utilitarian reasons, but yet I have a right not to do so, and no one else has a right to enforce the gift. It is this sort of right which orthodox moralists probably deny to the non-human.

Fully committed utilitarians, of course, must find such " rights of autonomy " suspect : there are no works of supererogation in utilitarian morality. If I ought to do ' x ' then I have no right not to, I am not in the right if I do not. And on the other hand, fully committed zoophiles, such as myself, can think of no good reason to deny such " rights of autonomy " at least to our closer kindred or even to any sentient being. If I have no right to force my fellow adults, children or mental defectives to serve the greater good against their will, I do not see how I could acquire such a right against a chimpanzee, a cat or a cow. To say that they have no wills is neither more nor less correct than to say that children and mental defectives have no wills. Incidentally, even non-utilitarians may agree that my rights or alleged rights cannot always hold out against the needs of the greater good : perhaps I have a right not to be robbed of my goods even to feed the starving, but if I have an enormous superfluity and the starving are desperate millions I do not suffer much injury from such forcible appropriation. (But where such gross inequality does not obtain, or holds in the opposite direction, I do not see that, for example, ten people have a right to seize on one to use his flesh or organs to aid their survival even if that one would be heroically virtuous if he exercised his right to self-sacrifice. And one further caveat : there may be moral rules of a non-utilitarian sort that forbid animal torture even for the greater good without attributing any rights of autonomy to the potential victims. But I am not now concerned with these.)

I myself then do not believe that chimpanzees, rats and the rest should be sacrificed even for an acknowledged greater good : such sacrifice infringes their right to refuse. In my morality, all creatures with feelings and wishes should be thought of as ends-in-themselves, and not merely as means.[114] We may remember the efforts men have made in the past to make it seem that their animal victims went consenting. Their intuition, though not their technique of " persuasion ", is also mine. However, I wish now to consider what moral effects follow from a determination to treat animals according to utilitarian, and people according to Kantian, morality.[115] Human beings must give their consent to operations either upon themselves or upon the human creatures in their tutelage and may not, at least in this country, give such consent in the latter cases unless the operation is, or is very likely to be, of direct benefit to the victim. We may not sacrifice our children even if assured that torturing one to death will enable doctors to save several. The child has a right to refuse, and since he cannot exercise his option in an informed manner we refuse on his behalf. My point is not that he *would* refuse if he were rational—we might know him to be good-natured enough to agree—but simply that as the operation cannot be carried out without his consent and as he has not consented, the operation cannot justly be carried out unless by failing to do so we infringe his right to our best help. Those who think, by the way, that children and mental defectives are not primary right-bearers, but are protected only for the sake of parental squeamishness, might like to explain why parents should not have the right to sell, say, brain-damaged or mongoloid or microcephalic children—you can see the posters already: " A Parent's Right to Choose ".

Let us simply stipulate, for no good reason that I can see, that creatures of human descent have rights of autonomy and creatures of non-human descent do not. I do not know if this is intended to licence acts of utilitarian violence against intelligent aliens: perhaps not, though if not, I do not see why, at any rate chimpanzees, gorillas and perhaps dolphins should not be allowed the courtesies we should afford to extra-terrestrials.

According to the view I am outlining, then, animals have rights in the sense that it is wrong to multiply their suffering, that their pain is an evil and their pleasure a good. If pain is not an intrinsic evil, nor pleasure an intrinsic good, by the way, much argument for, say, vivisection collapses, for it rests on the notion that (our) suffering is evil. But that *is* by the way. Animals do not have rights in the sense that once we have demonstrated to our satisfaction that a particular act leads to the greater good of the greater number, including animals, we are at once entitled to perform that act however much our victim objects. How, then, are we to perform this calculation and what, in general terms, could it justify?

Classical utilitarians do include animal pain and pleasure in their calculation, though they generally add some, rarely argued, clause to the effect that animals experience less intense or fewer pleasures. Correspondingly one would think, adult humans have more options open to them and suffer less from any single disappointment. Benthamite utilitarians work with a simple notion of quantity of pleasure or pain. Followers of Mill incorporate some notion of variety of pleasures, upon whatever excuse : better many pleasures than one pleasure, better a collection of entities variously pleased than a mass of the unanimously voluptuous. Better intellectual than sensual pleasures. These facts, with a little fudging, give a general bias towards the human, particularly the normal adult human. Better multiply such creatures than multiply, say, happy bees, and if we are to choose between having happily uniform animals and happily various humans, we should have the latter. Doubtless this point greatly exaggerates both human variety and non-human uniformity, but let it pass (particularly as it favours the vegan rather than the wholefood wing of ecologically-conscious politics).

Utilitarians make no difference between directly causing and merely allowing an event. To allow an event which one could have prevented is to be responsible for its occurrence. Common morality does not relish this : we think it one thing to save ten men at the cost of allowing another man to die, and quite another to kill one man in order to save the ten (unless the one man is himself the danger, potential assassin or plague-vector). The moralists I am considering allow this distinction amongst human objects, but not amongst non-human. If I forebear to experiment upon a baboon and thereby fail to acquire the knowledge that might enable me to save a human, I am guilty of that human's death, as I would not be guilty if the route to his survival was destructive experimentation on an unconsenting human victim. I repeat that I myself see no important difference between the cases, and do not consider myself or anyone else obliged to save any human being by causing pain, distress or death to an uncon-

senting " person "—where " person " is defined as a creature
with whom one can have at least as much of a personal relationship as one can with an infant, a brain-damaged adolescent
or a senile old man.

But let it be so. In judging whether an act of violence against
an animal is required I must see whether doing it or not doing
it will lead to an increase of pleasure, or variety of pleasure, or
a decrease of pain amongst those affected by my policy. In
calculating the matter I must employ simple decision-theory : that
is, I must attend both to the value and to the probability of the
outcome. If the value accruing, though great in itself, is very
unlikely, this may count for less in my calculation than a less
valuable, but more likely outcome. The peculiarity, though not a
failing, of utilitarianism is that I cannot perform the calculation
afterwards, in full knowledge of what *did* happen. Perhaps what
I did or failed to do resulted, by chance, in the greatest imagin-
able good, but unless I had some epistemological right to expect
that outcome with the appropriate probability my action was
not justified, and I ought not to have done it. Conversely
I may be justified in acting so, even though in fact history goes
against me. Neither the gains nor the losses of serendipity can
enter into my calculation, for they are, precisely, incalculable.
So in considering, say, whether or not to poison a baboon to
death, or smash his leg with a sledge-hammer, or drive her,
pregnant, into a brick wall, I must not simply weigh the distress
caused by so doing against an imagined benefit to other entities.
I must weigh the certain pain against the merely possible diminution of later pain. Otherwise I shall in the end simply be increasing pain (and we may note the steady increase in the vivisection
industry over the last century) : the less note is taken of the
relative improbability of certain outcomes, the more violent
actions are licensed, and the more often they result in no particularly valuable result. Of course some valuable results are in
fact obtained that could not reasonably have been expected at the
time, but that is not enough to justify the unreasonable act. The
same argument applies against any "rule-utilitarian" defence
of the institution of animal torture, that to require proper

discriminations of probability over any particular experiment would so hamper the scientist that the overall gains would not be as high as they might be if the scientists were allowed a completely free hand. Such an institution may increase profits: it also increases costs.

Strictly, there are two principles involved in utilitarianism: increase pleasure, and diminish pain. Or even four, for we might add: do not decrease pleasure, do not increase pain. There are no clear utilitarian reasons for judging between these principles when they conflict: we cannot assess the consequences in terms of " the greater good ", for it is the nature of this goal which is in question. Shall we increase pleasure even by increasing or failing to diminish pain? Or shall we diminish pain even by decreasing or failing to increase pleasure? The second option leads to the paradox of negative utilitarianism, that we should commit genocide. The first to the paradox of positive utilitarianism, that we should increase the population at every cost so long as that population has even a few more pleasures at each generation. Other problems of utilitarian population-control involve distinctions between the number of entities involved and the qualities of the lives they enjoy. All these problems, I think, require intuitionist solutions (that is, any solution has to be based on an independent assessment of several moral principles without any principled way of choosing between those principles, or at least without any utilitarian way: this is not Dr. Sprigge's sense of " intuitionism "), thus weakening the initial plausibility of utilitarian morality as an unambiguous and monarchical system. In particular, shall we cause pain in order to diminish pain or may we also do so in order to increase pleasure (where the absence of pleasure is no pain)? Shall we avoid pleasures in order to increase long-run pleasures or also to diminish pain? The second question seems plausibly answered by saying that we should forego pleasures in order to diminish pain, at least as long as there are some pleasures left. The first question may plausibly be answered by saying that we may cause pain in order to earn a long-run diminution of pain, but not so as to increase pleasure : if we decreed otherwise it would be *right* for a sadist to torture an animal to death if he thereby increased his own and his companions' sexual or gastronomic pleasures. Fortunately, these intuited answers agree.

So : as utilitarians we should forego pleasures if we thereby diminish or avoid increasing pain, and should not cause pains in order to increase pleasures. (Of course, this does not apply to a calculus over the agent's *own* pains and pleasures : if we like to pain ourselves now to gain pleasures later, very well. But even here there is something amiss with us if we take pleasures now at the cost of a later increase of pain : our " future self " should have more claim on what happens than that—he is entitled *not* to be pained. But this is to involve myself in the theory of rights once more.)

Utilitarians are also, of course and essentially, concerned with the choice between alternative courses of action. The incurably polar bias of our species suggests to us that in any crisis there are only two actions : to do or not to do. But of course in reality there may be non-denumerably many available acts. Do x or do y or do z or do something else entirely. So the calculus should not simply assess the costs and benefits of doing or not doing x, as if in omitting the one we are automatically barred from performing any other act. We must take the alternatives into account, as the Research Defence Society ably prevented Parliament from requiring of laboratory scientists.[116] Of course, " alternatives " are not merely those popularised by F.R.A.M.E. or financed by the various trusts recently set up by anti-vivisection societies (which may have their own costs) : the alternatives must include alterations in our diet and way of life, herbal remedies, and the application of elementary stoicism to the ills of the flesh rather than to the iatrogenic penalties of modern medicine. (Medical practitioners and experimentalists have until recently been strangely averse to submitting their success rate to objective study. It seems very likely that changes in social custom, wealth and diet have had an enormously more beneficial effect on the health of the developed west than laboratory science and orthodox medicine, even if particular cases have been unambiguously benefited by these latter.[117]) Some of these alternative courses of action, of course, are not directly in the power of, say, the individual scientist; he cannot decree that everyone stop smoking, and may consider himself justified in taking the actions of others and the way of life which they actually lead as providing the boundary conditions for his calculations. Given that people will go on smoking, how best can he hope to reduce the cancer rate? The answer is not obviously by *increasing* the cancer rate, among laboratory animals, particularly given our marked failure to solve the problem in this way so far. The laboratory scientist could perhaps use his knowledge to attack the given state of things: the more people realise the costs of their addiction, the more of them may stop.

One further difficulty: utilitarians are concerned with long-run advantage. But they cannot be concerned with too long a run, and there is no clear way of defining how many imagined consequences should be taken into account. Firstly, because on a long view it is difficult to say what *is* the consequence of a given act: the more time elapses between the act and the outcome, the more alternative courses of history could have generated just that outcome.[118] Blaming the blacksmith for the loss of a kingdom involves us in disregarding all the other agents, all the other causal factors that led to this denouement. Secondly, because once we do start reckoning long-run consequences we have no assurance that the value of the outcome will remain the same from one moment to the next. Perhaps the state of affairs at t^i is better than it would have been if action x had not been performed, but the immediately following state of affairs at t^{ii} is worse than it would have been if action x had not been performed. Probability theory will cope with some of these cases, of course: generally speaking, the more distant the consequence, the less ground could we have for expecting it.

Distant consequences of not performing destructive experiments must count for very little. But probability does not help us on one point: in the long run, as the saying goes, we're all dead. This is not an improbable, but an all-but-certain consequence of anything we do. In the long run any action will count for as much or as little good as any other. The differences of value will be ironed

out by the centuries, and in the end we're all dead. Experimentalists sometimes speak as if paradise is just around the corner: only
a few more acts of violence and we shall live, men and animals
alike, a pain-free idyll that will last for ever. If we could be sure
of this, and sure that the memory of our past behaviour would
not stain our felicity, their utilitarian calculation might be
justified. As I at least am sure rather of its opposite, that pain
and frustration will be with us till the day of doom, that in the
long run, nothing earthly lasts, their calculation seems far from
safe.

   Accordingly, as utilitarians we should think ourselves justified
in inflicting pain or deprivation on a sentient being only if we
are justified in believing that the amount of pain will thereby in
the not-too-long run be diminished to an extent that outweighs
(preferably appreciably so) the certain pain we inflict, and if
there are no alternative acts which would with equal or greater
probability lead to the same or nearly the same benefit. As far as
agribusiness and meat-farming in general goes, the answer is now
obvious: we are not so justified, since the benefits accruing in
terms of increased pleasure (to us) do not outweigh the costs (to
the animals) and there are other, incidentally healthier, diets.
(I am sorry to have to disagree with some earlier speakers, but
this is a practical point; it is no use complaining to an experimenter about the way he gets profit from a baboon, if he can
retort that one is oneself going home to chomp a battery chicken.
If the animals can be tormented for our purposes, they surely can
be for his.) As far as laboratory science goes, some acts of violence
might be hereby justified, but certainly no such act is proper
where there is an alternative available in a changed human life.
We can do without cosmetics and the like: we can reduce the
cancer rate by not smoking, eating more roughage, breast-
feeding (where appropriate), and so on.

   We can do this, and on utilitarian principles we should. But
I may now return to my beginning. Ought we to be forced to
prefer the option that is preferable? Do we have standing rights
in the matter entitling us to ignore the greater good? In claiming that we do, we entirely abandon utilitarianism as an ethical

policy, and reassert our rights, self-claimed, to treat non-human beings as we please. But if we are not utilitarians at this point we cannot make the distinction from which I began : we cannot claim to be considering animal pleasures and pains as morally relevant but denying them human rights of autonomy. In hanging on to our rights in this matter we implicitly deny animals all moral consideration.

I conclude that honest semi-utilitarians, even if their fundamental distinction between animals and men is allowed, must forego meat and other products of the factory farm and refrain from, or seek to halt, most vivisection. If they claim a continuing right to ignore the results of utilitarian calculations in this matter they are self-confessedly denying all rights to the non-human. And on *that* doctrine enough has already been said.

What has Sentiency to do with the Possession of Rights?

R. G. FREY

Can at least some moral rights be extended from human beings to animals? Plainly, this question presupposes that human beings *have* moral rights, and on a different occasion I should try to show—what many utilitarians and others have long argued— that a powerful case can be brought against the truth of this presupposition. Perhaps this case could be made to collapse; but the history of ethics teaches us that it is by no means an easy thing to show that human beings do have moral rights, and I know of no argument to this effect that commands general assent among philosophers. If human beings do not have moral rights, then the question of their extension from humans to animals simply does not arise; there is, so to speak, nothing to extend. And if there is nothing to extend, then arguments for animals' rights which turn upon such an extension are accordingly vitiated.

On this occasion, however, I want to turn to one of the means by which it is thought the extension in question can be carried out, namely, sentiency. If human beings have (certain) moral rights because they are sentient, then many animals, because they, too, are sentient, also possess (these) moral rights. So runs the extension, and it represents a powerful current in much recent thinking on the subject of animal rights. I am myself, however, inclined to think that sentiency has nothing to do with who does and who does not have rights, so that I obviously am at odds with a good many animal rightists, for whom sentiency is, if not the guarantor of, then at least the main hope for the inclusion of animals within the class of right-holders. This whole matter, of course, is a very complex one, and time allows for only a few general remarks at best; so I shall confine myself to bringing out and briefly enlarging upon a little-discussed assumption—an assumption about what has value—which seems to me to lie at the very basis of a sentiency criterion for the possession of rights.

The term " sentient " means " having the power of sense-perception ", and nearly all animal rightists go on to include under the term the " capacity to experience pain ".[119] We must not, however, get things in reverse: the higher animals are not sentient because they can have experiences of pain; rather, they can have experiences of pain because they are sentient proper, i.e. because they have the power of sense-perception. No creature which lacks the power of sense-perception can experience pain; indeed, in the appropriate sense, it cannot have experiences at all. Since almost no one today denies that at least the higher animals can, because they are sentient-proper, experience pain, it follows on this usage that they are sentient; and if we presume the truth of a sentiency criterion for the possession of rights, it follows that they have rights.

To this basic account of sentiency, one or two animal rightists want to make the odd addition. Joel Feinberg, for example, wants to include under the term " sentience " the various elements which make up a conative life, such as wishes and desires, which he thinks the higher animals have.[120]

Now I think what is common to all of these items included under the term " sentience "—to sense-perceptions, pains and the elements of a conative life—is, roughly speaking, that they either are or presuppose experiences, and experiences, clearly, are phenomena that are *had* by creatures. Creatures which have or can have experiences are sentient and are generally labelled " beings "; creatures which cannot have experiences are not sentient and are not generally labelled " beings " but " things ". Notice two points. First, a being is not sentient because it has or can have this or that *kind* of experiences—as if having experiences of this or that kind *constituted* sentiency—but rather because it has or can have experiences *per se*.[121] Second, the question of whether a being who has or can have experiences *prefers* some kinds of experiences to others, e.g. pleasurable to painful ones, is a secondary affair; for only if the creature has or can have experiences in the first place do questions of its preferring some kinds of experiences to others arise.[122] On the sentiency criterion, then, I think it is ultimately the fact that human beings and the higher animals have experiences which is used to distinguish them from everything else and is the fundamental basis of the claim that they are the possessors of moral rights. Thus, it is because rivers do not and/or cannot have experiences, not because they do not and/or cannot have experiences of a particular kind and because they do not and/or cannot prefer one kind of experiences to another, that they are not sentient beings. And, lacking sentiency, rivers have no rights.

It is ironic that this result of the application of a sentiency criterion, in part in order to combat speciesism, is itself blatantly speciesist in character. For, to put the matter rather pompously, it condemns the whole of non-sentient creation, including the lower animals, at best to a much inferior moral status or, as we shall see, at worst possibly to a status completely beyond the moral pale. In essence, non-sentient creation is "simply there" for sentient creation to do with as it sees fit. Animal rightists have objected to the Christian view of man as having dominion over the rest of creation;[123] but the only revolution they effect by means of a sentiency criterion is to give man and the higher animals dominion over the rest of creation. The criterion, then, does not eliminate speciesism; on the contrary, it broadens the category of those who can practise it, or, in the case of the higher animals, who can have it practised on their behalf. If one is going to complain about speciesism in the first place, why go on to practise it by means of a sentiency criterion?

But the matter goes deeper than this. For, lacking sentiency, the things which make up non-sentient creation lack not only moral rights but also what I shall call moral standing.[124] By this, I mean that, in the absence of sentiency, they are not themselves the bearers or repositories of value in their own right; they have, in other words, no value in themselves. Feinberg, for example, is emphatic about this:

" A mere thing, however valuable to others, has no good of its own. The explanation of that fact, I suspect, consists in the fact that mere things have no conative life . . . Interests must be compounded somehow out of conations; hence mere things have no interests. *A fortiori*, they have no interests to be protected by legal or moral rules. Without interests a creature can have no ' good ' of its own, the achievement of which can be its due. Mere things are not *loci* of value in their own right, but rather their value consists entirely in their being objects of other beings' interests."[125]

Non-sentient creation, in short, lacks even moral standing, since the things which comprise it lack a good of their own and are not *loci* of value in their own right. Sentient creation, therefore, is favoured, and whatever value non-sentient creation has lies in its usefulness or instrumental value to sentient creation, a speciesist but convenient conclusion, in view of the havoc we wreak upon non-sentient creation.

Now if the beings which comprise sentient creation are *loci* of value in their own right, then what is it about these beings that makes them *loci* of value? Clearly, on the sentiency criterion, it is their allegedly distinguishing feature, viz., their sentiency, their conative lives. And what is it that underlies and is presupposed by their sentiency, their conative lives? It is, as I have remarked, the having of experiences. Accordingly, if I am right, what appears to be at the very basis of a sentiency criterion, in the sense that this is what at bottom it involves, is the view that having experiences is valuable in its own right. It is just because the things which comprise non-sentient creation do not and/or cannot have experiences that they are not *loci* of value in their own right and are beyond the moral pale, whereas it is just because the beings which comprise sentient creation do and/or can have experiences that they have moral standing and so are in a position to possess moral rights.

What, then, is the support for the view that having experiences is valuable in its own right? The fact is that I have been able to find none in the writings of animal rightists;[126] the truth is, I think, that they *implicitly* assume that having experiences is valuable in its own right. Indeed, I think they have to assume this; for unless one argues or assumes that having experiences is valuable in its own right and suffices to confer moral standing upon creatures who have or are capable of having experiences, what reason has one for thinking that sentiency is a criterion for the possession of *moral* rights at all? Put differently, why are stones (a) not *loci* of value in their own right and (b) completely lacking in moral rights? It makes no sense to say, e.g., that it is because they lack this or that kind of experiences; for the whole point of stones, rivers, valleys, etc., is that they lack any and all kinds of experiences whatever. They are not sentient because they lack this or that kind of experience but rather because they lack experiences altogether; and it is this fact, I am suggesting, which on a sentiency criterion places them beyond the moral pale, that is, beyond the realm of those things, as Feinberg would have it, which have a good the achievement of which can be their due.

Thus, if I am correct, then the implicit assumption that having experiences is valuable in its own right lies at the very basis of a sentiency criterion and is used to confer moral standing and moral rights upon one part of creation and to refuse them to another. Quite simply, an assumption of this magnitude and importance requires argument in its support : it is by no means obviously true, nor can I see any immediate reason to give way in the face of it. For if asked to name those things one regarded as intrinsically valuable, I think many would reply that, *if anything* is intrinsically valuable (in order by this formulation to leave open the possibility that nothing is), then such things as deep and lasting friendship in the fullest of senses and the development of one's talents are. What I strongly suspect is that virtually no one would cite having experiences *per se* as among the class of the intrinsically valuable.

I should like to end on a different but closely-related note. Sentient beings have an enormous number of different kinds of experiences, and by no means all or even a substantial minority of these are experiences of pain; so why, as so many animal rightists do, single out experiences of pain from all the other kinds which sentient beings have? Because, it doubtless will be said, experiences of pain are themselves possessed of intrinsic value (i.e. are intrinsically evil). This answer warrants three observations here. First, argument is needed to establish that experiences of pain *are* possessed of intrinsic value; merely to assume that they are will not do, and appeals to authority (such as that Bentham and others have said that they are or that there is a noble philosophical tradition that they are) beg the question.[127] I assume in all this, of course, that arguments advanced by John Dewey and others to the effect (i) that there is nothing in the world possessed by intrinsic value and (ii) that the very notion is an incoherent one, can be defeated. Second, *even if* experiences of pain are possessed of intrinsic value, it does not follow that other kinds of experiences are not also possessed of intrinsic value; and if they are, why should not the sentiency criterion be formulated in terms of them? For example, G. E. Moore's *Principia Ethica* became well-known to a non-philosophical public partly through Moore's insistence that experiences based upon the contemplation of beauty were intrinsically valuable. But it would require a good deal of argument to show that even the higher animals engage in the contemplation of beauty. In other words, though only sentient creatures can have experiences of beauty, since such experiences presuppose the power of sense-perception, *not all* sentient creatures can have such experiences. Put succinctly, then, if one is determined to adopt a sentiency criterion, *why* should it be formulated around experiences of pain and so be animal-including instead of being formulated around, e.g., experiences of beauty and so be animal-excluding?[128] Third, if more kinds of experiences than merely experiences of pain are possessed of intrinsic value, yet if animal rightists nevertheless want to give moral pride of place to experiences of pain in the formulation of a sentiency criterion, on what basis—justified basis—do they do this? There is not time to speculate on answers here, except to remark that one important type of answer, the sort that focuses on the role experiences of pain play in generating the adaptive behaviour to their environment characteristic of higher sentient life, would amount to giving *moral* pride of place to experiences of pain for a naturalistic-cum-evolutionary reason that has, as far as I can see, no apparent moral status whatever.

Life, Liberty and the Pursuit of Happiness

MAUREEN DUFFY

When Thomas Jefferson drew up, as penman for his committee, the Declaration of Independence in 1776, he wrote:

> "We hold these truths to be self-evident; that all men are created equal; that they are endowed by their creator with certain unalienable Rights, that among these are life, liberty and the pursuit of happiness."

This was perhaps the first time that memorable prose had come from a committee, one which clearly believed that it had no need to present an argument: the truths were self-evident. I suspect they seemed so because the " certain unalienable Rights " listed are in fact the three basic impulses of a biological unit, of the individual of a species, rewritten.

The inalienable right to life is the urge to survive. Without it we sit down and starve or turn our faces to the wall. It can be overcome by psychic disorder, by some other deep-seated instinct (like the parental one which will cause a lapwing to feign lameness to lead a predator from the nest, or a human parent to fling itself between bullets and its child), or by a situation in which the pain of being alive, whether mental or physical, is greater than the pleasure. We are instinctively afraid, frightened to death, when our survival is threatened and we hope against hope that we shall live because, quite simply, while there's life there's hope.

But hope and fear are also bound up with the second inalienable, self-evident right: liberty. We may give up our liberty of our own free will and enter into a contract with someone else that curtails it, as a cat does when it agrees to live with us by returning home after its outing. This is, however, a very different thing from having our liberty taken away by imprisonment, however well- or ill-intentioned. We accept captivity, I suspect, because the survival instinct is the stronger but we will make every attempt to escape because the instinct for freedom is also bound up with survival, to be able to run from danger, to have the freedom to hide, to have the illusion of control over our own survival, which is hope.

The third inalienable and self-evident right, the pursuit of happiness, is closely and instinctually bound up with the other two. We may give up the struggle for survival if we are unhappy. Flint, the Gombe chimpanzee, pined to death when his mother Flo died. Humans in prison hang themselves. Individuals of over-populated species may destroy themselves by flight or their young by reabsorption or abortion of the foetus. Without the right to pursue and achieve a degree of happiness, life itself becomes not worth having, and happiness means primarily a degree of physical comfort and health.

None of these inalienable rights is uniquely man's. They are expressions of the basic drives of the biological unit, of mammals, birds, fishes and reptiles, to go no further through the biosphere. Yet we reserve our declaration of independence with its inalienable rights for homo sapiens. We deny the first part of the declaration to other species. We do not say it is self evident that all animals are equal, although the inalienable rights are in fact based on the common instinctual needs of all. We deny other animals equality with us because if we are basing our argument on reason, not on a revelation of man's dominion over the beasts, we deny them our intelligence. We believe that they don't understand when their rights to life, liberty and the pursuit of happiness are alienated, and therefore they don't suffer. We believe that their consciousness is qualitatively, and not quantitatively, different from ours: that they are merely Cartesian automata. I haven't (because of lack of time) an opportunity to suggest why, I believe, we do this.

I will say, though, that it's not their ignorance but ours which has led to this conclusion, and that it's based on a failure of communication and imagination. That failure is now being shown up for what it is by the language work being done in America with chimpanzees. The value of that work to our discussion is not that it proves that chimpanzees can recognise and use gestures and symbols syntactically as language, but the things that they say when they do, the sudden opening of the window into their consciousness. There is a story which suggests that even our denial of rights to other species is not particularly human but common-animal. Lucy, a pre-adolescent chimpanzee at the Institute for Primate Studies, Oklahoma, was given a kitten. She carried it everywhere calling it " my baby ". The cat resisted and in clinging on to the wire cage hurt the pads of its feet. The human foster parents took the kitten away from Lucy, who was stricken with grief. One of her trainers then explained to her that she had hurt the cat's feet. When it was eventually returned to her, Lucy cradled the cat and, pointing to its feet, signed, " Hurt, hurt ".

I hope that we are as capable of learning as Lucy, and that we shall now begin to grant those self-evident and inalienable rights to other species, perhaps by drafting at this symposium a Declaration of Mutual Dependence.

Section Four

THE THREE MAJOR AREAS OF CONCERN

Killing for Food

JOHN HARRIS

When I first started to think and write about vegetarianism seven years ago, one of the things I remember attempting in a lighter moment was a short story, to be entitled *The last meat-eater*. It was to be a tale of the not-too-distant future when humanity had come to its senses, everyone had read *Animals, Men and Morals*, and all but a few confirmed carnivorous criminals had seen the light and given up eating meat. Somewhere —perhaps in California—there was a last persistent band of carnivores, reviled and persecuted, but still clinging to a belief in the inherent superiority of homo sapiens, the moral rectitude of the slaughter of animals, and, of course, the potency of good red meat.

This story, like most, never got beyond the planning stage. Any of you here who have been vegetarians for a while will recognise a certain wish-fulfilment in our situation being reversed in such a satisfying fashion. I recall very well feeling a bit of a martyr to the cause at the time, and my frustration and aggression were very often near the surface. To my mind, at the time, being slaughtered was too good a fate for meat eaters.

Of course, it is very natural for us to envisage a future in which animals are no longer slaughtered for food, and not only because of wish-fulfilment. It seems more and more that meat-eating, which has always been something of a luxury, something that only the affluent Western nations could afford on a large scale, is becoming too expensive for us. The most important development since I became a vegetarian those seven years ago has been the emergence of the startling facts of the economics of

E

meat production. A vegetarian arguing a few years ago would have said " eating meat is wrong, therefore you shouldn't do it " —and now we say " eating meat is economic nonsense " as a first shot in debate. I am sure you all know at least some of those devastating statistics and calculations which show the colossal waste involved in large-scale meat production. They have provided the most forceful and effective new arguments against eating animals, and we should be duly grateful for this big stick that providence has placed in our hands. How would we have managed to continue the struggle, if it had turned out that by some mysterious process animals produced *more* protein than they consumed? Even now we should remember when we use this type of argument that some animals on a small scale can produce meat fairly economically, by eating rubbish, or by using land where crops could not easily be grown. In the end, the main argument must always be the moral argument—it is wrong to kill animals for food, and that is that.

Since, then, the economics of vegetarianism have begun to be an important field of study, and the facts are, on the whole, so favourable to the cause, the meatless heaven seems only a few years away to many. Utopianism has become realism in a remarkably short space of time.

My own guess, though, is that there is no prospect in the foreseeable future of anything like complete vegetarianism on the planet. The trouble with the new economic arguments, from the moralists' point of view, is that they continue to appeal to the same root cause of most of our difficulties on the Earth—selfishness. They say, in effect, " *You* will run out of food if you don't change your tastes ". And meat prices have risen dramatically, seemingly to illustrate the many over-simple arguments that vegetarians have used, but in fact for many complicated reasons. People may now eat less meat—and I am thinking primarily of Western society for the moment—but it is because they have to, not because they want to.

In many ways this does not matter. I should be grateful for almost any means if the end was fewer animals going to the slaughterhouse. It would be nice if people would suddenly realise the error of their ways, but it would be quite unrealistic to expect it. The individual force of selfishness, and the social force of conformity combine to make an enemy that the moral righteousness of an argument will almost never defeat. No one who has engaged in the grass roots work of talking to people about vegetarianism and trying to convert them by reason, can realistically see this as more than a token gesture towards the end of abolishing the slaughter of animals. A glance at the most obvious historical precedent confirms this apparently negative comment. I'm thinking of the slave trade, that classic example of the exploitation of humans by humans. By an odd, but fairly characteristic, twist of human nature, people now look back on this era almost with pride because of the satisfaction they get when they think of the way that awful trade was ended. We have come to believe that the force which ended slavery was the moral campaign lead by William Wilberforce, that upright, eloquent and above all persistent hero, guardian of the nation's conscience, etcetera, etcetera. The truth is that the slave trade in the West Indies ended when the sugar plantations which required the slaves as labour became bankrupt in the face of competition. When their monopoly of sugar production was broken, they collapsed, and with them the backbone of slaving. No credit in this for us, of course; and so the part played by the moralists has been exaggerated to the point where it is commonly held that public opinion became so revolted by the trade it would have no more to do with it.

Animal campaigners ought to be familiar with this hypocrisy, for it is very active in their field. Even though most people, including many farmers, profess to be against factory farming, the lure of cheap eggs is too great. So it's out of sight, out of mind—kept out of sight, of course. No pictures of hen batteries on the counter where you pick up your Sunnylay eggs.

Please do not think that my belief in the efficacy of economic pressures in altering well established situations, and my further belief in the weakness of moral pressures together, entail the conclusion that we talkers and arguers might as well pack up and go home. What I am asking for is a realistic and informed view of what arguments have achieved in the past, and may achieve in the future. I feel that vegetarians have not spent enough time putting their cause in a social and historical perspective, in comparing their movement with other similar ones.

If, as I have been saying, our relatively meat-free future will be reached regardless of the rightness of the end, why then should we bother to think and discuss and campaign? The first, practical, reason, is that telling people who are being forced to give up meat that it is the right thing to do, sugars the pill. The change is that little bit easier.

The second reason, more of a hope, I admit, is that as it becomes more difficult for society to afford to eat meat, people will start to re-examine their attitudes to animals. They will no longer need to be defensive, to rationalise and cover up. The problem of finding a place for animals in and alongside human society will lead to a wider questioning of accepted values, so more people will ask " What kind of animals are human beings? How do they differ from their fellow animals? What is the upshot of these differences with regard to inter-specific relationships?" And it is in offering the searchers a coherent philosophy and a clear moral code that those who are now vegetarians can take the lead. The outlines of this code have been given, especially in the last few years; this conference itself represents a significant step forward. It is not my intention, perhaps contrary to appearances, to give any aid or comfort to those who say " We'll all be forced to be vegetarians soon; why should I bother to make a stand now?" To those of you here who still eat meat, I have a couple of brief remarks. First, *give it up*. The practice is morally indefensible; that means, simply, you ought not to continue it. Don't fool yourself with all those rationalisations about social pressures, and your own unfortunate weakness of will; just take the plunge. It's really not as bad as you might think.

Secondly, as I've said, philosophising and campaigning still have an important place in guiding public opinion, and you will not be very successful if you do not practice what you preach. No one can claim to have a genuine interest in the welfare of animals if they continue to condone their unnecessary slaughter, not, at any rate, without being accused of hypocrisy. To continue to eat the object of your concern is a stunning piece of self-deception, one of those very contradictions in human nature that make campaigning such a frustrating business.

Ethical Questions Concerning Modern Livestock Farming

RUTH HARRISON

My brief is to deal with the situation as it exists.

A great deal has been spoken about pain in this symposium but there are other forms of cruelty which may be much worse.

In Britain last year around half a million sows were kept in stalls in which they were unable to turn round. They stood on an unbedded floor of concrete or slats. Some were kept almost continually in darkness.

Some 40,000 young calves were reared for the " white veal " trade in slatted floored crates, unable to turn round, unable to lie down freely, unable even to groom themselves freely. Some, again, were kept in near darkness.

If anyone kept a dog in these conditions he would be prosecuted and looked upon with horror.

Around forty-five million hens were kept in crowded battery cages, unable to spread even one wing and balanced permanently on sloping wire. An experienced countryman—a regular contributor to *Country Life*—described the sense of shock he felt when he saw their condition after some months in the cages. A farmer friend offered him some spent layers with which to stock up his deep freeze and he duly collected them from the battery house and brought them home.

" I didn't appreciate," he said, " how the inmates really looked until I had my two sacks of condemned prisoners away from their Sing-Sing galleries. The combs of the hens were grey. They were without feathers from their heads to their under bellies. Worse still, their claws were bleeding for these had grown round the wires of the cages and the hens had had to be pulled out forcibly. They hadn't stretched a leg since they had gone into the cell as ' point of lay ' pullets. They had lived in the gloom for nearly a year . . . I stared at the pathetic creatures . . . they toppled against the wall of the house. They looked like old women overcome by too much gin."

One of the problems is that during the last two decades the design of livestock systems has moved out of the hands of stockmen and into the hands of engineers and technicians in allied trades, men of great skill and ingenuity but with little knowledge of animals, and especially of animal behaviour. Perhaps the phrase " design of livestock systems " is misleading, for often there has been no attempt at any overall design. The systems have developed, rather haphazardly, with each firm trying to maximise the use of its own products. Innovation has followed innovation and the animals have been in effect, the guinea pigs of constantly changing techniques and fashions.

The design of housing and equipment has been directed towards ease of management rather than the comfort and wellbeing of the animals. It is a matter of some concern that firms are allowed to put a product on the market without prior testing in the field. They can then proceed to sell it widely with all the pressures of high-powered salesmanship and advertising and nobody can stop them. Anyone concerned with the humanity of the product, on the other hand, has to produce evidence of pathological damage before action is even considered, and this means that much suffering is likely to occur before the product is altered or taken off the market. In Sweden this situation is reversed and firms are not permitted to sell such products until they have been independently tested at the firm's expense.

We like to think that in Britain we have strict laws preventing cruelty, but how far do they protect the sow in the stall, the veal calf in the crate or the hen in the battery cage?

The most important thing in law is that the suffering of the animal must be substantial and observable. It sticks to the traditionally accepted forms of cruelty: the infliction of injury, neglected festering sores, emaciation, advanced and untreated disease. It also recognises certain concepts, again easily seen, such as terrifying, beating or overloading an animal. Our new Act covering farm animals—the 1968 *Agriculture (Miscellaneous Provisions) Act* has added " unnecessary distress " to " unnecessary pain " as an offence, and it was to be hoped that this would cover *behavioural* distress. In practice the situation is unchanged. The Codes of Practice which the Minister issues for the guidance of stockmen are voluntary and are honoured more in the breach than the observance. Farms are visited by the State Veterinary Service who are always willing to investigate complaints. I will come back to them in a minute.

In the spring of this year a case was taken by the National Society for the Abolition of Factory Farming against a firm of veal producers. It was pointed out in Court that the calves were kept in pens 22″ wide by 5′ deep, on wooden slats without bedding, that they could not stretch their legs freely when they were lying down, had difficulty in grooming themselves, were fed entirely on a milk substitute and denied the roughage normally given to young ruminants. It was further stated that the calves were kept in darkness apart from twice-a-day feeding. The producers were not complying with the Codes of Practice which stipulate that the width of the pen should be equal to the height of the animal at the shoulder (thereby enabling it to turn round and freely to lie down and groom) and that the level of lighting should be such that all the calves can be seen clearly.

The Chairman of the Magistrates was a West Country dairy farmer, a splendid man. He listened very carefully hour after hour to the arguments and then said he would like to see the unit. This was arranged for the following morning and he then made his judgement. He said that the system was one that obviously *could* cause suffering, but that he had not *seen* any suffering that morning.

What worried me was the emphasis, yet again, on *seeing* suffering. We were right back at having to have pathological evidence of distress.

Which brings me back to the State Veterinary Service. As you know, they carried out an extensive survey of farms in 1970 to see whether farmers were complying with the provisions of the

Codes of Practice and whether any evidence of pain or distress was apparent. Their Report came up with statements like this:

On veal units:

"In the majority of the units the calves were unable to turn round after the 6th or 7th week of life, and in their last two or three weeks of life many of them also had difficulty in grooming. We found no evidence of pain or distress in the calves attributable to these restrictions."

On pigs—and this will go down as a classic!

"In those cases where pigs were kept in darkness or where the lighting was so reduced as to be insufficient to enable the pigs to be seen clearly we found no evidence that these systems of management were causing any pain or distress to the pigs."

Now to be fair to the State Veterinary Service I must point out that the Report was based on the veterinarians' judgement of the *physical* well-being of the animals. Perhaps they did not feel qualified to judge whether inability to groom was distressful to an animal. But today, when behavioural research on farm animals has itself become somewhat of a growth industry, and when there are special courses in behaviour for the Veterinary Service, we still get the same sort of statements quoted soothingly by the Minister in answer to anxious questioners in Parliament.

May I just remind you of what the late Sir Julian Huxley and nine fellow scientists wrote to *The Times* when the Codes were first issued in 1969?

"It is obvious to us that behavioural distress to animals has been completely ignored. Yet it is the frustration of activities natural to the animal which may well be the worst form of cruelty."

Genetic breeding and improved nutrition have led to younger slaughter weights and often the animals are slaughtered before distress can result in clinical symptoms which could be questioned in law. The situation is further confused by the armoury of drugs now in use on farms. These can delay and mask the effects of imperfect systems. And if we have to wait for clinical manifestations of suffering before we can take action, aren't we in effect taking the animal *beyond* the measure of stress it can endure in its short life?

West Germany has been the first country to pass an animal protection law which takes account of behavioural suffering. Its 1972 *Animal Protection Act* takes a positive stand. It lays down that the Act " shall serve to protect the life and well-being of the animal ", and " well-being " is explained as being " based on the normal vital functions developing and proceeding undisturbed in a manner which is typical for the species and which does justice to the animal's behaviour." Amongst other things, the Act lays down that the person responsible for the animal " shall provide accommodation which takes account of its natural behaviour ".

The Council of Europe's *European Convention on the Protection of Animals kept for Farming Purposes*, completed in 1976, also takes account of behaviour. Article 3 states:

" Animals shall be housed and provided with food, water and care in a manner which . . . is appropriate to their physiological and ethological needs in accordance with established experience and scientific knowledge."

Although the Convention in itself is not legally binding, member states which ratify it accept the responsibility to include its provisions in their national law. (Britain is in the process of ratifying it.) A working party from ratifying states will then be formed to draw up detailed regulations based on these guiding principles.

What is the next step?

Some of us here today are vegans who do not take part in any deliberate killing for food; some are lacto-vegetarians who take part in the killing inherent in dairy farming and commercial egg production, but who do not eat the flesh of the animals; some of us eat the flesh of the animals but try to avoid that which we think has been inhumanely produced; some of us just eat flesh. But most of us here today would, I think, accept that if we rear animals specifically to use their products or their bodies for our food our responsibility to those animals is increased, rather than decreased—as so often seems to be the case in practice.

While there is greater interest in vegetarianism and veganism than ever before, I think that ethically most people will accept the position of eating meat on the assumption that the animal has some enjoyment in life while it lives and is then slaughtered as humanely as possible. This situation, as a previous speaker pointed out, is unlikely to change, except in degree, for some time to come. Now an animal's enjoyment of life is, as far as we know, largely in the exercise of patterns of behaviour inherited from the wild.

I spoke earlier of the sow in the stall and the veal calf in the crate, unable to turn round or to lie down comfortably, and I pointed out that if a dog were kept in these conditions its owner would be prosecuted. The young calf and pig are also active, playful and intelligent animals—why should the law be interpreted differently for them? Obviously there should be common welfare parameters for all animals managed by man whether they are used as pets, for amusement, food, research or education.[129] This should apply also to different classes of animal within each category. As far as food animals are concerned, for example, the same welfare considerations should apply whether the animal is for slaughter, breeding or showing.

Management implies some interference with an animal's natural inclinations. This interference should, however, be kept to an absolute minimum, and for every deprivation there should be an environmental compensation.

The well-being of the animal will be assured only if it is kept within the limits of that environmental range to which it can *adapt without suffering*. This must form the criterion for any future system.

Are we prepared to make the radical changes which this would lay upon us? So far there are few signs that we are, but I hope that my fears will be confounded.

This is a particularly apt time to pause and assess which way we are going. There are many other ethical issues the solution to which may well affect the type of system we use in future.

The mass production systems in use today were developed in the decades of plenty—the 1950s and 1960s—when imports of feeding-stuffs and energy were cheap and plentiful, labour was leaving the land and we were faced with a steadily rising population. We thought this situation would go on for ever and ever. Now we are faced with the reverse situation. The population of Europe has stabilised and may even be starting to fall, we have massive unemployment with agricultural schools bursting at the seams and people desperately trying to get back onto the land. We also face dwindling reserves of energy, foodstuffs, fertilisers and water.

One situation which remains the same today as it was twenty years ago is that the meat produced goes to feeding the overfed, especially in the west, and has little to do with the hungry in the developing countries. I regard the argument that we are robbing the starving of food by feeding grain to our livestock as grossly over-simplified, yet of course there is some truth in it. What seems to me just as serious is that we tend to be fashion setters for other countries and of course our commercial salesmen try their utmost to take over potential new markets whether or not it is in the interests of the people of those countries to use their products. Whereas in India, for example, the people were in the past mostly vegetarian, increased travel has brought them in touch with western standards to which they aspire and, sadly, included in these standards is meat eating. Some sixty per cent of the people of India are now prepared to eat meat. I say "sadly" because their country cannot support a food programme of increased meat eating. It cannot support, either, the use of battery cages which involve using precious grain for the hens, in place of the scavenging hen which did not compete for its food with the human population.

What does seem certain is that there is going to be an increasing demand globally for animal feed, and competition will increase prices so that production of food animals will have to be cut back. Obviously the first priority on land in all countries is the maintenance of sufficient supplies of basic plant foods to ensure an adequate diet for their populations. Only then can surplus land be used for animals.

These pressures—on land, the need to conserve dwindling energy supplies, the need for a fairer sharing of the world's resources—may make it easier for governments to make radical changes in the way food animals are kept. Remembering our special responsibilities as fashion setters, it is to be hoped that steps will be taken because we feel a moral responsibility to do so rather than because circumstances compel us to do so at a later date.

If we adopt as our aim systems which give the animal an environment to which it can adapt without suffering it will not be easy to maintain very large units and mass-production techniques. It will tend to take production out of the hands of the big monopolies and back into the hands of the farmer, which is no bad thing. Farming is not, after all, a conveyor belt industry churning out nuts and bolts, it is a biological process, self-renewing, the farmer being a husbandman for the future.

If we wish to develop systems which take account of the animal's behavioural needs they must be developed by stockmen and ethologists with knowledge of the animal's behaviour. Technologists, if needed, should work under their guidance. Something which we could do with much more enthusiasm than we appear able to muster at the moment, is to pick out those systems in use today which appear most advantageous from the animal's point of view, and to concentrate all the effort and ingenuity into making them viable, which has formerly been reserved for systems which do not now meet our criteria.

Even without the European Convention people all over Europe are rebelling against the more extreme systems and there must very soon be some effort to meet these criticisms by a run-down on veal crates (there can be no moral justification whatsoever for inducing an anaemia in an animal simply to produce white flesh for a snob market), sow stalls and piglet cages, and battery cages for hens, other birds and animals. Ultimately I think that progress lies in a return to balanced farming systems, and I suspect that it will be the ecological rather than humanitarian pressures which will prevail.

Meanwhile we must do all in our power to educate the public, for I believe that in the end only a change of heart is really effective.

Finally, may I register strong disagreement about the desirability of breaking into buildings, setting fire to vehicles, and other such acts of vandalism carried out in the name of "animal liberation" and "freedom fighting". I believe that if we encourage anarchy we will be working towards denying the animals the little legal protection which they now have. Our aim must continue to be to strengthen and improve that protection.

The Experts Say This Is Not Cruel . . .

PETER ROBERTS

We stand right now at a crossroads; factory farming is entering a new phase and the time is ripe for ordinary people to make decisions—decisions which will affect the future welfare of farm animals and which will also affect us. These animals are part of nature, part of *our* nature; they are part of an environment which will reflect back to us what we show to it—compassion or violence. It is within our power now to create for the future an environment in which we can peacefully co-exist, or to inherit a hostile environment, finding ourselves threatened on all sides by disease, hunger and pests: the implications are endless. We have to ask ourselves whether it is possible to rid our planet of famine by feeding more and more caged animals, devoting 370 million tons of annual harvest to them alone.

Ordinary people are made to feel unimportant these days; decision making seems to have been taken from them. *We* have to tell the ordinary people like ourselves that *WE CAN* decide the future. The assessment of suffering in livestock is not the domain of the expert, it is a matter of commonsense, a commodity more often found in the layman than in the expert. *The State Veterinary Service Report to Parliament* said that there was no suffering detected in the keeping of a calf in a 22″ wide veal crate night and day for all its life, and unable to turn round. Note the lack of commonsense.

They even say " it is not in the calf's interest to be able to turn round ". What they should have said was that if the calf turned round it might get stuck in its narrow crate and be forced to dung where its head should be and thus muck up the crazy system which the factory farmers had invented for it. These experts, among them the State vets, and a whole host of pseudo-scientific agronomists, tell us that we must not have feelings or try by subjective means to assess the degree of suffering in animals. Anthropomorphism is out they say, yet anthropomorphism may be the most valuable guide we have to assess suffering in factory farm animals.

Such agronomists despise talk of freedom, or justice, or the rights of animals, yet it has to be admitted that the values which they ridicule are those precise values upon which we have built our civilisation. We have to avoid the plausible arguments of the agricultural experts, we have to tell the *people* that *they* are the future, and that it is up to them, to all of us, to decide where we're going and what sort of a world we want, and then to create that world.

If we do not, then an increased number of livestock species will be subjected to battery farming. Massive cruelty both mental and physical is at the present time inflicted on some 300,000,000 animals every year in factory farms. By denying them light, movement, exercise, occupation and the social contact of their own kind, we reverse their evolution and in so doing we reverse our own. We, with them, are a whole, and when we damage them we damage ourselves.

In some areas there is hope. For instance, there is now no justification for the veal crate; calves can now more economically be brought to slaughter weight in communal strawed pens on the new Volac machines which feed milk gruel through artificial teats to them. There is no justification either for keeping them in veal crates nor for muzzling them. Another breakthrough is that only last week some members of the Aberdeen N.F.U. called for a ban on calf exports.

But elsewhere things look black indeed. The economics of the battery cage are no more to be confined to egg production; broilers (the oven-ready chicken in the supermarkets) will soon be reared in this country in light cages, four of them to the size of an L.P. sleeve. There are battery cages already in use in Ireland for the production of bacon heavyweight pigs, that are kept in wire cages, tier above tier of them, right through to bacon weight. There is black news also from Denmark where the farmers now want to revoke the ban on batteries which has been in force in that country since 1950. They say that if they do not have that ban revoked they will be unable to meet the demand for eggs from the people of Denmark and that battery eggs will be imported from the rest of Europe. But the editor of this month's Journal *Poultry Industry* says:

" I can't accept the argument in this context. Denmark's decline in egg exports has been most marked over the past two years but their anti-cage policy is much older " (27 years old, in fact).

He says that there has been a substantial cut-back in egg production and that it has been due to high interest rates and reduced returns to farmers.

The possibility of Denmark having her battery ban revoked, and all the agitation in this country to extend the use of the battery cage to fattening chicken and pigs, could not come at a worse time, for it is now that a big fight is going on in Europe to ban batteries. In Switzerland a £340,000 campaign is being waged to have batteries phased out over a ten year period. In an opinion poll conducted for the Swiss Federation for the Protection of Animals, 88% of those questioned considered that the keeping of hens in battery cages is an act of cruelty, and 65% said that the import of eggs from other countries which did not ban batteries should be prohibited also; 48% of those questioned said that they would pay as much more for eggs as it costs to have the hens living without discomfort. If this ban can be achieved in Switzerland the campaign will be extended to Germany and Holland, where much groundwork campaigning has been done. In conclusion let me say that we have listened to the veterinary experts and the agronomists for too long; the time has come for action. The first action that we should take, and that urgently, is to send a message of support to the organisers of the campaign to ban batteries in Switzerland. They do not know whether they have the support of the British animal welfare movement or not:

I ask, moreover, that a parallel campaign be mounted in this country. We want more action and less words. It is a time for decision and a time for action : this is an opportunity that may not come again.

Dietethics: Its Influence on Future Farming Patterns

JON WYNNE-TYSON

Ecological studies now embrace considerations unthinkable in orthodox circles a few years ago. Not only our use for, but our treatment of, animals is at last being seen as a legitimate area for investigation.

But of all the ways in which we have exploited and ill-treated other species, their use for human food has until recently been the most overlooked. Now, however, enquiry into our ethical obligations to the many creatures we directly or indirectly consume has become so strong a concern that it perhaps deserves the label (and I fear we live in a labelled age) of Dietethics. That is, the study of the ethics of diet.

These ethics, let it be stressed, relate not only to the animals we eat, but also to the world's malnourished and starving human millions. In order that the affluent nations may enjoy the meat and dairy products that have long been the focal point of their dietary patterns, vast quantities of grain must be fed to cattle. It is not an over-simplification to say that if we abandoned the grossly wasteful habit of eating our plants via the bodies of animals, there need be no starving people in the world today.

Thankfully, such facts are being recognised, not only by previously unconcerned laymen but also in academic and scientific circles. What is more, there is a growing tendency to correlate these various realisations, rather than treat them in isolation.

Indeed, there appears to be increasing acceptance of the view that the science of ecology stands—or should stand—for a concept of life and values in which the practical, the ethical and the philosophical elements are given equal weight. Now that our exploitation of the natural world is at last being seen to be inextricably bound up with the exploitation of our fellow men and women, we are possibly entering a new age in which the understanding we term " ecology " may have an effect similar in many respects to that compound of wonder, knowledge and fierce inner need for an explanation, a sense of direction, and a framework of behaviour, that in the past prompted notions of the Deity.

However, there are still many problems and mental blockages to be overcome. While convinced of the value of communication, and of the need to focus on points of accord rather than on our smaller differences, I think it relevant to warn that although ecological concerns have brought wider understanding of the inter-relationships of all species, progress—at least through what we now call the media—is being hampered and misdirected by those whose personal habit patterns influence them more strongly than any rational desire to accept scientific fact, or to arrive at an objective view of our obligations to other sentient life.

The current interest in self-sufficiency is in many respects very welcome, but among its more vociferous spokesman are those whose concern seems to be more with scale than with any genuine reappraisal of our basic attitudes to other species. These spokesmen include both urban sentimentalisers and pastoral ecomystics, whose determination to cling to the basic diet that until now has been made so easily available by the meat and dairy industries, has provoked their hot defence of " backyard " stock-rearing. That such regression may be possible for some during a transitional period is not denied, but in the long term it is an unrealistic dream for any but a tiny minority; a compromise aimed at reducing rather than eliminating unnecessary cruelty; a measure motivated more by expediency than by compassion.

Perhaps a more dangerous viewpoint needing identification is that expressed by those who conduct anachronistic but popular campaigns to justify the behavioural deficiences of the most miseducated members of our species. Commentators in this field would have us believe that the impulse to kill is an innate part of man's biological make-up, and that meat and many of its by-products are necessities, rather than mere wants for which there are ample alternatives. One comes across such nonsensical assertions as that "we should be doing something biologically unnatural if we all became herbivores" (Michael Crawford: *Earth in Danger*).

Most Aunt Sallies of this ilk are already flat on their backs. It is doubtful whether any balanced observer will leave this conference with the illusion that there can be any rational, scientific aesthetic, instinctual, moral or philosophical justification for our treatment of the creatures we wish to eat. Nevertheless, we must identify and deal with the specious arguments of those who at heart seek no fundamental alteration in long-established patterns of habit.

To turn to practicalities, what feasible alternative is there to the present dominant stock-farming economy governing our eating patterns in the West? I suggest there is no doubt that the only alternative in the long term (and it is the long term we must keep constantly in mind) is vegan farming. This is not to suggest that it is practicable to bring orthodox farming policies to a halt over-night, as some of the more hysterically anti-progress lobbies seem to fear. Today's butchers and farmers need not fear for their livelihoods now or in the near future. Fundamental change invariably comes slowly. But they, with us, should face that the only ethical and lastingly workable future economy must be based on farming methods which are solely directed to the growing and consuming of plant foods. There can be no eventual place in such an economy for animals bred under man's control to satisfy his acquired taste for eating their bodies.

These are the first brush-strokes of a rather different picture to that painted by those dinosaurian pragmatists who continue to seek solutions based on animal exploitation. The don't-knock-meat lobby plans actually to *extend* our cruelties by massive programmes for farming wild animals on top of a continuing policy of supporting domestic breeds on high protein foods that should go directly, and with far more responsible use of land resources, to humans. Such planning, if we take that vital long-term view,

is the opposite of what conservation and ecological studies should
be about. It is part and parcel of big agri-business that has
spawned such recent developments as the production of protein
for animal food from a derivative of natural gas, for the squalid
purpose that intensively-reared livestock may continue to bring
ever-greater profits to an industry still reluctant to read the
writing on its wall.

Many people associate the term " conservationist " with a caring and concerned regard for our environment. But conservationists' pleas for the preservation of wild species need rigorous
examination. Preservation for what? Too often, for man to crop
them with no more pity than he feels lifting turnips. When I
hear the word " conservation " I know that someone is reaching
for his gun. If our only motive in conserving certain species is
man's long-term benefit, then it would be more compassionate to
encourage their earliest possible extinction.

I see no realistic long-term alternative to a world whose
natural resources are regarded as factors with which we have
to collaborate—not dominate—in order to take our proper place
in the scheme of things. I suggest the reasons for this are not only
expedient, but evolutionary. The cold arrogance of those who wish
man to have self-interested mastery over everything he regards as
beneath him is an out-of-date and short-sighted perversion of
our responsibilities and potentialities.

However idealistic it may now seem to some, it is surely our
role to envisage and work towards a world which is sanely and
humanely controlled, not exploited, by those with the vision and
humility to question established *mores*. I say " humility " because
it is the arrogance born of long habit and entrenched prejudice
that seeks to defend behavioural patterns that have long been a
matter of comfortable acceptance for a privileged minority at the
expense of the rest of the world.

It seems inevitable that sooner or later nations must collaborate
to restrict populations to a size that will enable them to be fed
on the many and adequate forms of plant life, while at the same
time adopting those policies of deurbanisation and deindustriali-
sation that environmentalists are now recognising to be essential.

Indeed, although this is not the place to argue the matter, for it is hardly an arguable or neglected proposition, the fate of the whole world depends upon our species's success in controlling its numbers. No plague or pestilence is a greater threat than the infestation of humanity.

The symbiosis that could and should exist between man and his environment depends upon our adoption of a dietary system in keeping with our physiological structure. Whatever our spiritual potentialities may be (and I have no qualification to deny that they may be infinite), it is accepted fact that physically man is " by design " neither carnivorous nor omnivorous. He is a frugivore, " intended " to eat the fruits, nuts, shoots and other plant foods that form the basis of the normal diet of those great apes that are our nearest relatives. What habits some members of our species have got into since climatic and other factors supervened is neither here nor there. We know too much to suggest seriously that we can bring anything but benefit to ourselves and our environment by returning so far as is possible to that dietary system for which we are chemically and physiologically constituted.

In the gradual relinquishment of animal husbandry in favour of vegan farming methods, silviculture is an area of enormous potential. The important recent book *Forest Farming*, by J. Sholto Douglas and Robert A. de J. Hart, unfortunately failed to make clear that if we give up farming animals, a silvicultural/agricultural world economy could support even today's populations and provide such an abundance of land that a balanced and sane husbandry could be re-established, based on organic methods and bringing to an end the present vicious spiral of artificial fertilisers, herbicides and pesticides. Indeed, the book's findings may well be manipulated by those seeking ways of further prolonging an omnivorous economy by tapping sources of high plant protein for feeding to livestock. This is why the ethics of diet must lead, not be led by, the economics and expediences of the situation. Nevertheless, its findings confirm that the yields from farming food-bearing trees are far greater even than from conventional ground crops, and infinitely in excess of the meagre returns from farming animals. Responsibly employed, such facts can herald an age as near to the elysian as anything that man in his present state of evolution has any right to expect.

Can the people who are thinking along these lines any longer be regarded as impractical cranks? I think not. Compare the following extract from literature put out by the Vegan Society of the U.K. with what is currently being stated (often as though it were some astonishing new discovery!) by respected orthodox nutritionists, ecologists and agriculturalists:

" The age of man the ruthless predator is coming to an end. He is wasting his resources and fouling his nest. It is imperative that those who are alive to the enormous challenge of the environmental crisis, go forward (not 'back to nature') to pioneer a way of life that is attainable by all the world's people and sustainable within natural cycles. Wise land use is of primary importance. What is required is a change from traditional agriculture to intensive horticulture, with careful composting of all wastes with plant materials to keep the land in good heart without animal manure or artificial fertilisers. The landscape of a vegan world would show small fields of cereals, fruits, vegetables and compost-producing plants surrounded by shelter-belts of fruit and nut-bearing trees. Hill slopes and other areas unsuitable for cultivation would be used for trees of all types, as a renewable source of fuel and raw material for many purposes, as well as for their function in maintaining the environment. One-sixth to one-third of an acre per head would be required for the vegan diet. Even in densely populated England, which has nearly an acre for each inhabitant, wide areas would be left for wild life and recreation."

Let us consider for a moment what the habit of meat-eating involves in terms of the world's food supplies. It means the extensive growing of crops, notably grain, in order to feed them to animals from which, after an expensive interval, we take back in exchange an absurdly disproportionate quantity of food in a form that we hallow, quite incorrectly, as being superior to the plant life from which it was derived. In addition to being fed the corn that requires great tracts of the world's land supply, the animals themselves, even in these days of " factory-farming ", still need further huge areas for pasture. About four-fifths of the world's agricultural land is used for feeding animals, and only about one-fifth for feeding man directly. Most of the fertile land devoted to cattle could show a much quicker and more economical return if used for crops suitable for direct feeding to human beings. On average, animals eat twenty pounds of protein for every pound they yield as meat. In comparing plant with animal food production in terms of yields per acre in less developed and more developed countries, it has been shown that :

> " the plant protein production from cereals and pulses was three to six times the production of milk protein from the same area under the same conditions. For plant protein from leafy vegetables it was seven to twelve times. When these plant/animal ratios were measured against meat protein they were approximately doubled. On the average, about a fifth of the plant protein fed to animals becomes available for human consumption as milk, and about a tenth of it is turned into meat." (*Plant Foods for Human Nutrition*, Vol. 1, No. 2, Pergamon Press).

The ratios and methods of calculation vary a good deal, and I have discussed them in more depth in my book *Food for a Future*. But the conclusion is always the same—that the world's human populations could more responsibly and economically be fed directly on plant life. Meat can be phased out (a process governed by demand) just as other forms of food and consumer goods have come and gone in obedience to fashion and the fluctuations of climate and natural resources. So, too, can the trades that depend on animal foods.

So far from vegetarianism springing from the anthropomorphism of predominantly urban dwellers, as has been suggested by its more superficial critics, it and its inevitable successor veganism are increasingly being recognised as a logical, even inescapable, process, essentially relevant, essentially practical, essentially compassionate to all species; the province no longer of the so-called crank, but of scientists and philosophers and clear-thinking laymen.

The practical details of a switch to a farming economy based on plants as the immediate source of mankind's food are well within our competence to grasp and implement. We are within sight of the day when crop rotation, multiple cropping, and adequate land for resting periods, for green manuring, for cover crops, and for the supply of composting materials will have placed the whole sad and shameful practice of stock-rearing, with all its attendant evils, in the annals of an extravagant and barbaric past. The changeover requires only—or, at least, above all—a change of heart and a conscious decision to rethink our educational priorities.

And therein lies the key. It is only by education that these fundamental changes can come about. This has been mentioned during the conference, but too little stressed. Those of us now in adult life must surely recognise that it is the rising generations who most need to be convinced of such basics as the paramount necessity for preventing the infestation of our own species, and for a truly and less selectively compassionate regard for our total environment. The answers lie always with the young. We must educate them away from becoming yet another generation of dinosaurs—a species which, let it be remembered, abandoned flesh-eating for a herbivorous diet too late in the day to avoid extinction!

Humane Education

D. A. PATERSON

By definition, humane education aims to promote kindness and so to prevent cruelty to all forms of life: for this reason it is humane education which will provide the basic solution to almost every problem which we could discuss at this symposium.

My job is to help put this humane attitude back into the educational system itself—and I can legitimately include the entire adult population of the Country as being within that system: otherwise, since children are so influenced by adults (and vice versa) the work which we do for children would itself of necessity be undone.

There are some 33,000 schools in England and Wales. There are also some nine million children and young people in "the educational system", and something more than one million animals too! What on earth are the animals doing there at all? This question must not only be asked, but must be firmly *answered*. It is not an issue over which we in the animal welfare movement can continue to cultivate an "open mind". To quote Endymion, I fear that here "the cult of the open mind is a way of camouflaging a poverty of education which has no view of life at all to communicate". This is an issue on which all who have considered it *must* have views.

My own view of the educational system and of the way in which we who are concerned with animal welfare should work within it follows. You may not agree!

Very many primary schools keep pets, and our attitude here can reasonably easily be defined. Animals *are* there whether we like it or not, and I feel that we can continue to condone their presence, provided only that they are being *really well cared for*.

Animals give rise to a spontaneous and fascinated concentration of mind in young children : they provide an educational aid without parallel. That of course is *why* they are there in the first place, but what actually *happens* to them while they are there is a different question !

Children need to relate to animals, but they must do this in a *caring* situation : the keeping of animals always requires some justification, and animals can only be an effective teaching aid in the primary school if they help to cultivate, by being there, a sense of *responsibility* in both children and teachers. This objective is completely undermined if the classroom animals are at all neglected, or if there is an obvious lack of empathy between teacher and animals.

As far as secondary schools go, our attitudes should be more readily defined, since the issues are themselves much more clearly cut. Here, animals are present for one reason only : they are to be *studied*—alive when alive, and dead (for dissection) when they are dead. Our first criterion must again be the well-being of the animals. There is nothing against dissection of itself, so far as the animal is concerned. If an animal has been kept well and killed humanely prior to dissection, it feels nothing : it is dead. What happens to it *beforehand* is, however, a matter of concern to all of us. How did it live ? How did it die ? Did it need to be there in the first place ?

The R.S.P.C.A., the Royal Society, and the Institute of Biology, have all agreed that there need to be no dissection at all in schools prior to that which is laid down in ' A ' Level Biology Syllabuses. Hence, whatever the conditions of animal-care prior to their usage, there should be no question of dissection for most school pupils. Dissection is unwarranted, and so the keeping of animals for that purpose is also totally unjustifiable —the issue should not even arise.

As far as *children* are concerned, too, dissection not only confers no benefit, but may even be positively harmful—undoing the good work of the primary school, and desensitising the children to the needs and sufferings of their fellow creatures.

Inhumane attitudes towards animals in secondary schools are sometimes " justified " by saying that children " need to be taught to kill " in rural science : similarly they may be taken to hunting or coursing events " to form a balanced opinion on the subject " ! More often, though, cruelties in schools spring from ignorance or sheer thoughtlessness—killing pet animals in front of children, for instance. Direct experience of violence and cruelty must always be a cause for deep concern, but even more so where this is being inflicted, in our names, under the sacred mantle of " education ".

Humane education, therefore, must go far beyond the school system. We must teach and inspire others by our own attitudes, by our own example, and, perhaps above all, do this by setting universally *attainable* goals. There is little point in setting goals which people feel to be unattainable. In this context, therefore, we should not (yet) say " no " to *all* dissection in schools—we should limit our primary goal to one which is immediately attainable : confining dissection to sixth-form biology students. Similarly, our numbers are such that we cannot possibly teach *all* children a humane approach directly. But we *can* teach this to the relevant teachers—this *is* attainable—which is why we have started to do it!

To return to the beginning : we must make up our minds as to what education is : it is our foundation for living, but it also continues throughout life. The parameters of our educational system are laid down by our present day society and these are parameters within which we must ourselves work if we are to achieve our goals.

The field is open to us : there is a tremendous interest in animal welfare : let us take advantage of it. We must work out our own ideas and not, like Dr. Downey, " earn a high reputation for sobriety of judgment by resolutely refusing to have any definite view on any subject whatsoever." Our goals, on the other hand, must be attainable and our work co-ordinated across the animal welfare movement so that our messages are mutually compatible. We must lead, without being so extreme in our views as to be rejected before we are heard—one step will surely, steadily and more rapidly than we dream, lead to the next.

Let us, then, make up our minds as to what we are going to do about animal welfare and humane education for this generation and for the next—and do it!

Altruism and Aggression in Animals

W. J. JORDAN

In any discussion on animal suffering it is sometimes argued and often implied that if man carried the argument for animal rights to its logical conclusion he would have to prevent the cat from catching mice and predators from killing and eating meat. The essence of this argument is that nature herself is cruel and " red in tooth and claw ". This belief is not based on sound scientific study but on cursory observation leading to acceptance: familiarity breeds consent.

At the same time man ignores or is unaware of his need—aesthetic, moral and practical—to be a part of nature: aesthetically to nourish his soul, morally to benefit his gentleness and mental well being, and practically to preserve the fine balance of ecology.

In this paper we will consider briefly two aspects of the proposition that nature is not as cruel as we may think and that man needs for his own harmony to have a reverence for life. Biology and ethics are coming together—are we what we are because our genes demand it, and if we disobey are we in disharmony?

Altruism puzzled Darwin and he solved it by applying natural selection to the family as a unit. At first sight it might seem that the bully, the strongest man, or the cheat ought to secure more mates, gain more food and the safest place to rest, and so would ensure that he left plenty of surviving offspring with the same attributes as himself. More kindly, less aggressive, more co-operative animals would suffer and their off-spring would therefore quickly die out. Yet altruism persisted.

Many biologists ignored Darwin's theory and persisted in their contention that all animals were aggressive, especially Homo sapiens. It was not until the 1960s that altruism was considered again and Robert Trivers proposed the " evolution of reciprocal altruism " claiming that our sense of right and wrong is built into us, is in our genes. Man is not aggressive : rather was it the extreme development of kindliness and co-operation that accompanied or promoted the great leap from apes to humans.

If one comes across a man drowning in a canal, the normal human reaction is to jump into the water to try to save him. Why is this so? There is certainly no shortage of people in the world! Biologists have become greatly interested in this situation and they reason that if there is a fairly good chance that the man will die if he is not helped, and also if there is a small chance of the rescuer dying in the water if he makes an attempt to save him, then provided that the man was his brother he would certainly be obliged to try to save him, because the brother would be carrying many of the family genes. If he was a cousin he would be carrying fewer genes, and one would be less obliged to save him. If on the other hand the man is not a relative, then a different kind of reasoning comes into play. The rescuer may incur a considerable degree of risk, and yet on the other hand, in the future the situation may well be reversed : by rescuing this man now he could in turn rescue you when you got into trouble. This is the principle of reciprocal altruism which operates quite widely in human affairs. Obviously, if it benefits the genes, then this behaviour is capable of evolving. The theory of course suggests that our sense of right and wrong is built into us, a sort of basic need. Strange to say, many people find this proposition more unsavoury than the theory that aggressiveness is part of man's animal nature.

The decision whether or not to be aggressive or altruistic, certainly in so far as animals are concerned, has costs and benefits that can be quantified to explain why they are stable. In 1973 J. Maynard-Smith and G. R. Price[130] published their theory, the central concept of which is an evolutionary stable strategy (ESS) which is a gene-programmed behaviour pattern, not a conscious idea: thus, attack: if he runs away pursue him and if he fights back, retreat. Such a strategy must be stable under natural selection to survive. In which case most members of the population adopt it and no mutant strategy will give a higher reproductive fitness.

Suppose, said Maynard-Smith, that a population of a species of animals consists of two types—aggressive and placid individuals; he called them hawks and doves. Hawks will fight hard and get injured, doves will pretend to fight but will soon run away and so won't get hurt; of course they will also lose their prize—territory, food, mates, etc. Let us give a value of obtaining the prize, say 60, and of losing 0 and of being severely injured −100 and of wasting time pretending to fight −10. These values will of course vary according to species, but the theory remains the same.

If the population is all hawks, then an individual can expect to win half the contests and lose half, that is +60 and −100. So his payoff is −20 (half way between +60 and −100). A single dove in this population of hawks is better off, for although he loses half his fights his payoff is 0—considerably better than the −20 of the hawks. So doves will tend to multiply and spread through the population.

If the population is all doves, on the other hand, the dove will win half and lose half of his contests with a payoff of 60 and 0 respectively, but will also lose −10 for wasting time in the contest, a much better score than that for the hawk population. If a (mutant) hawk arrives in this dove population he has a field day, for he wins all his contests and stands no risk of injury, his payoff being +60 all the time! So hawks will multiply in the population and there will be a swing from doves to hawks and back until a stable ratio is reached. Of course if only all would be doves, every individual would benefit, but this situation is not stable.

There are of course other possibilities—the bully, the retaliator, prober-retaliator. Of all five possibilities the retaliator is the one that is evolutionarily stable.

The negative payoff may not always be injury—it can be time,

F

which is a valuable commodity in itself. So species that are well protected and unlikely to be injured may spend time in posturing to each other; since they can only afford so much time for it, the individual loses, for he has wasted time that could be spent on seeking food, etc. elsewhere.

This theory explains how altruism can exist and aggression be curtailed—they are simply selected for in time.

Going back to the first point that I wanted to make, namely that nature is not cruel, I have shown how extreme aggression is not an evolutionary stable strategy and fighting within the species is formalised—a type of jousting, that seldom leads to death and only occasionally to serious injury. It also explains how altruism, by that I mean those acts which increase the probability of survival of the social group at the expense of risk to the individual, can arise and become a stable strategy within a species.

Yet we look around and see nature cruel, man aggressive and hell-bent on his own destruction; pain, disease and suffering apparently without meaning. Perhaps we should look again. Though parasitism exists in wild animals there are few diseased animals to be seen in wild areas where there has been no interference by man. Wild animals live full lives, but though in constant danger do not " suffer ", otherwise their ability to survive would be affected. There are few aged, crippled, chronically sick animals. And when prey animals are killed naturally by predators other than man there is good evidence that often if not always no pain is felt. This sort of thing happens with humans too, and examples abound—men injured in the heat of the moment in a football game and feeling no pain until they return to the changing room; parents beating out the burning clothes of their child and feeling no pain until afterwards. Livingstone describes graphically how he was attacked and dragged away by a lion and felt no pain until after he had escaped : indeed a friend of mine was knocked down and severly mauled by a lion, and though he could feel his own blood running down his back he felt no pain until he reached the hospital and they began to suture his wounds. This is a physiological process called (when extreme) neurogenic shock, and we are only beginning to understand all its ramifications.

I have emphasised predators other than man because unfortunately man uses methods of killing and capturing that can and do cause extreme pain and suffering.

As we have seen, animals fight over territory or mates but this is generally no more serious than jousting. For example, the males of many snake species fight each other by wrestling without using their fangs. In some species of deer the bucks fight head on, antler to antler, and refrain from attacking when the opponent turns away though they could quite easily win the contest if they did so. This is a form of limited war. We have also seen that altruism exists in animals—parents to offspring, members of the flock who spot danger first and raise the alarm putting themselves at risk, and male baboons who turn to face a leopard giving time for the females and babies to escape. As Dawkins explains in his new book called *The Selfish Gene*,[131] these acts of altruism may be motivated by the genes' effort to spread in the population. A behaviour pattern can be altruistic and at the same time be motivated by the " selfishness " of the genes.

However, man has been able to alter the slow process of evolution by his ability to learn. Guided by culture rather than his genes he is changing the environment faster than he can cope with it, and he is losing his reverence for life. He is captivated by ideas which increase his rate of learning, though they are not necessarily correct. He has become dazzled by knowledge—the fallibility of Science is never questioned. Indeed if anyone wants to praise anything one calls it " scientific " and one can denigrate ideas or theories simply by calling them " unscientific ". The use of the word unscientific is taken by most people to mean unworthy. Indeed science has become the new religion, scientists the high priests, and their ritual attire the white laboratory coat. Science is shaped to some degree by social circumstances. It is a human creation rather than an autonomous non-human thing with intrinsic rules of its own. It is created, renewed and maintained by the human species by basic needs for food and safety, protection, affection and love, for respect and status, for self respect and self fulfilment. Therefore science is based on human values and is itself a value system.

We must not rely wholly on ideas whether they be scientific or otherwise; rather we must " listen " to our own inner natures.

When one says these things, there are those who immediately point out the benefits of science, and in particular medicine. Whilst not wishing to detract too much from all such benefits, it is a sobering thought that if one considers man from the biological point of view, in spite of the effort and money expended on medical services, the decline in early mortality other than through natural causes has slowed to almost zero. And with only a few exceptions the contribution of antibiotics and vaccines has been a minor one. Morris reviewed absence rates due to sickness in man and they showed no improvement from 1920–1960. In fact there has been a rise in chronic disease.

It is true that many infectious diseases have been controlled or are almost eliminated, but others have taken their place—nature does not like an empty ecological niche. Many now are degenerative diseases, diseases of maladaption which are increasing as mankind moves even further from his hunter-gatherer ancestors, and steps outside *his* ecological niche. Available evidence shows the importance of man's harmony with his environment. The major contributions of the medical and pharmaceutical professions have been the relief of pain and symptoms: real health has not improved.

One is captivated also by the idea of comforts—the protection of a house warmed and powered by fossil and nuclear fuels, the ability to travel rapidly from place to place, and so on. Does one need these? In hot countries the greatest pleasure is to sleep under the stars away from the noise and pollution of modern forms of transport. Of course there would have to be a lot fewer people, but I am persuaded that that might not be a bad thing. My happiness comes from wild nature, the liberty and loveliness, the crystal atmosphere and the landscape to myself with the feeling of wisdom all around.

Nature is necessary for mankind, his survival depends on it, that is the continual message of ecology. His growth and understanding depend on it too, and we have seen his genes demand that he does what they dictate for peace of mind and contentment. Man is motivated by basic needs such as hunger and thirst and when these are satisfied he becomes aware of other needs; for example to love and belong. Then other needs, such as to know and to learn, enter his awareness. Maslow describes this as a pyramid of self realisation. A basic component is the reverence for life.

Animal Exploitation in Human Recreation

J. M. BRYANT

We can look to the Romans as perfectionists in the exploitation of animals for human pleasure. Incidentally, they excelled at exploiting people too, since not only did they invent games involving the torture and slaughter of animals but they also revelled in the suffering and death of their criminals and members of minority groups on the sand of the arena.

The Roman games, which at their inception in 238 B.C., were innocent athletics expressing the spirit of a proud and hopeful civilisation, degenerated during the following five hundred years into incredible spectacles of cruelty and carnage. Thus Trajan gave one set of games which lasted 122 days, during which eleven thousand people and ten thousand animals were killed; Titus had nearly ten thousand animals slaughtered during a one hundred day " event " to celebrate the opening of the Colosseum.[132]

It seems that the depths of depravity and degradation enjoyed by all classes of the game-loving Roman citizens were probably in fact an expression of the despair of a once great civilisation sensing its impending doom—a symptom of hopelessness. In a desperate attempt to find a spirit of unity and national identity, the Romans found a place where the heavily-taxed rich, the unemployed and the starving poor could share a common experience. The arena became the focus of Roman life, where the people could convince themselves that the carnage, cruelty and courage which they witnessed was symptomatic of the invincibility of their race.

Despite the fact that the nation was being bled white by the cost of maintaining its gigantic armed forces and the heavy subsidies being paid to satellite nations, the Roman fleet was well occupied denuding whole territories of Africa of wild animals and shipping them to Rome for slaughter. Rome's politicians realised that great spectacles of sadism and perversion could keep the people anaesthetized from the reality of their troubles, and records show that when the fleet had the choice of returning from Egypt with either grain for the starving or sand for the arena, the order given was " Bring the sand!"

Rome showed us that even a great and mighty civilisation, which had taken man into a new world, which introduced law with a sense of individual and human rights, which opened up international trade and taught how to use the world's natural resources, could, despite fierce national pride, crash and disintegrate where the limited goals of materialism and conquest failed to sustain the people's inspiration.

Rome taught us that when communal man loses his sense of purpose, when disillusion, disenchantment and apathy break his spiritual heart, he swiftly sacrifices his individuality to " the mob " and degenerates into a cruel and sadistic being—unrecognisable even to himself.

And yet, amidst the despair and chaos of declining Rome we can find another, more hopeful message. Amidst the degradation the Christian church grew, offering a new spiritual meaning and hope to Rome's unhappy people. Gradually some of the more bestial diversions, such as the sacrificing of humans to wild animals, were outlawed, and finally Christianity in the form of a monk named Telemachus proved to be the instrument which killed the symptomatic sadism of the arena—the symbol of an old and discredited life style. In 404 A.D., Telemachus, on what has been described as a sacred mission, leaped into the arena and appealed to the people to stop the carnage. He was promptly stoned to death by the angry mob, but when Emperor Honorius heard of the murder, he became so furious that he closed the arenas. They were never to re-open.[133]

There are, I believe, two very distinct modern parallels to the Roman decline which I have just described. Firstly, we can observe all around us the symptoms of a crumbling materialistic idealogy. A desperate economy, inflation, massive unemployment and political corruption, shake the foundations of our civilisation. Disillusionment and apathy abound. Despite heavy taxation of the rich we still live in a society of "the haves" and "have nots", where the sales of champagne increase, and where old folk, unable to afford heat, die alone and neglected of hypothermia. The young receive an education based on the requirements of industrialisation, and yet we cannot offer them work when they leave the classroom. Vandalism and crime increase where people scratch out desperate lives in "battery houses", and the only relief we offer those afflicted by the national diseases of depression is *vallium et librium*, gleefully churned out by the ton by wealthy drug companies. In an attempt to find targets for our arrows of blame for impending bankruptcy, we begin to listen to the voice of "nationalism" and the arguments of the racialists. We squeeze the apparent luxuries of education and social services and debate the merits of euthanasia for the handicapped, abortion and capital punishment. In short, we compromise our conscience-born philosophy of reverence for life for a more logical one of reverence for what is apparently "useful".

It is the response to this degeneration of spiritual standards which brings me to the second similarity of our time to that of Rome. In an attempt to forget our problems and our seemingly hopeless plight, like the Romans, we turn to games, diversions and exciting spectacle. All sports, not only those involving animals, have now achieved a level of importance unprecedented since the days of Rome. Newspapers dedicate pages and pages to this peculiar human activity. One national daily newspaper recently filled ten pages with sport—the front page and two others featuring a game in which two women, cheered by thousands and watched by millions, knocked a ball over a piece of netting.

This addiction to the drug "competition", this love of spectacle, dominates the lives of millions, and our young are raised in the age of the "Super-star"—an example of success in a depersonalised world, shining in the media as heroic as a Roman gladiator.

As a frightening warning of the consequences of this worship of sport, the film " Rollerball " reveals with chilling realism the development of a sport which is itself more important than even the lives of the contestants. It shows how sport can once again degenerate to the level of the Roman games, where the ruthless survive the longest, cruelty succeeds cruelty until even the most sadistic practices become boring to spectators saturated with bloody spectacle. This search for excitement, this release from the boredom of a " challengeless " existence, has already brought to us the horrific possibility of public execution on the entertainment media of television, and worse, the news of the existence of pornographic films which in recognition that pornography has almost reached the level of respectability, use as their climax the real torture and murder of women before the camera and technician. If that is not Rome, nothing is!

Those of us involved in the animal welfare movement, like all others fighting for humanitarian causes, cannot afford to ignore these symptoms of degeneration. Already millions of animals and birds are sacrificed and abused in the name of human entertainment, and far from awakening human conscience to outlaw such needless suffering, we are hard pushed to prevent even more cruelty becoming acceptable. Despite the existence of religions teaching compassion, not only does the abuse and killing of animals for sport survive, but it is actually increasing in " popularity ". Not only does the shame of Caesar's bull-ring flourish in countries such as Spain, but we now hear that in Portugal the torture of the bull fails to satisfy the spectators and demands are being made for a change in the law so that the mob can witness the slaughter of these animals on the sand of their arena.

Most leading fox-hunts in this country claim to have waiting lists of people eager to join in the pursuit to the death of wild animals, and hunting, shooting and fishing are now huge industries supplying death and suffering for the entertainment of a large and growing section of the populace. Other areas of animal exploitation in human recreation, sometimes spiced with the additional "kick" of gambling, are all tremendously popular. Horse and dog racing, show jumping, rodeos, performing animals and zoos, all attract large numbers of people eager for excitement, spectacle or perhaps merely for "somewhere to go" and "something to do". I remember, a couple of years ago, attending an exhibition of "Yesterday's Farming" and noticing that the largest crowd was gathered around a demonstration of "thrashing" corn. When my wife and I pushed through the crowd, we found that the attraction was not the old machinery but the sight of children, cheered on by their parents, chasing after and stamping on mice as they fled from the machine. As my wife and I started to catch the mice and take them to safety, the spectators watched open mouthed and in silence. Even when we pushed their excited offspring to the ground to prevent them stamping on the terrified creatures, the only reaction from the parents was to gaze at us in utter amazement. Our compassion in action was so foreign to them that we might as well have been creatures from another planet. Admittedly, the teachings of religion and enlightened humanism have had some impact on the situation. Not so very long ago, bloodsports like dog fighting, cock fighting, bear and bull baiting were popular with all classes of people and were even patronised by Royalty. The reason that the old "fighting sports" such as bear-baiting were eventually outlawed, was that early anti-cruelty campaigners managed to convince the legislators that such events, so obviously pandering to the basest of human instincts, had a brutalising effect on the spectators and that such brutality might be extended to their fellow human beings. In fact this argument was shown to have some merit by some of the principal opponents of moves to abolish bull and bear baiting. In the early 1800s William Windham, Secretary of War, argued that his best soldiers came from the main baiting counties of Lancashire and Staffordshire, saying : "It is not unfair to attribute to their manly amuzements much of that valour which is so conspicuous in their martial achievements by sea and by land."[134]

However, for whatever reason, and we must hope that compassion at least played a part, the gruesome fighting sports were eventually abolished. The sports involving animals which have survived are those which offer pleasures connected more with the pursuit of animals or with competition between animals, rather than with their actual death. Of course there is still obvious suffering. Reginald Paget, Q.C., until recently a fox-hunting member of Parliament, says in his introduction to the book *In Praise of Hunting*: "Pain and suffering is inflicted on animals in the course of sport. Nobody who has seen a beaten fox dragging his stiff limbs into the ditch in which he knows he will die can doubt this proposition."[135]

We must accept, I think, that today such suffering is not the source of pleasure to the majority of its followers. Their pleasures are derived from other facets of the sport such as riding in the country, watching hounds work as a pack, the camaraderie of the hunt, the uncertainty of the chase and the excitement of seeing a wild animal on the run in the open. For some, the suffering and death of the quarry spoil the pleasure of the sport and they will deliberately avoid witnessing the digging out of a fox and the kill. By closing their eyes to the product of their sport, do they hope to escape responsibility too?

In other areas of animal exploitation in the name of sport such as horse and dog racing, show jumping and cross-country events, there is still obvious suffering although many of their supporters would never patronise any so-called bloodsport. In these less controversial sports, despite governing rules and etiquettes, suffering is only limited to a certain level—a level which is unlikely to affront the consciences of the spectators and which is unlikely to infringe vague animal welfare legislation. Whips and spurs are permitted but must not be used "excessively" or "unacceptably", but the judgment of these terms is tempered by the fact that *not* urging the animal to its maximum efforts can be interpreted as cheating. We have to accept that, like bloodsports, these areas of animal exploitation still pander to the old Roman love of spectacle, and although it is only incidental to the actual objects of the sport, still cause animals to suffer and die. The ghoulish gather in crowds around difficult fences in cross country events and derive sadistic pleasure from the spectacular falls of horses and riders. At races like the Grand National, many horses fall during the gruelling circuits. Some unmounted horses stagger to their feet and obediently and bravely race on, placating the consciences of the spectators, while behind them screens are rushed on to the track to hide the death throes of another expendable animal as it awaits a merciful bullet.

It is my sincere belief that the rapidly increasing popularity of sports and games, the fanaticism of participants and supporters, the trend towards hostility in games, and the insensitivity to suffering exhibited by participants and spectators alike, are all, as they were in the days of Rome, symptoms of the demoralisation of our civilisation. I submit that when the whole morale of a nation can depend on the success (or lack of it), of its national team in some game; when thousands jeer at the agony of an injured rival team member; when dogs are awarded points for the manner in which they attack hares; when wild deer are driven into the sea by hounds and left to drown; when tourists applaud the torture and death of bulls; and when horses are ridden and jumped to their death in the cause of human pleasure; then we are indeed approaching the depths of depravity exhibited during the fall of the Roman empire.

I further believe that such things are not only symptomatic of our spiritual decline but actually accelerate it, because by deriving pleasure from events which involve suffering, we allow ourselves to sink back to the subliminal instincts of " the pack ", retarding our evolution into a higher, spiritual and more noble plane. As the Venerable Edward Carpenter said of hunting for sport : " It is to fall back into that bondage, into that predatory system of nature, from which the Christian hope has always been that not only man but the natural order itself is to be released and redeemed."[136]

This grave warning to those who would seek recreation in activities which extinguish the lights of compassion and awareness, is only reinforced when we examine the writings of hunters. Christopher Sykes said he enjoyed hunting " because it ministers to obscure parts of our being, such as lie underneath reason and awareness."[137]

Pro-hunting Robin Page, in a recent article, " The Ethics of Field Sports " made the same admission, saying : " hunting helps to satisfy a subconscious urge that is very deep, and which goes way back to the very birth of man."[138]

It is my firm view that the most important of all human virtues is compassion, and that a civilised community should discard any area of activity which for its survival necessitates the rejection of compassion. Hunting is one such activity. In a famous book called *Hunting* published in 1885 we find the words : " It is not wise for the pursuer to analyse too closely the feelings of the pursued."[139] In another book, *The Art of Beagling*, Captain Otho Paget warns hunt followers to identify with the hounds' aims, saying : " If he allows himself to sympathise with the hare, his pleasure in the chase will be neutralised, and he might as well go home at once."[140]

So there we have it. While enlightened humanism and the advanced religions urge us to strive for awareness, to be conscious of our actions and thoughts, to cultivate reverence and compassion for all life—in fact to seek freedom from the shackles of our physical being—we are being urged by the hunting Peter Pans who refuse to grow up, to stay unconscious, to squash compassion, and to identify with the pack.

It is in the knowledge that those who gain amusement from suffering are in fact endangering Man's progress into an enlightened age of awareness, that we who oppose unnecessary suffering must present *our* colours. The bloodsports battle is a clash of philosophies in which there can be no tolerance or compromise, because the victory of either means the total defeat of the other.

Beware the arguments of hunters like David James, M.P., who says we need hunting to siphon off man's aggressive tendencies, and that the character built in the hunting field is that which " is necessary in dealing with domestic and business matters."[141] And Wilson Stephens who says poetically that those who hunt feel " a challenge and a release from the artificialities of living in the technological age, and share the ageless drama of the natural

order as it unfolds against the background of the fields and wood-
lands and clouds amid which their ancestry was forged."[142]

Regard instead these words of a child, recently penned to the
R.S.P.C.A.;[143] " I think foxhunting is cruel and stupid because
foxes are wild and should be left free." There surely is the Hans
Andersen child, who saw that the King was naked and said so !

And here, I believe, is the key to the type of battle that we in
the animal welfare movement must fight if we are to reduce the
cruelty and death that Man inflicts on the animal kingdom in the
name of sport and entertainment. We must grasp the basic truth
of that child's protest. Whatever the arguments of the hunters,
which in the case of foxhunting range from " control of vermin "
to " conservation of a wild creature ", and from " giving employ-
ment to thousands " to " providing training for Olympic show
jumpers ", we must fight from the knowledge that such exploitation is morally wrong and therefore indefensible.

It is essential that we see ourselves as part of the whole
humanitarian movement and ally ourselves with others fighting
injustice and suffering. Perhaps the time has come when there
should be a federation of all charities and similar organisations
battling against the apathy of our struggling civilisation. Such a
federation could present our legislators with demands for reform
across the whole spectrum of human and animal co-existence.
There may appear to be little common ground between say,
Shelter, Oxfam and the R.S.P.C.A., but if all see themselves as
battalions in the army against the front of evil, then co-operation
is possible. After all it is a case of " United we stand, divided we
fall ". The second route to progress is, I believe, a change in
attitude of the animal welfare movement itself. We must give
greater priority to prevention of cruelty rather than trying to cope
with the results of it. For instance the R.S.P.C.A. spends one and
a third million pounds running its 240 inspectors and under one
tenth of that amount in providing humane education. If we are
to win the young over to the ranks of the compassionate, we
must, through education, offer them the challenge and excitement of knowing and caring for the whole of creation. At the
moment, the child's need for challenge, the quest for adventure

and involvement in his world, is all too often answered only by that great school for the hunters of wild animals, the Pony Club. I believe that the R.S.P.C.A. should have an education officer in every county and an education centre attached to every animal home, where the young can learn some of the great mysteries of nature and the animal kingdom, where they can be helped through creativity to awareness.

Thirdly, let the animal welfare movement abandon its " pussyfooting " attitude to cruelty and suffering. There is too much compromise and too much effort being put into " being reasonable ". Let us be more vigorous and militant, and in an effort to reach the anaesthetized conscience of mankind, let us expose cruelty wherever it is found and by whomever it is perpetrated.

The fact that the animal welfare movement is failing is apparent in the actions of the young and impatient animal rights campaigners who, frustrated by lack of action and progress in the animal welfare battle, are burning boats used for hunting seals, rescuing animals from vivisection laboratories and factory farms, and damaging vehicles and buildings used for animal exploitation. I have no doubt that if the present animal welfare societies cannot find a way to wake up our people and our leaders to the plight of suffering animals, then organisations like the Animal Liberation Front will grow and their activities will extend into all avenues of animal exploitation.

If the hunting and killing of animals for sport continues at its present level unchecked by public conscience, then I predict that a young hunt saboteur will die in the hunting field in the very near future. Another Telemachus will come forward and leap into the arena of cruelty, to suffer death at the hands of the supporters and followers of death in the name of sport. You may think I exaggerate, but hunt saboteurs are being beaten and whipped every weekend by hunt supporters. The police either turn the other way or arrest the protesters for breach of the peace. Two hunt saboteurs have recently been gaoled, one for being attacked by hunt supporters and the other for trying to prevent hares from being chased by dogs for human entertainment.[144]

On 27th November last year, two hunt saboteurs in a car attended a meet of the Essex Union Hunt. They were recognised by hunt supporters who smashed the windscreen of the car, and despite the screaming of one of the occupants who had glass in his eyes, went on to smash all the car windows. The hunt saboteur had slivers of glass removed from his eyes in hospital and was lucky to retain his sight. The police took no action.

Consider this comment from the Master of the Hunt when questioned about the attack : " Horse-whipping a hunt saboteur is rather like beating a wife. They are both private matters." Perhaps *there* is the first common ground between two parts of the humanitarian movement—the anti-hunt campaigners and the battered wife protectionists—allies in the war against violence and cruelty.

NOTE

At the end of his symposium speech, Mr. Bryant played a brief tape-recording of the attack on the hunt saboteurs referred to towards the end of his paper. The recording was taken by an occupant of the hunt saboteurs' vehicle and the sound of glass being broken and a man screaming repeatedly " Oh my God, I can't see !" could be plainly heard.

The Management and Conservation of Carnivores: A Plea for an Ecological Ethic

DAVID W. MACDONALD
and
LUIGI BOITANI

"The wildlife of today is not ours to dispose of as we please. We have it in trust. We must account for it to those who come after."

King George VI.

Man's relationship to wild animals takes a variety of forms, including predation, competition, exploitation, and symbiosis. Of all the varied groups with which men interact, it is amongst the carnivores that almost universally we find species daubed as being pests or enemies. Sometimes this animosity derives from misplaced fear, as with the legendary but unfounded belief that wolves pose a threat to the safety of children; here the role of the conservationist is to replace fantasy with fact. In other cases, however, hatred against a predator emanates from a real conflict of interest between men and wildlife. It is the latter instance which presents challenging and sometimes urgent problems to the zoologist; it also gives rise to complex philosophical issues which are germane to any discussion of the ethics of man's treatment of other animals. Many contributors to this symposium are concerned with the principles of humanity which should govern our treatment of individual animals. In this paper we will draw attention to a different topic, namely the treatment of animal populations.

We draw principally upon examples of carnivorous animals because we have worked with them directly and because their predatory behaviour frequently leads them into obvious conflict with people. Clashes of interest between men and carnivores take many forms, and we ask whether there *is* one ethic or code of behaviour which is sufficiently robust to guide people faced with diverse wildlife management dilemmas.

The relationship between people and wolves serves to illustrate this problem. In different regions wolves provide examples of both of the two major categories of problem facing the zoologist : firstly, the case where conflict with people threatens the wolf with imminent extinction; secondly, the case where conflict poses no immediate threat to the survival of species or population, but nevertheless causes ecological disruption.

Historically, the end of the 18th century heralded the demise of the European wolf. During the 19th century the species was exterminated from region after region. In 1847 the last wolf was killed in the Bavarian forests. Alpine wolves soon followed them into oblivion and the Scandinavian population began to dwindle, although relict populations survived. Today only one wolf survives in the wild in Sweden. Last year two animals immigrating from Finland were killed within months of their discovery. Haglund (1975) reported that the annual toll of wolves in Sweden between 1856–1860 averaged 86, but this had crashed to only one by 1875. This decline across Europe seems to be linked with increasing industrialisation, reduction of appropriate prey species, and hence increased depredations on stock and a concomitant increase in hunting pressure. Zimen and Boitani have reviewed the process which led, by 1900, to the banishment of the European wolf to a few mountainous refuges. The wolf's status was reviewed by the I.U.C.N. in 1973 who found that the only viable populations outside Russia were in Rumania, Yugoslavia, Greece and Albania.

In the face of such declining numbers it may seem intolerable that the wolf is still freely hunted in many areas, given only game status (i.e. a closed season) in Spain and Yugoslavia, and hunted under a bounty of almost £100 a head in the C.S.S.R. Yet the wrath of the armchair ecologist might be tempered by the experience of a shepherd from a mountain village in central Italy who lost 264 sheep to wolves in one night. The slaughter of a fascinating and endangered species is intolerable to the conservationist, and the loss of his livelihood is intolerable to the shepherd. What is the ethical solution to this problem? In an attempt to resolve this impasse, the Italian branch of the World Wildlife Fund sponsored a study on which we have worked, together with Dr. Erik Zimen.

A survey of wolf numbers in Italy revealed that of the total population numbering under 100 individuals, the maximum concentration was in the Abruzzo Mountains with 20–25 wolves inhabiting Mt. Maiella and the Parco d'Abruzzo. This gave a density of 1 wolf/65Km² in an area with a human population of 29Km² (Zimen and Boitani, 1975). The obvious thought that human population density itself precipitated the wolf's decline was not borne out since settlement of the wolf-inhabited zone was actually denser than that in the surrounding land. Indeed, wolves have been exterminated in northern Sweden with a density of only 1.33 people/Km². When the project began the critical factors underlying the Italian wolf's decline were obscure; the only possibility of elucidating these factors was a detailed study which immediately raised an issue of practical ethics: the elusive habits of the species determined that the only feasible way to gather information on their behaviour was through radio-tracking, i.e. fitting wolves with miniature radio-transmitters which emit a 'bleeping' signal which enables the zoologist to plot the animals' movements. To attach a radio (mounted on a collar) to the wolf it must be caught. Clearly this involves a frightening intrusion into the wolf's world and one which includes some risk to the animal. Can such disturbance and risk be justified? Our answer to this dilemma was that without the knowledge potentially obtainable from a detailed study the wolf would almost certainly disappear from Italy, and even the tiniest possibility of avoiding this extinction was taken to justify our intrusion.

The study has revealed that the Abruzzo wolves often travel alone or in small groups, rather than in the larger packs that Mech (1970) has described for the N. American race. However, although the Abruzzo wolves often travel alone, members of a pack frequently meet at traditional sites. The entire pack probably consists of a pair and their adult pups of the year. Radio-tracking disclosed the location of the wolves' daytime lairs; these were invariably inaccessible to men, in dense forest amongst rocky outcrops. However, although inaccessible, these dens were often quite close to villages or bothies (Zimen & Boitani, 1977).

Depredations of livestock explain the mountain shepherd's dislike for the wolf; to assess the magnitude of these losses another member of the team, Poala Gnocci, analysed the food remains in wolf faeces and found that while garbage was very important, sheep were the most frequent prey. Mostly, sheep were taken in small numbers, but anachronistic shepherding practices favour occasional "surplus kills" where wolves kill sheep after sheep, apparently wantonly. The biological basis for this phenomenon, which underlies much animosity towards supposedly vengeful carnivores throughout the world, has been discussed by Hans Krunk (1972a; see also Macdonald, 1976) and relates neither to malevolence nor maladaptation on the part of the predator but to compromises in the prey's defence behaviour consequent upon captivity. During part of the study period the regional government of the Abruzzo compensated shepherds for wolf damage. Total claims amounted to $60,000 in 1974, but at least 50% of these were known to be fraudulent; in some cases shepherds even incited dogs to kill their own sheep! So, at the most, wolves cost the Abruzzo region about $30,000 per annum. The cost of each surviving wolf is thus about $1,200 p.a.

What benefits offset this substantial cost? Most are intangible, such as the aesthetic value of the species and its considerable scientific interest. Two benefits of very different types can be more rigorously defined; one is the " ecosystem argument " which stresses the complexity of natural communities which include predators and prey, plants and nutrients, whose properties are interwoven in such a way that interference with any one part of the complex rebounds through the entire system. Thus, in the famous case of the kiabab deer, when predation was removed the deer numbers escalated causing serious over-browsing and long-term habitat destruction and, ultimately, a dramatic crash in deer numbers through starvation. So, the wolf is part of the

Abruzzo ecosystem and we should not precipitate further imbalance by exterminating it. However, ecosystems change continuously and more species have become extinct in the past than exist today, so does it really matter if the Italian wolf joins the list?

At this point a second type of argument is relevant, and it is this one that is the most forceful with local shepherds: extinction is irrevocable; to kill the last wolf would be similar to slashing the Mona Lisa in the sense that neither could be put back together again later. In the past extinction has arisen through natural selection exerted by competition within ecosystems. When modern man precipitates extinction he does so knowingly. Industrial western man, unlike his tribal fellows, spans and exploits different ecosystems and has thus become, in Dasmann's (1977) words, a "biosphere man" and not an "ecosystem man". To devastate a species from this position of authority is not an honourable use of power. This point was summarised in Principle 4 of the Stockholm Declaration (1972) which states: "Man has a special responsibility to safeguard and wisely manage the heritage of wildlife and its habitat which are now gravely imperilled by a combination of adverse factors."

Beyond these arguments there is little that prevents the debate descending to the level of "I like wolves" versus "Well, I do not". Indeed, ultimately it is public opinion which will determine the fate not only of Italian wolves, but of other species too (see Boitani & Zimen, 1977).

Of the 13 wolves found dead in the Abruzzo in the winter 1975–76, nine had been killed by hunters or poisoned by bait set to kill foxes. To save the Italian wolf requires that people rapidly acquire an "ecological conscience" and we believe that this requires the teaching of an ecological ethic, stressing the importance of a diverse and self-sustaining fauna. Such a statement would be hopelessly pompous if it neglected the shepherd, for he is part of the mountain ecosystem; we seek methods of integrating the wolf and the shepherd, rather than permitting one to dominate the other. In our eyes, each wolf is worth $1,200 p.a., and if necessary this cost should be borne by the state.

However, the existence of the cost is in itself a reflection of historical failure to follow an ecological conscience.

The wolf's decline across Europe was heralded by the extermination of its prey species, such as the red deer, probably through overhunting by men. The wolf consequently turned to agricultural stock and incurred the wrath which has led to its widespread extermination. Ironically the archaic techniques of the Italian mountain shepherds are probably the sole reason for the wolf's survival there. Now the W.W.F. project is being extended, under Dr. Boitani's direction, to involve an attempt at reintroducing red deer and so re-establishing a balanced predator-prey relationship. Shepherding practices could be modified simultaneously. A regional national park with wild deer and wolf would attract tourism and allow the region to prosper through its own natural heritage. Of course such a park would require the establishment of undisturbed, secluded areas, but in general we believe that a genuine ecological conscience can only be built through integrating, rather than segregating, people and wildlife.

The future of the European wolf hangs in the balance and raises questions which are as much ethical as biological. We believe that studies of the ecosystem, including both humans and wildlife, provide the most constructive framework for tackling these issues. There are real conflicts which lead us to questions such as " who cares?", " who's responsible?" and, most critically, " who pays?" The answers to these questions spell either survival or extinction.

The wolf also provides us with a paradigm for a different series of ethical questions, where the stakes are not extinction but instead different degrees of ecological imbalance. For this example we turn to David Mech's (1970) study of the N. American wolf. Again, we are presenting complex issues, and not simply caricatures of "goodies" and "baddies". The Eastern timber wolf occupies about 5% of its former range in the U.S.A. However, between 1,000–2,000 wolves survive in Minnesota; so, depending on which State a person lives in, his idea of the wolf might vary from its being an endangered species to the role of pest. Certainly, some Minnesotans want to reintroduce a bounty on wolves, which was discontinued in 1965. In 1976 a federal bill provided for $500,000 to be paid as compensation to Minnesotan farmers over a five-year-period. So, while the Eastern timber wolf is in no danger of extinction, some taxpayers regard it as an expensive luxury. In the face of mounting controversy Mech and other biologists established the Eastern Timber Wolf Recovery Team to put together an ecologically sound scheme. Their solution (Mech, 1977) involved the establishment of " zones ". In three wilderness zones (totalling 10,000 miles^2) the wolf should be completely protected, giving an estimated wolf density of 1/10 miles^2. In a fourth zone (21,000 miles^2) wolves should be culled to maintain a density of 1/50 miles^2. The remainder of the State (zone 5) is currently devoid of wolves. The Team also advocated cutting and burning mature forest to encourage the growth of young trees, hence increasing its carrying capacity for deer, so augmenting the wolf's natural prey populations. They also aim to expand the overall range of the wolf, attempting reintroduction to Upper Michigan. The aims of this scheme can be quoted direct from Mech (1977):

" (1) preserve the wolf in Minnesota
  (2) decrease domestic stock loss
  (3) minimise public animosity towards the wolf and the Endangered Species Act
  (4) increase the base of support for the wolf to include more local citizens."

In summary, more than a decade of research into the wolf's biology and the social problems surrounding its conservation have led Mech to believe that the most ecologically auspicious stategy involves the slaughter of some of the wolves which he fought so hard to protect. This decision may be lamentable, but the point which we commend to the reader is that the only possible basis for such insightful planning is a deep understanding of the species biology and a regard to long-term ecological consequences. The sacrifice of some individuals, obviously as humanely as possible, may lead to the safeguarding and even the increase of the population as a whole.

Turning now more briefly to other examples where the relationship between men and carnivores raises different ethical questions, we will refer first to the Pribilof seal, *Callorhinus ursinus*. The introduction of an ecologically valid management policy has resulted both in the maintenance of a high population and a lucrative industry around this species. If the introduction of this plan had been delayed by only a few years it is doubtful whether the species would have survived. Now the main colony of northern fur seals on the Pribilof Islands during the breeding season constitutes the largest aggregation of wild mammals which can be seen anywhere.

The seals were discovered in 1786 by a Russian fur trader, Gerassim Pribilof. During the next eighty years the Russians took 2.5 million skins through indiscriminate slaughter, with the result that in 1806 and 1834 the industry ground to a halt through scarcity of seals. Just when Russian sealing practice was becoming more enlightened, they sold Alaska to the United States. In 1870 the Alaska Commercial Company took control of sealing, and fixed an annual quota of 100,000 animals.

The idea of setting a limit on the cull was an illusory advance since the numbers and selection of victims was not based on knowledge of their ecology. Indeed, the seal population began to dwindle and poachers took to the open sea where no restrictions operated. These open sea hunters made huge profits, but three-quarters of the slain animals sank before they could be recovered and about 60% of the victims were cows. By 1883 the Alaska Commercial Company had taken 2,000,000 skins; in tax and royalties these alone offset the cost of purchasing Alaska! The seal population was decimated. In 1911 pelagic sealing was outlawed and the scientific management of sealing began. The most important advance was an understanding of the animal's mating system. Bull seals fight amongst themselves to maintain small mating territories in the rookery. Within his territory the successful bull serves a harem of cows. Other males live in bachelor herds and do not contribute to the production of the population. A survey of more than 200,000 tagged seals by biologists of the Fish & Game Department yielded data on migration, mortality and age composition of the herd. Using this information a plan was proposed enabling 60,000–70,000 bachelor males of given ages to be harvested annually, without diminishing the breeding population. Under this scheme the herd was increased from 150,000 at the turn of the century to 1,300,000 just before the birth of pups, of which 4,000,000 are born each year. The population has reached its maximum size, being limited not by sealing, but by the availability of summer food (Johnson, 1968).

The study has shown that 15% of pups may succumb to hook-worm infection. Recent trials have attempted to reduce this mortality using disinfectants. An ecologically based management scheme has raised the Pribilof seal from the abyss of extinction to the centre of an industry which yields $3 million annually. The animals which are killed are surplus males, many of which would die through natural selection anyway. We are not discussing here whether it is right, or desirable, that 6,000 seals be killed annually to provide furs. Rather we are stressing that while economic forces dictate that seals be killed, it is possible to do so with the appropriate knowledge, in a way that minimises the ecological disruption. Such a strategy keeps our future conservation options open since the population, even if manipulated, is at least extant. Some might maintain that rather than managing wildlife for human exploitation we should change our own behaviour. Of course we endorse this view, but point out that in many instances there simply isn't time for such profound changes in thinking; the zoologist has to act rapidly if there are to be survivors left to benefit from future changes in attitude. The success of the Pribilof seal scheme has been summarised by the biologist G. C. L. Bertram : " One can give no higher praise than sincerely to hope that planning and agreement for the future may be as beneficial and rational as have been the administration and conservation of the herd during the last forty years." In this context one can contrast the appalling mismanagement of other groups of marine mammals, e.g. the whales (see Gordon Clark et al, 1975; and FOE, 1976), and the dolphins (Norman, 1976).

Of course, whatever policy is adopted towards wildlife it should be pursued with a minimum of inhumanity. In the case of sealing, the methods used are open to question and Jordan (1978) has pointed out that young Harp seals may not be killed outright when clubbed. Care should be taken that the search for what is effective should not obscure what is humane. For instance, there is some evidence (Delany *et al*, 1978) that cyanide gas pumped into badger setts infected with TB may not reach all parts of the tunnel system and that some animals may subsequently suffocate in exhausted air pockets. Donal (1976) has studied practices to reduce the cruelty in fur trapping while Englund (1978) has meticulously documented unnecessary cruelty in gin-trapping and proven that a leg-snare is infinitely more humane. Studies like Englund's herald a welcome new approach to animal trapping. Considering that the draft declaration of human rights was only ratified in 1948 it is perhaps not surprising that we have been so late in turning attention to unnecessary suffering in wildlife.

The intense selection on a certain social class within the Pribilof seal population raises another issue : is the management scheme possibly altering the genetic constitution of the surviving population and what are the ethics of maintaining or manipulating the genetic integrity of wild populations? This issue is particularly relevant to conservation schemes which involve moving animals from one population to another in attempts to boost numbers in an area where a species is losing ground. For instance, bears could be imported into the Alps where only a few survive (Roth, 1977) and the idea of releasing wolves in Sweden has been mooted. However, the imports will be genetically different from the local population, and subtly adapted to slightly different conditions. The question of whether this matters, both biologically and ethically, has been discussed by various authors in Boitani (1977).

Lest the armchair conservationist be lulled into some sense of security by the geographical distance separating him from the problems we have mentioned, let us conclude with two further cases of carnivores in conflict with people where the dilemma is literally in our back garden. First, consider the fox in its role as a vector of the disease rabies. A fox-borne rabies epizootic has been moving westwards from Poland since the late 1930s. This raises two problems; what can be done on continental Europe to impede the spread of the disease and ideally to eradicate it and, secondly, what should be done if, as is thankfully improbable, rabies became endemic in our British wildlife? The problem has been concisely reviewed by Lloyd (1977) and approaches to it from the basis of an ecological ethic have been considered (see Macdonald, 1977 and 1979). Briefly, a solution should be sought which minimises ecological disruption whilst maximising the chances of controlling the disease. Such a solution may or may not involve killing large numbers of foxes, which may be regrettable but necessary.

An ecological conscience would demand that we strive to avoid the disruption caused by killing if an equally effective alternative can be devised. A candidate in this case is the immunisation of wild foxes with anti-rabies vaccine. Similarly, where foxes prey on livestock there may sometimes be alternatives to traditional gamekeeping. For instance, fox visits to a tern colony were reduced to about 16% of their former frequency by erecting an electric fence (Patterson, 1977).

However, the relative merits of alternative schemes can *only* be judged on the basis of detailed behavioural and ecological studies. Our suggestion to the members of this symposium is that where real problems of this nature exist, careful thought must be given to the management of populations (understood in terms of the biology of the individuals composing them) which may involve conflict with our humanitarian principles concerning individuals in the population.

A second problem on our doorstep concerns the role of the badger, *Meles meles*, in the transmission of bovine tuberculosis. Again the conflict between people and wildlife has a significant and measurable cost: in southern Dorset 626 cattle have been slaughtered since 1970 because of TB and the indications are that badgers may be instrumental in maintaining the infection (see Anon, 1976). For instance, of 160 outbreaks of bovine TB in Avon and Gloucestershire, 113 were within 0.75 Km of places where infected badgers had been found. Farmers will not tolerate these losses and so the Ministry of Agriculture's " firebrigade " actions of gassing infected badger setts may at least serve to placate agriculturalists whose wrath might otherwise drive them to personal campaigns against the species.

However, just as slaughtering foxes may not be the ecologically optimal strategy for rabies control, so also present policy towards badgers may not sufficiently incorporate ecological insight (Coffey, 1977). The right approach can only be selected on the basis of understanding the species' behaviour and ecology. The preliminary work of Cheeseman and Mallinson (reported in Anon, 1976 and 1977) represents an attempt to achieve this end: they are studying the badger's behavioural ecology, with the aim of understanding how this may link with TB transmission, and also the efficacy of different control measures, which can thereafter be evaluated in terms of ecological and agricultural merit.

While badgers are implicated in the transmission of bovine TB, there are many anomalies: the incidence of TB in cattle is now a fraction of its pre-war level, when the disease spread nationwide. Why, then, is TB only found amongst badgers in the SW? Why also do some setts remain free from infection when their neighbours have contracted the disease, and why do some herds remain healthy when local badgers are tuberculous, and vice versa? These questions must be answered before sensible management can be undertaken, and in the meantime 1464 setts had been gassed by August 1977.

To conclude, there are many wildlife problems which stem from genuine conflict between the interests of men and other species. The solution to each of these involves both biological and ethical decisions. In assessing alternative attitudes and policies toward wildlife we suggest that an ecological ethic provides a robust framework within which to make judgements (see Lockie, 1977). To behave properly within this framework demands an emphasis on detailed and expansive study of each problem so that predictions can be made regarding the probable outcome of alternative policies. Such a dictum outlaws all " blanket " approaches to wildlife management, since ecological circumstances vary from region to region and flexibility to accommodate such variation must be incorporated into management policy. The most persuasive evidence for this point comes from studies revealing the huge differences in behaviour of the same species in different habitats; an example being Kruuk's (1973) demonstration that the social organisation of two populations of spotted hyaena differed dramatically as a consequence of differences in their food supply. In fact, Kruuk used these data in a discussion of the management of carnivores in African national parks. Recently, several excellent accounts of the behaviour and ecology of British Mammals have been published and these will form a firm groundwork for future management. Examples include Mitchell *et al* (1977) on red deer, Kruuk and Parish (1978) on badgers, and NCC (1977) and King *et al* (1978) on otters.

Of course, detailed scientific enquiry is not only useful in relation to wildlife problems, it also helps us to assess our treatment of domestic animals, as Dawkins (1977) has shown with her pioneering work on the behaviour of farmyard chickens. Hopefully, future controversy surrounding our relationships with wildlife will not be resolved on the basis of supposition, but rather on knowledge derived from an objective science of wildlife management.

Animal Experiments:
Time for a New Approach

BERNARD DIXON

What I have to say starts really from the point that I am not, in any sense, a card-holding anti-vivisectionist. As a biologist I am convinced that some experimentation using animals is inevitable at the present time, if we are going to safeguard the health of the community by, for example, developing and testing vaccines, and for pursuing research into frequently devastating forms of disease in both man and other animals. But I am impressed by the way that the climate of opinion has changed in the last ten years or so from a time when there were battle-lines drawn between the anti-vivisection bodies and the scientific establishment, who more or less did not speak to each other or at least made rather rude noises in each other's direction.

Times have changed since then, and one or two landmarks in this period, I think, have been the setting up of the International Association against Painful Experiments on Animals in 1969 and, shortly after that, the establishment of F.R.A.M.E., Fund for the Replacement of Animals in Medical Experiments. Both of these organisations have been notable for the restrained way in which they crusaded not for an overnight ban on all laboratory work with animals, but for solid initiatives in the search for alternative approaches. Over the same period the other anti-vivisection bodies have adopted, I think, an increasingly positive rather than negative approach to the problem. One example of this would be the Lord Dowding Fund which has been spending money directly to fund research into alternative methods of experimentation.

A complaint, though, that one still hears quite frequently from orthodox scientists is that people in the opposite camp (I am labelling them anti-vivisectionists for shorthand) do not appreciate the complexity of investigations for which guinea pigs, rats, mice, beagles and other animals have to be employed. This accusation, I think, used to be well-founded until a few years ago. One was often told with alarming naïvety that all the problems of animal experimentation could be overcome simply by using tissue culture. Indeed, some methods of this sort are being used already in research laboratories as alternatives to living animals, but it is equally true that, at the moment, isolated tissues provide such simplistic models of the behaviour of whole animals that they can solve only a very tiny part of the problem.

So, from the standpoint of an outsider, the work of the anti-vivisection societies has changed in recent years. They have begun to argue on matters such as tissue culture and computer modelling and so on with rather more rigour and rather more selectivity about what is feasible and what is likely to be achievable. In some cases, they have begun to fund research in that direction. The rewards so far have been modest, but there is no doubt in my mind that the change of policy has been to the good, and in the long-term this change will be infinitely more potent in effecting change than some of the tactics of sensationalism and misrepresentation of which we used to hear so much about ten years ago.

How, then, has the scientific community changed in response to this shift of emphasis? I think one should distinguish between the scientific community as a whole and the various bodies, organisations and individuals who, in one way or another, represent it. One could, for example, merely quote as evidence the initial response of the Research Defence Society last August to the Paper *Experiments on Living Animals* (The " Houghton/Platt Memorandum ")[145] which was produced by Lord Platt, Lord Houghton and their colleagues. The Research Defence Society was extremely angry about the document. They commented that "research workers should not be lectured by this group" and claimed that the memo showed " consistent denigration of the research worker ". This was not, in fact, true, and was an altogether intemperate reflex reply to a very carefully considered set of proposals. Even more astonishing was the vitriolic response of Colonel R. S. Vine, until recently the Chief Inspector under the Cruelty to Animals Act—a person one also might assume to be representative of orthodox science in these matters. But to take views of this sort as typical would be unfair. The Research Defence Society did appear to have second thoughts about the Houghton/Platt Memorandum. In a statement issued two months later in October, 1976, Professor William Paton, the Society's Chairman, said that the concluding proposals of the Houghton/Platt Memorandum contained " much that the R.D.S. would support ", including the need for more information and, if thought necessary by the Government, some enlargement of the Advisory Committee and Inspectorate. So one should perhaps concede that the intemperate conditioned reflexes of a former Chief Inspector under the Cruelty to Animals Act do not accurately reflect official policy today. Indeed one can take heart from the assurances given by Mr. Merlyn Rees to a deputation including Lord Houghton, earlier this year, about the need to amend some aspects of the 1976 Act. In particular one must welcome the Home Secretary's promise to reconsider the constitution and enlargement of the Advisory Committee, and his offer to consider names offered by the Houghton group.

I would now like to turn to what many see as a paradox. From the standpoint of the animal anti-vivisection lobby, an institution like the Medical Research Council's Laboratory Animals Centre at Carshalton must symbolise all that is most hateful about animal experimentation. Its sole purpose is to help scientists in their work with animals. Yet, as I know personally, and also from their contributions to the scientific literature, the staff at the L.A.C. are acutely concerned about animal welfare, about conditions under which laboratory animals are kept, about the way in which they are used, and above all, about the need wherever possible to reduce the numbers of animals that are required for both research and toxicological screening. It is not they but the majority of working scientists, I believe, whose consciences need to be stirred. Indeed, the work of the Laboratory Animal Centre—much of it directed towards reducing pain and discomfort inflicted upon animals—is far too little-known amongst the medical and biological scientists up and down the country.

One senior member of the L.A.C. staff, Dr. Michael Festing, has been particularly outspoken in his comments about the misuse of laboratory animals. He believes that, even without the extreme restrictions that are favoured by some anti-vivisectionists, both the numbers of animals used in research and their suffering could, and should, be greatly reduced. Areas in which he has highlighted a great deficiency are the training of staff and the design of experiments. No British university teaches laboratory animal science and, in Dr. Festing's view, many researchers in this field have a " totally inadequate training ".

One of the main consequences of this lack of proper regulation over animal experimentation is that a high proportion of what are called " dirty " or " unsuitable " animals, purchased from disreputable dealers and from unspecified sources, are used in laboratories. This is a point that has been made by Dr. Festing, by somebody who is, in a sense, a member of a scientific establishment. But he has been much concerned to publicise the fact that, for example, disease amongst laboratory animals can itself be very costly if it confuses the results of experiments and thereby makes a greater demand upon the number of animals which are used. I realise, of course, that on an occasion of this sort an argument for better quality of laboratory animals will seem like special pleading on behalf of orthodox science. Many people will feel that the real goal is to abolish animal experimentation altogether, and I would accept that as a long-term goal—but one that may never be achieved fully. More immediately, however, enormous reductions in the numbers of animals used in research laboratories could be achieved simply by substituting high quality animals, well looked after, for those which are still very widely used.

As a practical goal for the immediate future, efforts to insist on the highest standards to be used in rearing laboratory animals could have an astronomically greater influence on reducing suffering than a campaign to abolish animal experiments overnight.

This, I think, is one reason to regret the extraordinary decision, made by the Medical Research Council in 1976, to withdraw its

G

financial support from the accreditation scheme which is administered by the Laboratory Animal Centre. This scheme which came into effect in 1969 involves staff from the L.A.C. in examining animals from throughout the country and screening them for various parasites. It is an important scheme in providing assurances for research workers that animals are of reliable quality. Yet the Medical Research Council has decided that it wishes to recover the £70,000 annual cost of this scheme, and this, in the view again of people like Dr. Michael Festing and others (and I support them in this), is that it is very likely that this withdrawal by the Medical Research Council will mean that many more animals will have to be used in research, and that animal welfare will, to that degree, suffer.

One of the things that I would like to speak about briefly is that one often hears from the scientific " establishment " that arguments against the use of animals in research are misplaced, because, purely on the grounds of cost, animals are indeed replaced wherever possible, by non-animal techniques in laboratories. But I believe that there are other pressures acting on research scientists, the effect of which is to discourage them from exploring alternative methods; one such pressure is simply habit. A biologist who has always applied a particular method in assessing some aspect of metabolism is thoroughly familiar with the way in which that system behaves, and is therefore likely to go on using it as a tried and tested procedure. Secondly, there is the question of reproducibility. Despite the fact that well-known tests with living creatures give more variable results than those with inanimate chemicals, the research worker may stick to established technique because he or she is able to make strict comparisons of results with his or her earlier data and, even more importantly, perhaps, with those recorded by other investigators. Thirdly, and perhaps most important of all, there are simply the demands of time. A biologist or medical scientist, working in a particular field, may find it inconvenient to stray from the main path of his or her research in order to spend, perhaps, several weeks or months developing an entirely new method of conducting tests.

I think these pressures are most clearly shown in the case of the apprentice scientist or the research student—somebody who is doing a postgraduate course directed towards an M.Sc. or a doctorate. He has a period of time in which to do this research, two or three years, and quite honestly he is not going to go down byways and seek out new methods of pursuing his research. His main objective is to get his degree and to become qualified as a research worker.

What I would argue, therefore, is that many research workers are caught up passively in a situation which does not encourage— indeed it inhibits—radical thinking about means of replacing conventional methods. I do not believe that the country's research laboratories are populated by scientists malevolently torturing animals. On the contrary, Britain's scientific community has high standards and an unwritten consensus making it unlikely that some of the types of experiment reported abroad would ever be carried on here. One example would be a study which was reported from the University of Oregon a few years ago—an investigation of the degree to which face grooming movements in mice are inherited. This scientist studied six litters of mice and the day after birth he severed one foreleg on each of the three mice out of each litter of six to nine animals. Between one and three of the remainder, in each case, had both of their fore-limbs excised. The research worker then observed all of the mice, both normal and defective, and he recorded their grooming movements with a cine-camera. Well, normal mice lick their forepaws by extending the tongue as they bring their paws together towards the face, by rotating their shoulders in a particular way. The amputated mice made every effort to do this, but their movements were ineffective as the limbs had been severed. I think the results of this research would have been predictable. I accept that an instinctive behaviour is a fascinating topic for scientific scrutiny, but it seems to me that this type of experiment, which appeared in the American Journal *Science* published by the American Association for the Advancement of Science, was *not* a legitimate type of experiment. I believe it would not be conducted in Britain.

It is not pleasant to describe abuses of this sort, but I have done so to emphasise what I believe to be one area which calls for attention by all organisations who are concerned with experiments on living animals

Science is an international activity, one within which professional contacts and friendships have endured, despite political and military conflict between different countries. The world-wide scientific fraternity operates by conferences, symposia, learned societies and the publication of research reports in scholarly journals. Each of these provides a route through which research workers can exert political and moral influence on their colleagues in other countries. In the realm of animal experimentation it is surely not too much to ask that, for example, individual scientists, editors of journals, officers of learned societies and so on, from countries with rigorous rules governing animal experiments, should seek to influence practices in countries where standards are more lax. I do not need to say which countries they are. Editors could, for example, refuse to publish papers: they could reject papers, however outstanding, in which there was evidence that animals had been treated badly or used unnecessarily. Scientists employed as referees by such journals could advise strongly against publication, and scientific societies could insist on high standards in this area from people delivering papers at international conferences.

You will notice that I have not, during this lecture, argued a logical case for replacing animal experimentation as far as possible by alternative techniques. It would, I think, be even impudent of me to do so in a gathering such as this. I feel in the final analysis that this case does not rest upon rational argument. It arises from sensibility rather than deductive reasoning. So I have avoided the underlying justification and instead I have reviewed what seemed to me some welcome changes in the tactics of the anti-vivisection movement in recent years: I have also tried to draw attention to further moves which could be made by the other side, by the scientific community and, in summarising what I have to say, I would add that two of these, I believe, would have considerable impact.

Firstly, enormous reductions in the numbers of animals used

in laboratories could be achieved by an insistence on the highest standards in the breeding and care of such animals.

Secondly, scientists who feel strongly on these matters could, through their international societies and journals, bring pressure to bear on their colleagues in countries abroad, where those standards and attitudes towards such work, are so far behind our own.

Many of us were deeply disappointed when 1976 passed without any movement by the Government to consider a review of the century-old Cruelty to Animals Act. Despite the very welcome assurances given to the Houghton group very recently by the Home Secretary, to which I have already referred, I still believe that the Act needs updating to bring it in line with modern circumstances. The pressures for such a review seem to me irresistible, but I also believe that any political moves ought to be preceded by a comprehensive and factual survey of the field —one which could marshal the vast amount of complex evidence and present it as a basis for discussion. This would help to raise the level of political debate on the subject; something which, in my view, is of variable quality, to say the least. Whenever, for example, the subject is discussed in the House of Commons, one finds erroneous and totally misleading statements being made on all sides. I think some sort of survey will help to provide a solid basis for that sort of debate or discussion.

There are various possibilities, and I do not have any particularly strong feelings as to what form such an enquiry could take. The British Association for the Advancement of Science could, perhaps, man a study. An alternative idea could be that the House of Commons Select Committee on Science and Technology could take animal experimentation as a subject for study.

I do believe that an exercise of this sort, which would really take the outline of the very excellent Houghton/Platt Memorandum, and go into the question of alternative methods and the need for investment in research in those areas, could take this in very much more detail and, in my view, would be essential before further legislation could be introduced on a sensible basis.

Perhaps for the first time, the climate is now such that spokesmen on all sides would be able to co-operate in such an inquiry in a constructive spirit. I am saddened that 90% of the impetus towards the changed climate, of which I have talked, in fact has come from one side of the debate—from the critics, the anti-vivisectionists, the animal welfare bodies and so on—rather than from the scientific establishment. But I believe it is heartening today to be able to discern some signs of movement too, even in the corridors of scientific orthodoxy.

Controversial Aspects of Current Animal Experimentation

LOUIS GOLDMAN

Because we are meeting in Cambridge in August 1977, I think it appropriate to begin this paper by referring to a book published earlier this month by a very distinguished Cambridge scientist, Colin Blakemore. His book is entitled *Mechanics of the Mind.* Dr. Blakemore is the Royal Society Locke Research Fellow of the University here, an experimental physiologist and director of studies in medicine at Downing College.

His book is a slightly expanded version of the Reith Lectures he broadcast last year at the invitation of the B.B.C. I don't think anyone could read this book without being impressed by the width of Dr. Blakemore's knowledge, by his lucid ability to communicate even complex scientific information, and by his critical and, in my opinion, perceptive approach to some of the ethical problems in medicine.

He is, for example, highly critical of psychosurgery. Psychosurgical operations like pre-frontal leucotomy were often done in the 1950s in an attempt to treat emotional disorders, even though there was no evidence of organic disease of the brain tissue. The benefits were questionable and the consequences sometimes disastrous. Dr. Blakemore sardonically observes that, while current psychosurgical techniques are more sophisticated and surgical lesions in apparently healthy brain tissue more discrete, the lack of moral restraint as well as the lack of theoretical background to justify these operations are just as serious.

What, you may be wondering, has all this to do with controversial aspects of current animal experimentation? It so happens that the same Dr. Blakemore has for the past ten years been carrying out a series of animal experiments that give rise to considerable controversy. His research field, not surprisingly, involves the brain and particularly the mechanism of sight.

During some experiments, kittens were housed for several weeks in a totally darkened room. Others were deprived of any pattern of visual experience because their eye-lids were sutured (stitched) together. Yet another group of animals received a distorted visual impression of the world because they wore goggles that permitted separate control of the visual input to the eye. For example, they might wear goggles fitted with powerful bi-convex lenses for as long as nine weeks.

In 1975, Blakemore and his colleagues described a new set of experiments. They took three kittens less than three weeks old, another kitten reared in total darkness for five and a half weeks, and an adult cat. An operation was done on these five animals in which the muscles which control the movement of the right eyeball were cut and the eyeball rotated. Care was taken not to damage the blood supply to the eye or to put stress on the optic nerve.

The rotated eye apparently remained in its new position without stitching. The animals were then housed in a colony room for several weeks before undergoing behavioural and neurophysiological tests. More recently, animals were housed for longer than a year after the operation before testing was carried out.

The investigators reported that the rotated eye was able to mediate behaviour to visual input, but the animal's responses were not very accurately directed in space. They commented that this wasn't perhaps very surprising in view of the rotation of one eye, and the conflicting information which the animal was receiving from the other eye.

Now I'm sure you will remember that a few minutes ago I quoted Dr. Blakemore's opinions on psychosurgery and the lack of moral restraint exhibited by psychosurgeons. And I can't help wondering why experimental physiologists don't exhibit moral restraints as well. Sight is after all such a vital function for all animals that deliberately to place it at hazard or damage it seems an offence against nature.

I am not, I hasten to add, a neurophysiologist and can offer no informed opinion about the scientific worth of these studies. But even if they are regarded as important by the scientific community, I would question the cost in animal suffering needed to obtain such information. Speaking merely as a physician with some experience of scientific investigation, I can only say that reading the description of the experiments aroused in me an intense feeling of distaste and repugnance.

Let me make it clear that I make no personal attack on Dr. Blakemore. He is, after all, following the same experimental path that has been taken by many other scientists in the field of animal experimentation. But few of them are as literate as Dr. Blakemore and even fewer, I suspect, possess the deep critical insight that he manifests in his book.

Yet, clearly, he regards experiments on man and experiments on animals as belonging to entirely separate moral categories. I find this difficult to understand. True enough, I value a man's life much higher than I do an animal's. I still cannot believe that we are entitled to ignore completely the fact that we have some moral responsibility to animals—unless we choose to regard them merely as "animal machines" without the capacity to feel pain or suffer from cruelty.

Perhaps, though, it is time to leave Cambridge for a while, at least in spirit, and visit a few other experimental laboratories in the country. If you had gone to Newcastle-upon-Tyne last year, you might have seen twelve cats who had been living for at least a year with a gastric fistula—a hole in the stomach with a cannula (a tube) coming out through the abdominal skin. The fistula permitted the investigators to study directly the effects of stimulating gastric secretion by means of such agents as histamine and pentagastrin. I cannot believe the animals found it comfortable to live with a gastric fistula. I cannot help wondering why it is necessary to keep them alive in this state for a year.

Or we could have paid a visit to King's College in London to watch a group of investigators pumping a mixture of room air and an alcohol (ethanol) vapour into a perspex chamber housing a group of mice. Over a period of eight or nine days, the investigators increased the concentration of alcohol in the air. Early on the animals were apparently stimulated and moved about a good deal; later they became lethargic and exhibited signs of an unsteady gait. Between five and ten per cent died, presumably from alcohol poisoning. When the experiment was stopped, the remaining animals showed a pattern of alcoholic withdrawal symptoms. So it seems that even *breathing* alcohol in high concentrations can do harm, but the *relevance* of this observation either to social custom or to clinical medicine escapes me.

While in London we could have studied another addiction experiment, this time at the Institute of Psychiatry. I rather like the way the work was described when it was published early this year, for the opening sentence reads:

> " Naive rats do not normally drink solutions of morphine, possibly because they are bitter-tasting (to man) and possibly because of the post-ingestational effects of the drug."

Are rats really *naïve* not to prefer morphine solutions to plain water? However, sophistication lies within their grasp, for the experimenters showed that you can train rats to prefer morphine solutions if you repeatedly force the animals to drink them to relieve their thirst. Once again, the clinical importance of this work is not immediately apparent, at least to me.

At several centres around the country we might have been able to watch so-called behavioural studies on animals. These studies almost always involve stress of some kind, starvation and electric shock being most commonly used. For example, rats might be subjected to electric shocks in a cage. One investigator a few years ago reached the interesting conclusion that electric shocks to the feet consistently resulted in the animals avoiding that part of the cage where shocks had been given.

Are experiments like these cruel? If you believe that animals feel pain in much the same way as we do (and I have seen no convincing evidence to the contrary), then these experiments are certainly cruel. Can they be justified? That seems to me a much more difficult question to answer, unless you happen to belong to the anti-vivisectionist movement or to the right wing of the

Research Defence Society, the organisation which Dr. Dixon mentioned in his paper.

The anti-vivisectionist argues that any experiment which causes suffering is morally wrong; so strong is the repugnance which he feels to the idea of experimenting on animals that he presses for laws to prohibit *all* of these experiments. Ranged against him are the legions of devoted scientists who claim that almost *any* experiment which could increase our knowledge and lead to a possible medical advance is justified, even if it causes pain.

I find it impossible to sympathise with either view. Absolutism is a doctrine that has no appeal for me. The anti-vivisectionist who would prohibit all experiments on animals is, whether he admits it or not, jeopardising the future and well-being of mankind. On the other hand, the arguments of the Research Defence Society strike me as equally unconvincing. Because some cruel experiments can perhaps be justified doesn't mean that all of them can be justified.

Very well, then—how *is* one to justify cruelty in animal experiment? (I am uncomfortably aware at this point that I am sailing close to those treacherous seas in which moral philosophers abound and in which there is much esoteric argument about good and evil and even more about ends and means. I pretend to little knowledge about moral philosophy and haven't learned to swim in deep water—though I have a worrying suspicion that some of my criticisms could land me in hot water.)

So the only way I can deal with the moral dilemma is to find a pragmatic solution : if you like, a simple utilitarian solution.

Experiments which cause pain and suffering demand special justification. That special justification cannot merely be that scientists are entitled to do anything that might increase the sum total of knowledge or bring about a medical advance in the remote future. There has to be a direct benefit, a good and immediately relevant reason—one which most people would accept as adequate.

I believe that most people accept the use of animals to test a new vaccine or a new drug before it is given to man. I believe that most people accept that new surgical procedures like transplant operations should first be tested on animals. But I question experiments like those which I have cited earlier, because their aim is too indirect. Indeed, it seems to me that some scientific problems are not really worth solving. We don't really need proof that inhaling a mixture of air and alcohol produces a state of addiction in mice. Nor do we need proof that animals can be trained to avoid a part of a cage where they received electric shocks to their feet. The link between the experiment and a possible benefit to mankind is so remote as to be almost invisible.

In his book, Dr. Blakemore rather gives the game away, for in the last chapter he writes about " the promise that research on the brain will provide a genuine basis for the treatment of mental disease ". That's an exaggerated statement, because a hope should not be construed as a promise.

Dr. Blakemore then goes on :

> " But much more than that, it will give a greater under-
> standing of the nature of man himself . . . For without a
> description of the brain, without an account of the forces
> that mould human behaviour, there can never be a truly
> objective new ethic based on the needs and rights of man."

With all due respect, most of this strikes me as intellectual pie in the sky. It sounds impressive, but it doesn't bear close scrutiny. What on earth is a " truly objective new ethic " anyway? Such high-flown ideas are just about as remote as you could possibly get from a laboratory where investigators carefully rear kittens in total darkness and operate on them to rotate one eye so as to distort visual function.

Perhaps what we need isn't so much an " objective new ethic " as an old one in which we pay more than token respect to the mystery and wonder of life, whether human or animal.

References:

Abu-Murad, C. *et al*   *Journal of Physiology*, 1977, 266, 10P
Albinus, M. *et al*   *Ibid*, 1977, 266, 801
Blakemore, C. and
    Van Sluytens, R. C.   *Ibid*, 1975, 248, 663

Blakemore, C. *et al*   *Nature*, 1975, 257, 584

Blakemore, C.   *Journal of Physiology*, 1976, 261, 423

Blakemore, C.   *Mechanics of the Mind.* Cambridge University Press, 1977.

Kumar, R. *et al*   *British Journal of Pharmacology*, 1977, 60, 276P.

Research

JENNY REMFRY

Philosophical and ethical debates are important in determining long-term objectives. But while we gather here expounding the theory that animals should not be exploited in laboratories, the fact is that animals *are* being used in great numbers and will go on being used into the foreseeable future. How can the situation of these animals be improved?

One way is to learn more about the animals themselves, so that by understanding their needs we can provide them with greater comfort. Not enough work has been done on the behaviour of laboratory animals: Chance and Mackintosh in the 1950s showed how the response of mice to certain drugs could be influenced by the size and type of cage, and by the numbers of mice in the group, but only recently has the importance of this been recognised as reactions to drugs in safety-testing programmes come to be more and more accurately and sensitively recorded.

Domestication has the effect on animals of making them more placid than their wild forebears, so that they are content to live under man's control. This is true of cattle, sheep and pigs, which have been selectively bred by man for thousands of years, and is also true of laboratory animals. Domesticated rats and mice can develop relationships with people, as many a child will attest. Moreover, they have lost their wild, protective colourings, so that if they are released into the wild they are ready targets for predators such as owls, cats and foxes. I suggest that it is not a kindness to " liberate " such animals.

Some (though by no means all) experiments involve inflicting suffering on animals. The ways in which this suffering may be reduced were summarised into the 3R's by Russell and Burch in 1959 and they still hold true, namely: Refinement, Reduction and Replacement.

Refinement of experimental technique should be the constant concern of the experimenter, whether it concerns the size of needle to be used for giving inoculations or the details of a complicated surgical technique. More attention should be given to post-operative care and the use of analgesics.

Reduction in the number of animals being used in a particular experiment can be achieved by the use of better animals, that is, healthy animals of a species and strain chosen specifically for that experiment, and also by proper statistical design of the experiment itself.

Replacement of animals by non-sentient material may be achieved in several ways: the scientist could re-phrase his question so that the problem can be solved with mechanical or mathematical models; a part taken from a dead animal, such as the nerve axon of a squid, may replace the whole animal; an organ or tissue may be maintained or grown in a culture medium. For the biochemist, bacteria can be used to answer many questions. Indeed man himself is the ideal experimental animal for testing drugs intended for man, and the micro-techniques now available make it feasible for small amounts of test substances to be safely and ethically given to human volunteers so that their pharmacology and metabolism can be studied. Many people maintain that modern medicine is over-dependent on drugs; if new forms of medicine could be developed, the saving in terms of animal suffering could be enormous.

There is a saying at the Cavendish Laboratory in Cambridge which goes: " We do not have much money so we have to use our brains instead." We should not be afraid to ask biologists to use fewer animals: they too can use their brains instead.

Finally, we need more training in animal care at all levels, from the technician in the animal house to the scientist performing experiments; we also need specialist training for the curators or managers who have overall responsibility for the animals themselves.

Scientists and their Experimental Animals

DAVID SPERLINGER

I believe that animal experimentation is one of the most important areas of animal exploitation that we are examining at this symposium. It seems to me that it is one of the few areas of animal exploitation where there can be a genuine ethical conflict arising—that is, a conflict involving important interests for humans, which have to be balanced against the suffering and death caused to experimental animals. (I am dealing here, of course, with some medical and scientific experiments. Many of the animal experiments conducted for commercial reasons would appear to involve no important human interests at all). Dr. Goldman has already clearly outlined the issues and dilemmas which face us in this area.

What I would like to do in this short paper is to make a few simple comments on what is possibly the most fundamental issue facing this symposium. That is, what can be done to make scientists, and other animal exploiters, change their ways of treating animals. There is clearly no simple answer to this problem, and a variety of approaches on the political, economic and educational aspects of animal experimentation will be necessary. What I want to examine here are some approaches to this problem from a psychological point of view.

I strongly believe that if change is to come, an important impetus will have to emerge from the animal experimenters themselves beginning to question what they are doing. I am, therefore, very encouraged by several recent signs that there is in fact a growing concern amongst scientists about this issue. To give just three examples: (1) There is the sympathetic coverage that the *New Scientist* has given recently to issues such as the Houghton-Platt Memorandum and to Angela Walder's case. Obviously Bernard Dixon's attitudes and influence have played an important role in fostering this change. But in view of the attitudes often held towards anti-vivisectionists by scientists, I think this is a striking and significant development. (2) Nearer to my own home territory, the British Psychological Society (the professional body for psychologists in Britain) recently set up a working party to enquire into the ethical issues arising from animal experimentation by psychologists. I am pessimistic about this working party producing any radical recommendations, but nonetheless its very existence is I think encouraging, particularly in view of psychologists' sorry record as animal experimenters. (Some of the horrifying examples given by Dr. Goldman were experiments performed by psychologists). (3) There is the growing number of eminent scientists who are now involved in research using (or seeking to find) alternative techniques which do not involve the suffering and death of animals which is produced by so many current research methods.

How then can we encourage this trend amongst scientists away from animal experimentation? Unfortunately the Animal Liberation argument is, I think, at it weakest on this crucial issue. The most successful recent examples of liberation movements—in the Third World countries, by blacks in the United States, by the Women's Movement, etc.,—have all begun with the oppressed group liberating themselves. That is, as a first step the oppressed group had to free themselves from the oppressive definitions and constraints of the dominant group. Once this had been achieved they could then turn to the problem of forcing, or attempting to force, the oppressing group to change *its* attitudes and behaviour towards them. This clearly cannot happen in the case of animal experimentation—since animals themselves are powerless to change their own situations or to exert any pressure on their oppressors to alter their ideas or actions towards them.

I think it is also not helpful if we start off with the attitude which seems to have been shown by some speakers at this symposium—namely that animal experimenters, people who hunt, factory farmers, etc., must be people very different from ourselves, with attitudes and beliefs about animals very different from our own. I cannot accept this.

In our culture there are various ideas, models, metaphors, etc., about animals that we are exposed to as children—these ideas or models are complex and often contradictory. This is nicely illustrated in Susan Isaacs' classic book *Intellectual Growth in Young Children*, published in 1930. She writes of

> " the extraordinarily confused and conflicting ways in which we adults actually behave towards animals, in the sight of children. What children make of our injunctions to be ' kind ', and our horror at any impulse of cruelty on their part, in the face of our own deeds, and the everyday facts of animals' death for our uses and pleasures, would be hard to say. There is probably no moral field in which the child sees so many puzzling inconsistencies as here."

Think, for example, of the range of ideas about animals that one learns from one's parents' attitudes to pets, the insects who are attacking dad's vegetables, injured animals, spiders, farm animals, etc., or from fairy tales or cartoon films. These different ideas about animals, and our relationship towards them, do not disappear as we grow up—although they may become altered or elaborated.

Scientists who experiment on animals have also been exposed to this range of ideas about animals. In their laboratories their main view of animals, as Cora Diamond (1977) has recently pointed out, is as delicate pieces of research equipment. That is, within certain limits, the scientist regards his experimental animals as like any other of his research tools : providing certain minimal standards are met, their fate is of little more concern to him than the fate of the chemicals in a chemist's test-tube. (This is, of course, not the only model which scientists who experiment on animals use; the most striking exception being ethologists who show much more concern to learn *from* or *about* the animals they study). Yet the scientist, who treats animals as mere research tools in his laboratory, will, on his return home, be as capable of treating his pets or an injured animal humanely as the most fervent liberationist.

Thus what I am arguing is that : Firstly, scientists who experiment on animals are *not* people with a completely different mentality from the rest of us. They do certainly act towards animals, when inside and outside their laboratories, in ways which may appear to us to involve an inherent contradiction. In this I think that they are an accurate reflection of the complex attitudes to animals which are found in our culture generally and which most of us at this symposium also still probably show in some degree. That is not to say that these attitudes on our culture must be accepted as unalterable, only that it is important to consider the actions of animal experimenters in a wider context. Secondly, in a sense the availability of a whole range of ideas concerning animals in the culture generally, and in scientists who experiment on animals particularly, gives some (small) grounds for hope. For it is precisely in the possibility of getting scientists to reconstrue their experimental animals, to see them more as creatures deserving of concern and with interests of their own, and less as merely pieces of experimental equipment, that I believe the hope for change lies. And they already *do* see some animals in some situations (outside their laboratories) in precisely this more humane way.

As a clinical psychologist, much of my work involves helping people to change themselves. I know the problems that can arise in the process of change, particularly (as with many scientists on this subject) when the people concerned themselves have little desire to change. My first task in the clinical situation is to try to understand the world from the point of view of the person who has come to me for help. In the case of animal experimenters too I think it is important, as a first step, to try to understand *their* view of animals. There is no simple solution to the question of how to get them to *change* these views, but I believe that this has to be our starting point. We do not aid the cause of animals by over-simplifying the complex ideas of, and relationships to, other animals which we all (including scientists and other animal exploiters) hold.

Examining the parallels between our own ideas about animals and the ideas of animal experimenters may be important in another way. For perhaps the richest source of ideas, in the struggle to develop ways of encouraging change in animal exploiters, is for each of us to ask ourselves what were the main factors which led us ourselves to change our attitudes towards other animals? Most of us at one time or another have exploited animals in the various ways which we have examined at this symposium. Perhaps by looking at the development of our own attitudes and feelings towards animals we can begin to develop ideas about how to go about encouraging change in others. What I am arguing is that by understanding the potential animal experimenters in ourselves, we can perhaps start to understand more clearly those scientists who experiment on animals, and begin the process of getting *them* to change.

References:

Cora Diamond   *Some philosophical questions raised by animal experimentation.* Paper read at the Annual Conference of the British Psychological Society, Exeter, 1977

Susan Isaacs   *Intellectual Growth in Young Children,* London : Routledge, 1930

Section Five

POLITICAL AND LEGAL PERSPECTIVES

Animal Welfare Year in Retrospect

CLIVE HOLLANDS

Animal Welfare Year marked the centenary of the oldest legislation now remaining on the British Statute Book, the *Cruelty to
Animals Act 1876*.[146] The marking of a centenary may have
some importance, but Animal Welfare Year was much more
than this, as it saw the coming together for the first time in
history of nearly seventy Animal Welfare Organisations throughout Britain to express their growing concern over the plight of
animals in our modern technological society, and the suffering
being deliberately inflicted upon those animals.

It can be said that considerable progress has been made during
the past hundred years in securing legislation for the protection
and welfare of animals. Certainly a review of the number of Acts
of Parliament and Regulations would indicate this to be the case,
but careful reading makes it abundantly clear that almost invariably the protection granted is minimal, particularly where commercial profit is involved.

If animals merely had to die for us—humanely and without
pain—it is probable that there would not be an animal welfare
movement or, for that matter, an Animal Welfare Year. It is
a fact that animals suffer for us—and wherever and whenever
animals are exploited for commercial profit, almost invariably
suffering is involved. It is what is known as " necessary suffering ", since most protective legislation provides penalties for the
infliction of " unnecessary suffering ".

Animal Welfare Year (August 1976/August 1977) was the
greatest opportunity ever presented to animal societies in Britain
to get their message across to the public, Press and Parliament.

It was an opportunity to present to the uncommitted majority the progress made in animal welfare during the past hundred years—the situation as it now stands and the trends likely to occur in the next hundred years unless there are reforms.

Previous speakers have already discussed some of the areas of particular concern on which Animal Welfare Year has concentrated and I propose therefore only to make brief reference to these and the progress which has been made during the Year.

Since the 1876 Act became law, the number of experiments on living animals has steadily increased from some 350 to well over 5,000,000 annually, many of which in the present day are not for medical purposes, but for purely commercial undertakings. Reforms have already been achieved during Animal Welfare Year through the work of the Houghton Group which has now been formalised as the Committee for the Reform of Animal Experimentation (C.R.A.E.) which represents members from both Houses of Parliament, scientists, the R.S.P.C.A. and the Anti-Vivisection Organisations.

Intensive methods of farming may, in the short term, produce more food and greater profits, but apart from possibly affecting the quality of the end product, these methods, which deny animals the basic rights due to any creature capable of suffering, should be questioned. The Farm Animals' Welfare Co-ordinating Executive (F.A.W.C.E.), formed during Animal Welfare Year, represents twelve organisations and other experts in Great Britain concerned with the welfare and protection of farm animals under the Chairmanship of Robin Corbett, M.P.

The destruction by animal welfare societies of over 2,000 dogs and as many cats every day because there are not enough homes to be found is not only a heavy financial burden placed on these organisations but is also a figure which reflects the suffering imposed on abandoned and unwanted animals. The Joint Advisory Committee on Pets in Society (J.A.C.O.P.I.S.), formed prior to the commencement of Animal Welfare Year, represents the Pet Animal Societies, the R.S.P.C.A., the veterinary profession, and pet food manufacturers. There is also great concern over the slaughter of horses and ponies for human consumption (a trade which has increased nine-fold in the past three years), and those Societies concerned with the welfare of equines have come together as the National Joint Equine Welfare Committee.

In the march of progress, we destroy wild places and wild creatures on an alarming scale, and although it may be impossible to put the clock back, at least thought should be given to the ecology of areas devastated in the name of progress. Additionally, wild animals which have commercial value are still being hunted, trapped and destroyed on a horrifying scale—the whale providing a good example of the effect of man's greed. It is known, although expert estimates vary wildly, that many species of whale are endangered, and the International Whaling Commission quotas give nominal protection to only the most severely threatened. Britain does not hunt the whale, but we are responsible for importing over 8,500 metric tons of sperm oil annually, almost a quarter of the world's total annual production, for no greater reason than for the softening of leather (for which alternatives are available). We must therefore accept equal responsibility with those countries which still harpoon this magnificent animal on the high seas.

I am not basically a conservationist. When the last great whale is slaughtered, as it surely will be, the whales' suffering will be over. This is not the whales' loss, but man's. I am not concerned about the wiping out of a species—this is man's folly—I have only one concern, the suffering which we deliberately inflict upon animals whilst they live.

Britain is now the only European country which provides no legal protection to the otter, whose numbers diminish every year. During Animal Welfare Year, and as a result of the efforts of the Joint Otter Group, the Nature Conservancy Council and the Society for the Promotion of Nature Conservation, the Minister of the Environment is considering protecting the otter under the *Conservation of Wild Creatures and Wild Plants Act 1975*.[147]

The legal use of the poison strychnine for killing moles, which causes a slow and painful death, and frequently kills other animals further along the food chain, is also a matter of great concern, particularly as there is evidence that this poison is also used to control other animals illegally; Animal Welfare Year has pressed for a total ban on the use of this particularly cruel poison.

Animal Welfare Year was primarily a publicity campaign, and in this it has achieved a considerable measure of success. Perhaps, however, the most important contribution which the Year has made has been in bringing the Animal Welfare organisations closer together, both at national and local level. At a time when commercial organisations spend vast sums of money on promoting products, and when highly organised pressure groups like the trade unions and the student bodies can call upon their enormous manpower resources to exert pressure on public opinion and for political lobbying, the animal welfare movement must come to terms with the fact that it is only by joint effort that it can really succeed. It is therefore essential that a spirit of co-operation between organisations should be encouraged and, even at some cost to themselves, societies must be prepared to sink their differences in order to work together to ensure that real protection is given to animals.

Those present at this Symposium represent a good cross-section of the whole animal welfare movement from the moderates to the extremists and to the militants; I would like to make a plea at this point—not a plea for moderation, but for co-operation. I am not a moderate and I am too old to be a militant, but I do represent what is considered to be an extreme organisation.

There have been some indications during the past two days that some of us take the view : " If you don't do it our way, then you are against us." There is room in the animal welfare movement for all of us—we are all needed. God knows, we need all the support we can get. Do not turn away all the meat-eaters who oppose vivisection, for example, merely because they eat meat. When vivisection has been abolished, we can exhort them to become vegetarians.

Do not belittle the work of other groups because they are too moderate, too extreme or too militant. We must all go our own way, but we must also learn that although we travel by different roads, our destination is the same.

Animal Welfare Year was not an end in itself—it was a beginning. When the history of the twentieth century comes to be written it may not be the economic or political upheavals of the present day which will be recorded as having great importance, since such upheavals have marked man's progress throughout the ages; although having importance to those who live through them, they have little historical significance.

Perhaps this century will be recorded as seeing the dawning of man's first acceptance of the other species who share the earth with him, a point in history when the rest of creation is seen to have a significance and—dare one say it?—to possess rights equal to those of man himself.

This century has seen the publication of a number of books which propound a new approach to our relationship with animals. *Animals, Men and Morals*[148] was followed by Richard D. Ryder's *Victims of Science*[149] in which he coined the word " speciesism " (relating to animals as " racism " relates to man). Professor Peter Singer in *Animal Liberation*[150] and Stephen R. L. Clark in *The Moral Status of Animals*[151] both take this concept further in a damning condemnation of what we do to other species whether for food, clothing, research, sport or pleasure. The Rev. Andrew Linzey in *Animal Rights*[152] has made a valuable assessment of man's treatment of animals from a Christian viewpoint.

Animal Welfare Year has put forward a proposal to establish a Standing Commission on Animal Protection, which if accepted by Parliament, will ensure that the whole question of animal welfare and protection in every field will be kept under constant review.

Professor Georges Heuse of the International Institute of Human Biology in Paris has been the guiding light behind the Universal Declaration of the Rights of Animals, which is now nearing its final draft.[153]

This Symposium has also now been asked to endorse " A Declaration Against Speciesism ", and in paying tribute to Lord Houghton for his magnificent support during Animal Welfare Year, I would like to quote his words as its President:

" The concept of Animal Welfare Year is inspired by a challenge to the selfish creed of the rights of man to the exclusion of all others. It is a recognition of the claims of all living things to their place in the continuing evolution of the inhabitants of the earth."[154]

Perhaps the dream of those who saw Animal Welfare Year as a beginning will become a reality, if future historians record this century as being the time when man first accepted his place in the Natural Order—not as master, but as an equal partner with all living creatures.

Animals and the Law: Moral and Political Issues

LORD HOUGHTON

At the end of a Conference like this we naturally want to know what happens next. Is there an action point somewhere, or are we only a spur to action? What is the message? There are several: mine isn't the only one. My message is that animal welfare, in the general and in the particular, is largely a matter for the law. This means that to Parliament we must go. Sooner or later that is where we will *have* to go. That is where laws are made and where the penalties for disobedience and the measures for enforcement are laid down.

There is no complete substitute for the law. Public opinion, though invaluable and indeed essential, is not the law. Public opinion is what makes laws possible and observance widely acceptable.

I have been reading again the Papers given at the Universities Federation for Animal Welfare in September 1974, and the concluding address by Brigid Brophy on the question: " Is there a need for animal legislation?" She replied :

"Yes, if there is a need for human welfare legislation. It may be there are no such things as rights and morality : we may have no moral choice : everything may be a mechanical power-struggle, in which non-human animals have no power-base, just as they have no votes. However, if that is so, it applies equally to humans who have little or no power-base : to all the weak. Certainly, we can't escape believing we have moral choice, though we may be deluded. Most of us now believe we owe recognition to the rights of other humans, whether or not they can speak up for themselves. As evolutionists we cannot rationally withhold recognition from the rights of the other animals."

That I believe to be the conclusion which this Conference is coming to.

If we tend to be discouraged by the length of time it takes for this point of view to become generally accepted we should remember that the United Nations Declaration of Human Rights was made less than thirty years ago and is not universally observed even today.

Animal rights, like human rights, are what people of influence and power declare them to be. Rights are born out of strength, the strength to assert. the strength to insist, and the strength to enforce. The meek do not inherit the earth. The establishment of rights may entail insurrection, revolution, or war. In more peaceful conditions it becomes a matter of the law.

Take, as an obscure and not too serious example, the right of our pets to a decent burial. I say " not too serious " although *The Times* devoted three-quarters of a column to a report of the recent planning inquiry on that subject in Lancashire.

While it appears to be lawful to bury our pets in our own back garden, the use of land for a pets' cemetery requires planning permission. A recent public enquiry in Lancashire revealed strong resistance from neighbouring residents to such a proposal, though the sponsors referred to the need for it, and what was more the availability locally of clergymen willing to conduct burial services.

That brought protests from some clergy who could not countenance the extension of Christian burial to animals. But, the applicant retorted, they were approved by the Catholic Church in Italy and, as objectors would be aware, in places like India they worship cows . . .

In a democracy all laws should rest upon *consent*. Moreover, public consent usually reflects some *moral* judgment, whether it be social justice, equity, compassion, the achievement of public benefit, and so forth.

It is well over a hundred years since one moral question related to animals was resolved and written into Statute Law—and that was unnecessary cruelty. Ever since then, cruelty has remained the outstanding feature of animal law.

Next to cruelty, and much more recently, comes health and the protection of particular species in special danger. This, for all its value (which is considerable), represents a narrow concept of the rights of animals. It has to do with suffering and the danger of extinction. Not many " rights " in that.

If we now aim to widen the area of animal rights far beyond the present, we are moving into a new epoch of man's relations with animals almost as important, difficult, and prolonged as the struggle for human rights.

The battle, even in enlightened communities, has scarcely begun. When it has begun, been fought and won—when, I say— among the casualties will be, to mention only a few :

1. all blood sports
2. factory farming
3. the killing of animals for human adornment
4. the erosion of the land and the habitat of other species by the ravages and exploitation of their resources by increasing numbers of human beings with more and more demands.

In fact little has been said at this Conference about the biggest threat to the animal kingdom, which is the rising human population.

There is a growing awareness of the multiplying of our problems, rather than the solving of them. We are very much at a turning point in thought and action on the place of human beings in the world of living things. There is widespread concern for the future of Western civilisation and material standards; about the supply of the world's energy in the next century; the rate of exhaustion of our finite resources; the dire consequences of population-pressures almost everywhere; and man's endangered peace with himself and his environment in a world which is changing out of all recognition. Are animals in the wild doomed by this global infestation by mankind ? The problems are so vast and so complex that we contemplate the future in a somewhat helpless frame of mind.

Yet we must persevere. The concluding lines of the poem by C. Day-Lewis " Keep faith with nature " come to mind at this point :

Now more than ever we need
True science lest mankind
Lording it over nature's
Territories, by greed
Or thoughtlessness made blind,
To doom shall have consigned
Itself and all earth's creatures.

This is the field for international co-operation. It should find
a place on the agenda of every Commonwealth Conference, be
the unremitting concern of the U.N., the E.E.C., and other
forms of regional associations in Asia, Africa and South
America.

We in this country have a full part to play in all that. What
is more, we can do a great deal to get things right here.

What can we do that is at hand for us to do? What is our
part in promoting the harmony of man and other species whom
you might say God hath joined together? In this regard we can
take some pride in achievement and approach a wider task with
hope and courage. Within our nation-state we have achieved
much to outlaw, and we punish the sort of basic cruelty which
the R.S.P.C.A. and other bodies were formed to stop. Many
disgusting and degrading practices which I needn't enumerate
have been suppressed, though new ones come to light all the time.
It would be misleading to suggest that this was an easy conquest
a hundred or even seventy-five years ago. One has only to read
the history of the R.S.P.C.A. to realise that.

Today, however, if we are to make any advance at all we
must move forward into a territory which is heavily defended
by those of noble birth and lofty purpose, by the cheap food
brigade, the men of science and of medicine, and sundry mer-
chants and mercenaries. This is where we move from the land of
the sadist, the fiend and the half-wit, to assault the vested interests,
the fashion and beauty specialists, the cattle men, the hunting
men, the hare coursers and the rest. While public opinion is
pretty clear on what may be thought to be wanton, avoidable, or
unnecessary cruelty, it is by no means so positive about cruelty
inflicted on animals in the course of satisfying human needs: in

attitudes towards killing for food, or even for sport, towards painful experiments in our laboratories, or even to the merciless trapping of wild animals for their skins or furs—areas where the moral issues are blurred by material gains or by the pleasures involved.

Organised cruelty or harsh treatment within the law, condoned by some, justified by others, or ignored by a public shielded or actively prevented from learning the truth—that is also part of the battleground lying ahead. This challenge calls for an entirely new initiative, a fresh drive and an entirely new unity, involving a choice of priorities for public and Parliamentary action. Areas of concern need to be identified, researched and documented. Parliament and the public should be presented with as much evidence as possible on those matters demanding investigation, preferably by a permanent Commission on Animal Welfare. A new legal concept of cruelty and welfare should therefore be drafted here; Norway can already give us an example, and Congressmen in the United States are working on something similar in a proposed law of animal rights.

Within the three main areas of concern in the treatment of animals in this country, the E.E.C. and in Western Europe, I would specify six priorities:

1. *The transportation of live animals for slaughter,*
      especially the traffic to Europe
2. *Intensive husbandry,*
      with echoes from the Brambell Report of 1965
3. *Experiments on living animals,*
      with echoes from the Littlewood Report 1965 and the growing abuse of the meaning of the word "experiment" and other sophistries under the Act of 1876
4. *Killing for sport,*
      to grasp the nettle of nettles and purge the soul of many an animal lover
5. *Methods of slaughter,*
      for food and otherwise
6. *Protection of wildlife.*
      Imports of live animals, furs and skins.

H

There are others, but there is a full programme of action in these six priorities alone. None can even be touched without changing the law. The law cannot be changed until there is the Parliamentary will to do it, and Parliament has long since surrendered its sovereignty to the Party machines. The existing farce of Parliamentary procedure on non-Government Bills must be exposed, showing up the wastefulness and frustration which occur as a result of the discredited procedures relating to Private Members' Bills.

At the beginning of every Session the Government commandeers almost all available Parliamentary time and leaves a few Fridays as a sop for back-benchers to occupy. By imposing restricted facilities for Private Members' Bills they stand little hope of becoming law, if at all controversial. The outside chance of the ballot and the scope for successful obstruction of any Bill which a Ministry does not like, effectively destroys any hope of changing the law. It is to this contemptible area of Party-gamesmanship that governments usually consign Bills on animals.

M.P.s have therefore to be convinced that although animals have no votes, many humans who care for animals do. The kid-gloves of respectable middle-class campaigning will have to come off for the next round in this contest. What is known as " the animal lobby " needs a new dynamism, a militancy which springs from the crusading spirit. Have we got it? Have we got the resources for it?

Determination and resources: these are imperative. Fragmentation of effort, and differences of outlook, if not of policy. weaken the forces of reform. When it is new laws we are after there is only one place to get them and that is the place we go for—Parliament itself. This calls for constituency work, for education, and for daring methods of exposure. It will cost money, a lot of money, and it will take a lot of courage.

We may lose the support of some who have come with us this far but who will have no part in this new endeavour. So be it. If we choose and name the targets and show signs of aiming to hit them, we shall get the money. We must awaken the people. This is the age of exposure and pressure, and Parliamentary opinion is not insulated against it. Trinity College, Cambridge, is probably not the right address to deliver this message. I have all the right addresses and I want to deliver the message. What I want to know is—will there be anybody in?

Political Perspectives:
The National Petition for the
Protection of Animals

BILL BROWN

A great question remains even at the end of these proceedings, and it is this: What can be done in practice to bring our idealism into effective operation? I would suggest that given certain prerequisites, reforms which would both transform the laboratory animal scene and raise the general status of animals, could be achieved in the foreseeable future by political action.

Apart from dictatorship, law reform can be initiated by Government or by the voice of the people, which can itself produce a government committed to reform. We know, to our sorrow, that successive governments have largely remained indifferent to the pleas of private members, and so our main effective hope lies in a government policy which reflects the voice of the people and is capable of overcoming powerful vested interests.

One of the main motivations of the mass of the people appears to be selfishness—hence our sick society. In the animal context, the people say: " We come first, animals second." However, many then say: " Provided that we are not disadvantaged ourselves we don't see why animals should suffer more than is necessary." At least 80% subscribe to this view. In practical political terms this means that these people are the only hope available of achieving reform; it means similarly, that any laboratory-animal-reforming movement, to have any hope of success at all, must be structured so as to correspond with the views of these 80% of the people.

We would all dearly like to eliminate the use of the laboratory animal immediately, but the unhappy fact is that the reforming potential at our disposal does not share this desire, and immediately melts away as soon as instant abolition is canvassed. The only hope of substantial improvement in the lot of the laboratory animal is gradualism, as dictated by 80% of the population, paralleled by greatly intensified research into alternatives.

For the sake of the animals alone, I therefore beg for the total co-operation of all organisations here represented in support of this Petition, which represents a positive and practical weapon for reform.

To those who claim that petitions are ineffective, I would reply.

1. It depends upon the size of the petition.

2. The declaration of the wishes of such a vast number of people cannot fail to strengthen other steps towards reform, such as the work of the Committee for the Reform of Animal Experimentation.

Appendix I

BIBLIOGRAPHY AND PRINCIPAL NOTES

The Struggle against Speciesism (Richard D. Ryder)

1. *Introduction to the Principles of Morals and Legislation,* written in 1780 and published in 1789. Chap. XVII, para. 4. footnote. (Chap. XIX, para. 4. footnote of Bowring edition).

   Personally, I doubt the validity of computing a Calculus of Pains and Pleasures by adding or subtracting *across individuals.* Each sentient individual (whether human or non-human) is a subjective universe. Therefore pain inflicted upon an unwilling individual can only be justified by a greater pleasure accruing to that *same* individual. For example, 1,000 units of pain inflicted on one sentient cannot be justified by single units of pleasure accruing to 1,001 others.

   Also, pain should count for more than pleasure, in that even the most intense pleasure will not excuse the infliction of severe pain. Furthermore, pains which are certain to occur and those which are artificially induced should have a higher negative value than pains which are still uncertain to occur or those which are naturally occurring. So, for example, attempting to justify an experiment which is certainly painful on the grounds that it may provide a means of alleviating natural disease at some time in the future, and in other individuals, would seem a highly dubious exercise. (See Ryder : *Speciesism. The Ethics of Vivisection.* Pub. Scottish Society for the Prevention of Vivisection, 1974. Reprinted R.S.P.C.A., 1978).

2. See *Minor Morals for Young People* by John Bowring. London, 1834, vol. I, pp. 78–81.

   In another version of this story, the cat is named as the Reverend Doctor John Langborn. See *The Works of Jeremy Bentham,* ed. J. Bowring, 1843, vol. XI, pp. 80–81.

   Bowring himself lays great emphasis upon humanity to animals. See *Minor Morals,* pp. 74–90.

3. Boswell's *Life of Johnson.* Oxford University Press, 1953, pp. 1216–1217.
4. *Essais.* Book II, chap. XII. "An Apologie of Raymond Sebond." (Translation by Florio. 1890 edition, p. 144). See also, chap. XI " Of Crueltie " and chap. XXVII " Cowardize, the mother of Crueltie."
5. *The Utopia of Sir Thomas More.* (Translation by Ralph Robinson. Edited by George Sampson, London, 1910. Book II, p. 181.)
6. Ibid., pp. 128–129.
7. *History of European Morals from Augustus to Charlemagne,* by W. E. H. Lecky. London, 1869, vol. I, pp. 256–258. Lecky is a most insightful writer on the history of humanity to animals : see Ibid., vol. I, pp. 47–51, 256–258, 297–307, 340–341 and vol. II, 171–188. Probably he was the " Mr. Lecky " who signed Frances Power Cobbe's antivivisection Memorial in 1874.
   (The word "zoophilos " was, as far as I am aware, first used in English by Rev. Henry Crowe in a booklet of this name published in London in 1819. Frances Power Cobbe, the antivivisectionist, founded the magazine the *Zoophilist* in 1881. We are indebted to Dr. Stephen Clark for reviving this useful term.)
8. *Speciesism,* a pamphlet published in 1970. My first published comments in this field were letters to the *Daily Telegraph,* April 7th, May 2nd/3rd, and May 20th, 1969.
9. *Animal Liberation: A New Ethics for Our Treatment of Animals.* Jonathan Cape, London, 1976. See especially Chap. V. "Man's Dominion, A Short History of Speciesism." This important work is a necessary starting point for all students of the subject.
10. *The Anatomie of Abuses.* London, 1583. (See Colliers Reprints of Miscellaneous Tracts, pp. 177–182.) " It is a common saying amongst men, borrowed from the French, Qui aime Jean, aime son chien; love me, love my dog : so love God, love his creatures."
11. *Enchiridion.* London, 1641. Century 2. No. 100. Quarles advocates hunting as " most proper to a commander . . . the chase is a faire resemblance of a hopefull warre, proposing to the pursuer a flying enemy." (Century 1. No. 80.) But he also enjoins : " Take no pleasure in the death of a creature; if it be harmless or uselesse, destroy it not : if usefull, or harmefull destroy it mercifully." (Century 3. No. 23.)
12. *The Counsels of a Father* (written circa 1662). London, 1817.

It was said of Sir Matthew Hale that the only time he was known to be thoroughly angry was when a servant allowed a pet bird to starve (p. 17). Hale puzzled about the rightness of eating flesh. (See also pp. 77, 161–165, 190.)

13. *The Countryman's Companion.* Circa 1683 (p. 140.) See also Tryon's *Wisdom Dictates,* 1691—" violence and killing either Man or Beasts is as contrary to the Divine Principle as light is to darkness " (p. 94). " Man's Soul nor Body can never be at rest or peace, until he do suffer the inferior creatures to have and enjoy that liberty and quiet they groan to be delivered into . . ." (p. 125). Thomas Tryon (1634–1703) was a vegetarian and extensively wrote about diet. He also wrote against slavery. He was widely read in his day and was admired by Franklin, despite a highly repetitious style.

14. Humanity towards animals is only one possibility. It has often been alleged that the motive was anti-hedonistic. Sir George Clark has suggested it may have been a tactic to prevent Royalist assemblies. (Personal Communication.)

15. *Animals and Their Legal Rights,* Emily Stewart Leavitt *et al.* Animal Welfare Institute, 1968. (See pp. 13–14.)

16. *The Statutes at Large, passed in the Parliaments held in Ireland.* Dublin, 1786. Chap. XV, pp. 168–169.

17. Op. cit., vol. 2, p. 188 (see Note 7).

18. See *English Fox Hunting: A History* by Raymond Carr. Weidenfeld and Nicolson, London, 1976. Page 213, note 2.

19. *The Analogy of Religion,* by Joseph Butler, 1736. Part I, chap. I.

20. *Free Thoughts upon the Brute Creation,* by John Hildrop. London, 1742.

   This work is subtitled *an Examination of Father Bougeant's Philosophical Amusement Upon the Language of Beasts.* G. H. Bougeant's essay had been published in London in 1739; the title page notes that Bougeant is " now confined at La Fleche on Account of this Work."

21. *An Essay on the Future Life of Brutes, Introduced with Observations upon Evil, its Nature and Origin,* by Richard Dean. Manchester, 1767.

   Dean refers approvingly to the writings of John Hildrop (note 20) and the Chevalier Ramsay. " As Brutes have sensibility, they are capable of Pain, feel every Bang, and Cut, and Stab, as much as he himself (the reader) does, some of them perhaps more, and therefore he must not treat them as Stocks, or Stones, or Things that cannot feel," writes Dean (pp. 106–107).

22. Letter to Henry More, 5 February, 1649, and *Discourse on the Method*, volume 5, by René Descartes, Leyden 1637.

23. Hildrop, op. cit., pp. 8–9.

24. "An Apology for the Brute Creation or Abuse of Animals Censured; In a sermon on Proverbs XII, 10. Preached in the Parish Church of Shiplake in Oxfordshire, October 18. 1772. By James Granger, Vicar." London, 1772.

25. *Letters Between the Rev. James Granger, M.A., Rector of Shiplake, and Many of the Most Eminent Literary Men of His Time* : ed. J. P. Malcolm, London, 1805, p. 68.

26. *A Dissertation on the Duty of Mercy and Sin of Cruelty to Brute Animals*, by Humphrey Primatt, D.D. London, 1776.
This work was republished in an abridged form by Rev. Arthur Broome in 1831. Broome's footnotes are quite extensive and give classical and other early references.
The full work was republished in Edinburgh in 1834.

27. See *A Century of Work for Animals, The History of the R.S.P.C.A., 1824–1924* by E. G. Fairholme and W. Pain. London, 1924.
Valiant Crusade. The History of the R.S.P.C.A., by A. W. Moss. Cassell, 1961.
Who Cares for Animals by Antony Brown. Heinemann, 1974.

28. Christoph Christian Sturm's *Reflections Upon the Works of God* was first published in English in 1788. See Lessons XXXV and CXLII.

29. Mrs. Sarah Trimmer (1741–1810) was a noted educationist. She edited *The Guardian of Education* (1802) and *A Help to the Unlearned in the Study of the Holy Scriptures*. (1805).

30. For example *The Hare or Hunting Incompatible with Humanity. Written as a Stimulus to Youth Towards a proper Treatment of Animals*. John Gough, London, 1799 and Dublin 1800; *The Youth's Magazine*, e.g. vol. 8. 1813; *The Picturesque Primer*. W. Fletcher, 1837; *Holiday Amusements*, W. Belch, c. 1828.
Serious works such as William Mavor's *The Elements of Natural History*, 1799, are more humane in approach than are later school textbooks.

31. For example, *The Adventures of a Donkey* by Arabella Argus, 1815; *Further Adventures of Jemmy Donkey* by Arabella Argus; *The Life and Perambulations of a Mouse*, 1850; *Keeper's Travels in Search of his Master*, 1850; and *Tuppy*, 1860.
I am grateful to Miss Diana Daniels for her helpful comments on this subject.

32. (See also Note 61). Steele principally was attacking the Shrove Tuesday practice of tying a cock to a stake and throwing sticks at it until dead. He was also writing against violence portrayed in the theatre : " I hope that my dear Countrymen will no longer expose themselves by an Effusion of Blood, whether it be of Theatrical Heroes, Cocks, or any other innocent Animals, which we are not obliged to slaughter for our Safety, Convenience or Nourishment. Where any of these Ends are not served in the Destruction of a living creature, I cannot but pronounce it a great Piece of Cruelty, if not a kind of Murder." (*The Tatler.* No. 134. 14–16 Feb., 1709).

33. Addison describes "a very barbarous Experiment" on a dog, referring to it as "an Instance of Cruelty". (*The Spectator.* No. 120. July 18, 1711). This is not the principal subject of his essay, and is only alluded to.

34. Pope quotes Plutarch, Ovid, Montaigne and Locke, concluding : "there is certainly a Degree of Gratitude owing to those Animals that serve us; as for such as are Mortal or Noxious, we have a Right to destroy them; and for those that are neither of Advantage or Prejudice to us, the common Enjoyment of Life is what I cannot think we ought to deprive them of." *Guardian*, May 21, 1713.

35. Pages 146–158 of 1714 edition. Pages 187–197 of 1723 edition. Mandeville is very much aware that man, despite his pretensions, is an animal among animals.

36. *Dictionnaire Philosophique*, see "Bêtes".

37. *Idler*, 5th August, 1758. Johnson chastises the "race of wretches" who perform such experiments : "It is time that a universal resentment should arise against those horrid operations, which tend to harden the heart and make the physicians more dreadful than the gout or the stone." See also his *The Plays of William Shakespeare*, 1765, vol. VII, p. 279.

38. *Enquiry Concerning the Principles of Morals.* Chap. III.

39. *Boswell's Life of Johnson,* ed. Chapman, O.U.P., 1953, p. 753.

40. Bowring, *The Works of Jeremy Bentham*, 1843; *Principles of Morals and Legislation*, printed 1780 and published 1789, ch. XIX, pp. 142–143 of Bowring edition; *Principles of Penal Law*, ch. XVI, p. 562 of Bowring edition; Letter to the *Morning Chronicle*, March 4th, 1825, vol. X, pp. 549–550 in Bowring; *Deontology*, pub. posthumously in 1834 by Bowring, vol. I, p. 14.

   In line with his principles, however, Bentham apparently saw nothing wrong in despatching a cat that was "despotic" and "clamorous"—"means were found to send him to another world " (Bowring, vol. XI, p. 80). There is little objection to the taking of life provided it is humanely done.

Bentham, as a boy, had burnt some earwigs in a candle flame and had been reprimanded for this cruelty by a servant called Martha. His uncle also had occasion to rebuke him for teasing his dog, Busy. He never forgot these two experiences (vol. X, p. 17, Bowring). Bowring recalls Bentham's claim that he had been impressed by the fondness for animals shown by Cowper, George Wilson and Romilly. Bentham had shown affection for " a beautiful pig at Hendon " and " a young ass of great symetry and beauty " at Ford Abbey (ibid., p. 81). His genuine warmth for animals is most convincingly displayed by the several stories of mice being allowed amazing liberties by modern standards.

" I became once very intimate with a colony of mice. They used to run up my legs and eat crumbs from my lap. I love everything that has four legs : so did George Wilson. We were fond of mice, and fond of cats; but it was difficult to reconcile the two affections " (ibid., p. 81).

Bentham was opposed to baiting, hunting and fishing (Bowring, Chap. XVI, p. 562).

41. *Disquisitions on Several Subjects.* I, p. 6, and II, pp. 12–26. 1972.

Jenyns describes desensitisation (or habituation) to bloodshed with memorable metaphor—" The butcher knocks down the stately ox with no more compassion than the blacksmith hammers a horse-shoe; and plunges his knife into the throat of the innocent lamb with as little reluctance as the taylor sticks his needle into the collar of a coat " (pp. 14–15).

42. Broome, the founder of the world's largest animal welfare organisation, seems to have been especially influenced by the writings of Plutarch, Hale, Cowper, Dean, Primatt and Jenyns.

43. *The Cry of Nature, or An Appeal to Mercy and Justice on behalf of the Persecuted Animals.*

44. *On the Conduct of Man to Inferior Animals.* Manchester, 1797. This is an essential text for the historian of the vegetarian movement.

Other eighteenth century writers include *David Hartley* (*Observations on Man.* London, 1741, vol. 2, pp. 222-4) who argues that " taking away the lives of animals, in order to convert them into food, does great violence to the principles of benevolence and compassion ". Flesh eating, he suggests, is not a necessity and should be left to individual choice. *William Paley*, although justifying flesh-eating on religious grounds, emphasises that it is not necessary and is poor economy : " A piece of ground capable of supplying animal food sufficient for the subsistence of ten persons, would sustain, at least, the double of that number with grain roots and milk." (*Moral Philosophy*, 1785, book 2, p. 599).

45. *An Essay on Humanity to Animals*, 1st ed., 1798, with an " Ode to Humanity " by Rev. C. Hoyle, amended in a contemporary hand in the Bodleian copy (2nd ed., 1809, abridged).

46. *A Philosophical Treatise on Horses, and on the Moral Duties of Man towards the Brute Creation*. Two vols. London, 1796 and 1798.

Lawrence's favourable view of certain forms of hunting and cock-fighting—he justified two animals fighting *voluntarily*, and the hunting of *ferocious* (rather than timid) animals which, he believed, feel no fear—lays him open to the charge of inconsistency. (But does inconsistency or even hypocrisy invalidate an argument? If an habitual murderer says " Murder is wrong ", then surely he is still right? The problem of inconsistency is one that specially afflicts the zoophile.)

Lawrence also wrote under several pseudonyms, notably that of William Henry Scott for his *British Field Sports*.

47. *Ibid.* Lawrence proposed " the jus animalium, or the rights of beasts to the protection of the law, on the ground of natural justice in the first instance, and in sequel, on that of expedience, regarding both humanity and profit ". He gives a whole chapter the title " The Rights of Beasts ". Thomas Young in 1798 actually used the phrase " The Rights of Animals ", op. cit., p. 3.

48. Edward Byron Nicholson (Principal Librarian and Superintendent of the London Institution) published his own work *The Rights of An Animal: A New Essay in Ethics* in 1879. " Lawrence, Bentham and Helps have each of them laid down the principle that feeling (by which I mean the power of feeling pleasure and pain) gives rights . . ." (p. viii). In a letter attached, Nicholson complains of the lack of interest in his book from the " well over 100 " Societies for the Prevention of Cruelty to Animals, to whose officers he had only sold seventeen copies.

By about 1860 the large animal welfare bodies in Britain had lost any real intellectual interest in the ideal of animals rights. They had become upper class and conservative. John Stuart Mill wrote to the Secretary of the R.S.P.C.A. on 26th July 1868 :

" Dear Sir,

I do not feel it consistent . . . to identify myself to any greater extent with the management, while it is thought necessary or advisable to limit the Society's operations to the offences committed by the uninfluential classes of society. So long as such scenes as the pigeon-shooting exhibitions lately commented upon in the newspapers take place under the patronage and in the presence of the supposed elite of the higher classes, male and female, without attracting the notice of your Society, this respect of persons, though it may be prudent, is too foreign to my opinions and feelings to allow of my sharing in any, even indirect, responsibility for it." (Quoted in *John Stuart Mill: A Logical Critique of Sociology*, ed. Ronald Fletcher. Michael Joseph, 1971, p. 416).

I am grateful to Dr. Brendan McLaughlin of New College, Oxford, for drawing my attention to this reference.

Twenty years earlier, in *The Principles of Political Economy*, Mill had written firmly on behalf of " those unfortunate slaves and victims of the most brutal part of mankind—the lower animals ".

49. Lawrence pays tribute to a number of politicians for their humane attitudes towards animals, among them Lord Erskine, Sir Charles Bunbury, Sir Samuel Romilly, Sir Richard Hill and the black Haitian leader, Toussaint L'Ouverture.

50. E. S. Turner, *All Heaven in a Rage*. Michael Joseph, 1964.

51. Especially in " The Seasons ", 1726–30.

52. See, for example, George Nicholson's *On the Conduct of Man to Inferior Animals*, and Thomas Young's *On Humanity to Animals* (pp. 26–27).

53. See Richard D. Ryder, *Victims of Science*. Davis-Poynter, 1975, pp. 201–204.

54. Bernard Shaw, *Against Vivisection*, an answer to H. G. Wells, *Sunday Express*, Aug. 7th, 1927.

Shaw on Vivisection, ed. Bowker, Allen and Unwin, 1949. John Galsworthy, *For Love of Beasts*. Animals' Friends Society, 1912.

The Slaughter of Animals for Food. R.S.P.C.A., 1912. *A Talk on Playing the Game with Animals and Birds*. R.S.P.C.A., 1926.

The twentieth century has seen a growing number of strongly anti-vivisection novels, notably : *Crowleigh Hall* by Emily Robinson, 1906; *The Difficulties of Dr. Deguerre* by Walter Hadwen, 1926; *Morwyn on The Vengeance of God* by John Cowper Powys, 1937; *Doctor Rat* by William Kotz-

226 APPENDICES

winkle, Aidan Ellis, 1976; *The Plague Dogs* by Richard Adams, 1977.

55. Salt was a friend of Shaw. See *Salt and his Circle* by Stephen Winsten, 1951.
His main zoophile works are: *Animals' Rights and Social Progress*, 1892.
Animals' Rights Considered in Relation to Social Progress (with an essay by Albert Leffingwell), 1894.
The Humanities of Diet; Some Reasonings and Rymings, 1914.
The Story of My cousins, 1923.
The Creed of Kinship, 1935.

56. See John Vyvyan. *In Pity and in Anger*, Michael Joseph, 1969. *The Dark Face of Science*, Michael Joseph, 1971.

57. Major C. W. Hume founded the Universities Federation for Animal Welfare. Originally named the University of London Animal Welfare Society, it started in 1928.

58. Brigid Brophy, *The Rights of Animals*. *The Sunday Times*, October 10, 1965; reprinted as a leaflet by the Animal Defence and Anti-Vivisection Society.
See also Brophy's contribution to *Animals, Men and Morals*, ed. Godlovitch and Harris, pub. Gollancz, 1971 and to this publication.
"The Silent Victims", *New Statesman*, 28 Feb. 1975.
"The Zoophile Case", *The Listener*, 30 June, 1977.
Brophy indisputably has become one of the intellectual leaders for the movement and has helped to soften the unthinking and dismissive attitude of many socialists towards the rights of animals.

59. See Appendix of *Animals' Rights Considered in Relation to Social Progress*, 1894.
Simon Butler has drawn my attention to Samuel Butler's mockery of Animals' Rights in *Erewhon* (1872), chapter 26. This just precedes the spate of late Victorian publications in the field. One cannot help feeling that Butler shows ambivalence to the subject.

60. See also Broome's footnotes to Primatt (*op. cit.*, see note 26), pp. 15 and 41.

61. *Tatler*. No. 134. 14–16 February, 1709.

62. Turner, *op. cit.*, p. 73.

63. *Op. cit.*, (see Note 45), p. 20.

64. Singer, *op. cit.*, chapter 5 (see note 9).

65. *Op. cit.*, p. 514. Lawrence's observations so often hold true to the modern situation.

66. Some of the few important findings of modern experimental psychology are those of Dr. Stanley Milgram, who has shown that a majority of ordinary citizens will perform apparently painful and even lethal experiments upon other unwilling human beings; they do so, not because they are sadistic freaks, but merely because they follow what they believe to be the conventions of the system in which they find themselves.

67. A Study of L. T. Brown *et al* at Oklahoma State University indicated "that people who express little affection for dogs also tend to manifest little affection for other people". (*Psychological Reports*, 1972, 31, 957–958). The psychiatrist Anthony Storr has pointed out that several psychopathic murderers, including the "Boston Strangler", were extremely cruel to animals : "What," asks Storr, "is the predictive value of extreme cruelty to animals? I suspect it to be highly significant." (*Sunday Times*, 19/9/76). My own experience with disturbed adolescents bears out the connection between cruelty to animals and cruelty to humans.

68. See Mary Wollstonecraft's *Original Stories*, 1788. These were probably influenced by Mrs. Trimmer's *Fabulous Histories* published two years earlier.

Mrs. Despard spoke at the great International Anti-vivisection and Animal Protection Congress held at the Caxton Hall, London, in July 1909, and seconded a motion declaring "vivisection to be morally unjustifiable". (See *The Animals' Cause*, ed. Lind-af-Hageby, vol. 1, pp. 11 and 15).

69. The idea of "natural sympathy" or "natural compassion" was frequently expressed by eighteenth-century writers. In the twentieth century there has appeared the assumption that kindness is motivated only by acquired cultural values, and the conception of man as innately aggressive has been over-emphasised. Man is both naturally aggressive and naturally sympathetic; certain stimuli (e.g. frustration or the pathetic cries of an injured child or animal, respectively) may trigger aggression or compassion. In addition, of course, such behaviours may also be acquired, and in any event will inevitably be modified through learning.

It is incredible that modern psychology (one of the century's most uncreative as well as cruellest sciences) has ignored the very powerful phenomenon of squeamishness—that is to say the emotional reaction to the sight of blood, injury, etc. Those attending a surgical operation for the first time very often experience feelings that are strange and strong; some faint, some feel nausea, few are unmoved. In a small sample of adolescent female biology students, 55 per cent disliked dissecting a mouse and a third found such procedures made them feel sick or ill (R. D. Ryder, Paper read to the British Psychological Society, A.G.M., Exeter, 1977). Such natural aversion to the sight of injury has had survival value for the species and counter-balances the argument that "man is naturally a hunter/killer/exploiter of animals". It would seem that man is only the latter when he overcomes, through hunger, fear, anger or custom, his natural fellow-feeling for other sentients.

70. The chairman of Animal Welfare Year, Clive Hollands, as well as its President, Lord Houghton, must be credited with having helped to bring together the previously fragmented factions within the animal welfare movement. The Rt. Hon. Lord Houghton of Sowerby (previously Douglas Houghton, Cabinet Minister and Chairman of the Parliamentary Labour Party) is Vice President of the R.S.P.C.A. and chairman of several co-ordinating committees, notably the Committee for the Reform of Animal Experimentation (C.R.A.E.) which produced an important Memorandum to the Home Secretary in 1976. See also his "Without Pity", *The Spectator*, March 1, 1975.

Animals and Moral Theology (Andrew Linzey)

71. Karl Barth, *Dogmatics in Outline*. S.C.M. Press, 1966, p. 54.
72. See Gen. 1. 26ff; Cf. Ps. 8, 4–8 and Ecclus. 17, 1–4.
73. Charles Raven, *The Creator Spirit*, 1927, p. 120. See A. R. Kingston's "Theodicy and Animal Welfare", *Theology*, November, 1967, p. 485.
74. Karl Horrman, *Introduction to Moral Theology*, Burns and Oates, 1961, p. 274.
75. John Hick, *Evil and the God of Love*, Fontana, 1968, p. 350. See also C. F. D. Moule, *Man and Nature in the New Testament*, Athlone Press, 1964, p. 13f.
76. Joseph Rickaby, S. J., *Moral Philosophy*, Longmans, 1889, p. 248. C/f Henry Davis, S. J., *Moral and Pastoral Theology*, vol. 11, Sheed and Ward, 1958, p. 258.
77. See for example J. A. Baker's *Biblical Attitudes to Nature, Man and Nature*, ed. Hugh Montefiore, Collins, 1975, p. 92ff.
78. K. Fichtelius and S. Sjolander, *Man's Place: Intelligence in Dolphins, Whales and Humans*, Gollancz, 1973, p. 34.
79. C. S. Lewis, *The Problem of Pain*, Fontana, 1957, ch. IX. "Animal Pain."

80. John Burnaby, *The Belief of Christendom*, S.P.C.K., 1963, p. 40f.

81. *Man and Nature, op. cit.*, p. 67.

82. *Man and Nature, op. cit.*, p. 8off.

83. Some Christians maintain that we should never talk of moral rights, natural, assigned, relative or otherwise. I have sympathy for this view and I think it is certainly clear that Christians cannot accept that any being holds absolute rights. Nevertheless, if we are going to continue to hold that rights-terminology, for all its difficulty and ambivalence, has a place in moral theology, then I see no reason why we should accept them in the case of fellow humans and then quibble about terminology in the case of animals.

84. I have given a fuller treatment of these questions in my *Animal Rights*, S.C.M. Press, 1976, in which I argue that the best criterion for the possession of rights is sentiency, instead of the criterion of persons, rationality, etc. Nevertheless, I am aware that this criterion too has limits (clearly for example in the case of comatose patients, as Professor R. G. Frey has kindly pointed out in his *Interests, Animals and Vegetarianism* —as yet unpublished). While it is possible that an absolute criterion may be found for attributing moral rights, I judge that a good case can be made out for arguing that sentient beings *ipso facto* have moral rights.

85. Cited by Stephen R. L. Clark, *The Moral Status of Animals*, O.U.P., 1977, p. 38.

86. Hans Hass, *Development Forum*, May, 1973.

87. Victor Hugo, *The Relationship Between Men and the Animals*, reprinted in *The Ark*, Catholic Study Circle for Animal Welfare, August, 1967, p. 116.

88. Message read to the A.G.M. of the R.S.P.C.A., 24th June, 1977.

Animal Rights and Nature Liberation (M. W. Fox)

89. *The Findhorn Garden* by the Findhorn Community, Harper and Row, NY; and Dane Rudhyar, *The Planerarization of Consciousness*, The Seod Press.

90. Lawrence Blair, *Rhythms of Vision*, Viking, NY., and M. W. Fox, *One Earth One Mind*.

91. Davis Poynter, London (1975).

92. *Animal Liberation*. Random House, New York (1975).

93. W. Leiss, *The Domination of Nature*. Braziller, New York (1972).

Exploring the Idea of Animal Rights (Tom Regan)

94. A longer version of this essay was originally presented in the Spring of 1976 as part of a series of lectures on the general theme of "Technology and Value" at the Fredonia campus of the State University of New York. I am especially grateful to my colleagues at North Carolina State University—W. R. Carter, Alan Sparer, and Donald VanDeVeer—for their helpful criticisms of earlier drafts of this essay.
95. St. Thomas, for example,. seems to hold a position like Kant's. See selections from his work in *Animal Rights and Human Obligations*. Edited by Tom Regan and Peter Singer (Prentice-Hall : Englewood Cliffs) 1976.
96. Immanuel Kant, *Lectures on Ethics*. Translated by Louis Infield (New York : Harper & Row) 1963, p. 240.
97. *Ibid.*
98. As quoted in John Vyvyan : *The Dark Face of Science* (London : Michael Joseph) 1971, p. 29.
99. W. D. Ross, *The Right and the Good* (Oxford : The Clarendon Press) 1930, p. 49.
100. See, for example, H. J. McCloskey, "Rights" (*Philosophical Quarterly*, vol. 15, 1965). For a critical examination of McCloskey's attempt to exclude animals from the class of right-holders, see my "McCloskey on Why Animals Cannot Have Rights" (*Philosophical Quarterly*, vol. 26, 1976). A defense of McCloskey is offered by R. G. Frey, "Interests and Animals Rights" (*Philosophical Quarterly*, vol. 27, 1977, pp. 254–259). But see also my "Frey on Interests and Animal Rights" (*Philosophical Quarterly*, vol. 27, 1977, pp. 335–337).
101. I am not sure that even this much should be granted. What needs to be examined are the *grounds* on which art-objects and plants are said to be excluded from the class of right-holders. It is not enough merely to assume them out of membership in this class. On this matter, see my "Feinberg on What Sorts of Beings Can Have Rights" (*Southern Journal of Philosophy*, Winter, 1976.) See also Alan Tormey, "Aesthetic Rights" (*Journal of Aesthetics and Art Criticism*, vol. 32, 1973), and David A. Goldblatt, "Do Works of Art Have Rights?" (*Journal of Aesthetics and Art Criticism*, vol. 35, 1976).

102. Ross, *op. cit.*, p. 50.

103. Such a view seems to be implied by the theories of Kant and St. Thomas.

104. Since it at least seems arguable that some higher animals *can* reason, have a concept of their own identity, etc., it could be that these animals have basic moral rights, given these criteria for right-possession.

105. This way of disputing theories of right-possession recently has come under attack. See both R. G. Frey, "Animal Rights" (*Analysis*, vol. 37, 1977, pp. 186–189), and Jan Narveson "Animal Rights" (*The Canadian Journal of Philosophy*, March 1977.) For replies to both see Dale Jamieson and Tom Regan "Animal Rights : A Reply to Frey", (*Analysis* vol. 38, 1978, pp. 32–36); and Tom Regan "Narveson on Rational Egoism and the Rights of Animals" in this same issue of the *Canadian Journal of Philosophy.*

106. In his "Animal Liberation : A Critique" (*Ethics*, January, 1978), Michael Fox advances such a position. For more detailed criticisms of his essay see Peter Singer's "The Parable of the Fox and the Unliberated Animals" and my own "Fox's Critique of Animal Liberation" in this same issue of *Ethics.*

107. Richard Ryder, *Victims of Science* (London : Taplinger), 1976.

108. Peter Singer, *Animal Liberation* (New York : Random House), 1976.

109. For a more comprehensive attempt at an answer, see my "An Examination and Defense of One Argument Concerning Animal Rights," *Inquiry* (forthcoming).

110. See my essay on Feinberg, *op. cit.*

111. John Vyvyan, *op. cit.*, p. 108, quotes Galsworthy as writing that " (w)hether or no animals have what are called ' rights ' is an academic question of no value whatsoever in the consideration of this matter . . ." Similarly, Salt states that " the controversy concerning ' rights ' is little else than an academic battle over words, which leads to no practical conclusion " (*Animals' Rights*, London : The Humanitarian League, 1912, p. 2.)

112. "The Parable of the Fox and the Unliberated Animals," *op. cit.*

How to Calculate the Greater Good (Stephen R. L. Clark)

113. See L. C. Rosenfield, *From beast-machine to man-machine,* Octagon : New York, 1968, 2nd ed., pp. 16ff. 52.

114. See D. D. Raphael, " The standard of morals," *Proceedings of the Aristotelian Society* 96. 1974–5, pp. 1ff.
115. See R. Nozick, *Anarchy, state and utopia*, New York, 1974, pp. 34f.
116. P. Singer, *Animal Liberation.* Cape, London, 1975, pp. 83f, quoting *Bulletin of the National Society for Medical Research* 24 (10), October 1973. West German law is well in advance of ours on this point : see R. Ryder, *Victims of Science*, Davis Poynter, London, 1975, p. 141.
117. See Robin Bates, " Why Medicine has a Health Problem," *Listener* 98, pp. 130ff., 4 August, 1977.
118. See Arthur Prior, *Papers on time and tense.* Clarendon Press : Oxford 1968.

What has Sentiency to do with the Possession of Rights (R. G. Frey)

119. See, for example, Andrew Linzey, *Animal Rights.* London, S.C.M. Press, 1976, ch. 3.
120. Joel Feinberg, " The Rights of Animals and Unborn Generations," in William T. Blackstone (ed.), *Philosophy and Environmental Crisis*, Athens, Georgia, University of Georgia Press, 1974, pp. 49–51. I consider the question of whether animals can have desires in my paper " Russell and The Essence of Desire," *Philosophy*, forthcoming.
121. My point here may be put in the form of an example. Suppose an operation were performed on a rabbit as a result of which, *ex hypothesi*, though the rabbit could no longer feel pleasure and pain, its other experiences remained unaffected : would not the rabbit nevertheless remain a sentient being? For it still eats, sleeps, hops about, etc.
122. I disagree, therefore, with Mary Ann Warren's account of sentiency in this respect; see her article " Do Potential People have Moral Rights?", *Canadian Journal of Philosophy*, vol. VII, 1977, pp. 283–86.
123. See, for example, Peter Singer, *Animal Liberation*, London, Jonathan Cape, 1976, ch. 5; and Andrew Linzey, *op. cit.*, ch. 2.
124. I coin this phrase as the moral analogue to the legal notion of " legal standing ", but all I mean is that it is " possessed of value in itself " in this context.
125. *Op. cit.*, p. 50. Feinberg's position here is this : mere things are not *loci* of value in their own right because they lack interests, and they lack interests because they lack a conative,

life, which, as we saw earlier, Feinberg includes under "sentience"; ultimately, then, it is because mere things lack sentiency that they have no "good" of their own and are not *loci* of value in their own right. An interesting and useful critique of Feinberg's position on what can and cannot have a good of its own is to be found in Tom Regan's paper "Feinberg on What Sorts Of Beings Can Have Rights," *Southern Journal of Philosophy*, forthcoming.

126. This is not surprising, of course, once one comes to realise the status of the view as an *implicit* assumption, as I go on to note.

127. I should not like to be misunderstood on this point. In saying that pain is an intrinsic evil, people sometimes mean that it is undesirable in itself. Without going into complex philosophical detail, my point is this : either the proposition "Pain is undesirable in itself" is true solely by virtue of the meanings of the words it contains, or experience is necessary in order to establish its truth. Since I cannot see how the former can be the case, though I am willing to be persuaded otherwise, I suggest that its truth must be argued for on the strength of experience.

128. I have used Moore and the example of beauty here because his work is likely to be known to a non-philosophical public. But the point I am making can be developed around any kind of experience which is such that (i) it is held to be possessed of intrinsic value, (ii) it is had only by sentient creatures but not by all such creatures (i.e., the higher animals), and (iii) it is other than and does not amount to feeling pain.

Ethical Questions concerning Modern Livestock Farming (Ruth Harrison)

129. *Animals and Ethics.* Working Group. London, 1977.

Altruism and Aggression in Animals (W. J. Jordan)

130. J. Maynard-Smith, G. R. Price (1973) *Nature,* vol. 246, pp. 15–18.
131. R. Dawkins, *The Selfish Gene.* Oxford University Press, 1976.

Animal Exploitation in Human Recreation (J. M. Bryant)

132. "Rome and the Romans," by Showerman—quoted as source in *Those about to die by* Daniel P. Mannix, Mayflower, 1972.
133. *Those about to die,* Daniel P. Mannix, Mayflower.
134. House of Commons library. Bibliography No. 61. "The Abolition of Certain Field Sports."
135. *In Praise of Hunting.* A symposium edited by David James and Wilson Stephens. Hollis & Carter, 1960.
136. *Against Hunting.* A symposium edited by Patrick Moore. Victor Gollancz, 1965.
137. *English Fox Hunting.* By Raymond Carr. Weidenfeld & Nicolson, 1976.
138. "The Ethics of Field Sports" by Robin Page. *Shooting Times,* 1977.
139. *Hunting* by Mobray Morris and the Duke of Beaufort, 1885. Badminton Library.
140. *The Art of Beagling* by Captain Otho Paget. H. F. & J. Witherby, 1931.
141. *In Praise of Hunting.* Hollis & Carter, 1960.
142. *In Praise of Hunting.* Hollis & Carter, 1960.
143. *Animal Ways* No. 48. April 1977 (R.S.P.C.A. magazine for children.)
144. Mrs. Valerie Waters, aged 45, of Birmingham appeared as a witness against four hunt supporters who ambushed her car and was herself ordered to be bound over. She refused and after appeal at Leicester Crown Court was jailed for a month.

Mrs. Susan Hough, aged 33, from Middle Barton, Oxfordshire, was arrested for running onto the field at the Waterloo Cup Hare Coursing event and also refused to be bound over. She was jailed for a week. July 1977.

Animal Experiments—Time for a New Approach (Bernard Dixon)

145. *Experiments on Living Animals* (The Houghton/Platt Memorandum), May 1976. Obtainable from R.S.P.C.A., Causeway, Horsham, Sussex RH12 1HG, England.

Animal Welfare Year in Retrospect (Clive Hollands)

146. *The Cruelty to Animals Act 1876*—the Act governing the use of animals for research purposes in Britain. Other than for the

purpose of attaining manual skill, the Act does not place any restriction on the use of animals for research purposes providing the experimenter holds a Home Office Licence and the relevant Certificates, and performs the experiment in premises registered for the purpose, and that the experiment is performed with a view to the advancement by new discovery of physiological knowledge or of knowledge which will be useful for saving or prolonging life or alleviating suffering.

147. *Conservation of Wild Creatures and Wild Plants Act 1975*— the Act provides protection from the killing or taking of wild creatures or taking or uprooting plants which are listed in the Schedule of the Act. Animals and plants can only be added to the Schedule where it can be shown that this is necessary in the interests of proper conservation. The otter was added to the Schedule from 1st January, 1978, and is protected in England and Wales (not in Scotland).

148. *Animals, Men and Morals*, edited by Godlovitch & Harris. Victor Gollancz, 1971.

149. *Victims of Science*, by Richard D. Ryder. Davis-Poynter, 1975.

150. *Animal Liberation*, by Peter Singer. Random House, 1975.

151. *The Moral Status of Animals*, by Stephen R. L. Clark. Clarendon Press, Oxford, 1977.

152. *Animal Rights*, by Andrew Linzey. S.C.M. Press Ltd., London, 1976.

153. Professor Georges Heuse, Professor of Human Biology, Hospital Archard, Paris, France, and founder of the International League for Animal Rights.

154. The Rt. Hon. Lord Houghton of Sowerby C.H. Former Member of Parliament and Cabinet Minister, Chairman of the Parliamentary Labour Party 1967/1974, created Life Peer in 1974, Companion of Honour and Privy Counsellor.

Appendix II

BIOGRAPHICAL NOTES

John Aspinall
Founder of Howletts Zoo Park and Port Lympne Wildlife Sanctuary in Kent. Author of *The Best of Friends* published by Macmillan in October 1976. Breeder of rare animals.

Rev. Jack Austin
Born in Caerleon, Gwent, Wales, Mr. Austin went to Llandaff Cathedral School and Bristol Grammar School. While at the latter he began studying other denominations, and joined the Roman Catholic Church.

During the war he extended his studies to other faiths, and became especially concerned with Buddhism, professing that faith at the end of the war. Ordained in 1952, he was involved with the Zen Sect of Mahayana Buddhism, and with the Shin Sect. He is now Chairman of the Shin Buddhist Association of Great Britain. As a Buddhist, he prefers vegetarian food, taking the view that it is kind to animals not to eat them if it can be helped.

Brigid Brophy
Born in 1929 and is a professional writer of both fiction and non-fiction. Her most recent novel, *Palace Without Chairs*, was published in 1978. She is an active campaigner for the rights of animals and, via her trade union (The Writers' Guild of Great Britain), for the rights of writers. She lives in London with her husband, Michael Levey who is also a writer and Director of the National Gallery.

Bill Brown, BSc.
Two years after graduating in Communications Engineering Bill Brown formed his own company specialising in the design and development of radio test equipment. During the war and until 1972 he served with the Radio Department at the Royal Aircraft Establishment, Farnborough. A member of the District Council since 1962 and of Berkshire County Council since 1973, Bill Brown

there first raised the question of the suffering of laboratory animals. In 1975, believing that the only hope of reform for laboratory animals lay in drawing on mass feeling against their unnecessary suffering, he decided to launch the National Petition for the Protection of Animals. His watchword at all times has been : " Reform through Co-operation "; he is still seeking it.

John Bryant
Born in Yeovil, Somerset, in 1942 and after a Technical School education became an aircraft engineer. He was elected to the R.S.P.C.A. national Council in 1972 and made a detailed study of foxes and fox hunting. He is Manager of the Ferne Animal Sanctuary, became a vegetarian in 1973, and is now a vegan.

Stephen R. L. Clark
A Fellow of All Souls College, Oxford 1968–75; Lecturer in Moral Philosophy at the University of Glasgow since 1974. Publications : *Aristotle's Man*, O.U.P., 1975; *The Moral Status of Animals*, O.U.P., 1977. Married with two children, Stephen Clark is a vegan of the Episcopalian faith.

Bernard Dixon, BSc., PhD., MIBiol
Born in 1938, educated at Queen Elizabeth Grammar School and the University of Durham and Newcastle. Dr. Dixon was Assistant and then Deputy Editor of *World Medicine* (1965–68) and is now the Editor of *New Scientist* (1969 ff). Author of *Journies in Belief* (1968), *What is Science For* (1973), *Magnificent Microbes* (1976), *Invisible Allies* (1976), *Atoms and Humours* (1978), together with numerous scientific articles.

Maureen Duffy
Born in 1933. She wrote poetry from the age of six and had her first poem published at the age of seventeen. At King's College, London, Maureen Duffy wrote plays and she has continued to write for the stage and television. She taught in assorted state schools for five years and gave a creative writing course at the City Literary Institute, Drury Lane, for four. Novels are *That's How it Was, The Single Eye, The Microcosm, The Paradox Players, I Want to Go to Moscow* and *Capital. The Erotic World of Faery* was her first non-fiction book, and she has published three books of poetry. In 1972 with other writers she founded Writers Action Group and has since played a large part in writers' movements, in particular the opening up of a trade union for all writers. A biography of Aphra Behn, *The Passionate Sheperdess*, was published in 1977, and a new novel, *Housespy*, in 1978.

Michael W. Fox, DSc, PhD, BVetMed, MRCVS
Born in 1937. Dr. Fox is married and has two children. He studied at the Royal Veterinary College (B Vet Med MRCVSM 1962) and later in the United States. He was awarded a PhD (Medicine) by London University in 1967 and was associate Professor of Psychology from 1969–1976 at Washington University. He also received a DSc (ethology/animal behaviour) from London University in 1976. A member of many distinguished societies. His published works include *Canine Behaviour* and *Canine Pediatrics, Integrative Development of Brain* and *Behaviour in the Dog, The Behaviour of Wolves, Dogs and Related Canids* and *Concepts in Ethology, Animal and Human Behaviour.*

R. G. Frey, MA, DPhil
An American, working in England, Frey is Senior Lecturer in Philosophy in the University of Liverpool. He is the author of a number of papers on moral philosophy in the philosophical journals, and he has written extensively on animal rights and related subjects. His book *Interests and Rights: The Case Against Animals* is forthcoming in the immediate future.

L. Goldman, MB, BCh, MRCOG
Born in 1922. Qualified originally in Johannesburg and then moved back to this country. Worked for N.H.S. for 10 years. Medical Director of pharmaceutical company for several years. Now engaged in medical journalism and clinical practice. Member of the R.S.P.C.A's Animal Experimentation Advisory Committee and the Committee for the Reform of Animal Experimentation.

John Harris, MA
Was a lecturer in Philosophy at Manchester University from 1971 to 1975; he is now a social worker in Salford. Co-editor of *Animals, Men and Morals* (Gollancz, 1971), he has been a vegetarian for eight years.

Ruth Harrison
The author of *Animal Machines* (1964), and contributor to many other books and journals, both here and overseas. She is a member of the Ministry of Agriculture's Farm Animal Welfare Advisory Committee and a Council member of the World Federation for the Protection of Animals. She served on the Council of the R.S.P.C.A. from 1969 to 1975.

Clive Hollands

Born in 1929. Director of the Scottish Society for the Prevention of Vivisection; Secretary of the St. Andrew Animal Fund, Chairman, Animal Welfare Year 1976/77; member of the Committee for the Reform of Animal Experimentation; Vice-Chairman of the Humane Education Council.

The Rt. Hon. Lord Houghton of Sowerby, CH

Elected MP for Sowerby (West Riding), 1949/74, he was Minister for the Social Services from 1964/67 and Chairman of the Parliamentary Labour Party 1967/74. Lord Houghton was President of Animal Welfare Year 1976/77 and is Chairman of the Committee for the Reform of Animal Experimentation (C.R.A.E.) and a Vice-President of the R.S.P.C.A.

W. J. Jordan, MVSc, BSc, MRCVS

Born in 1925. Consultant to Persian Government, employed by Ministry of Overseas Development. University lecturer for $6\frac{1}{2}$ years (Surgery and Anaesthesia). Honorary veterinary surgeon to Chester Zoo for 16 years. Local veterinary inspector for MAFF for 15 years, now Chief Wildlife Officer to the R.S.P.C.A. Co-author of *The Last Great Wild Beast Show*.

Andrew Linzey, BD, AKC

Born in Oxford in 1952 and educated at King's College, London; University College, Cardiff and St. Augustine's College, Canterbury. Ordained an Anglican priest in 1975, he served his curacy at the Parish of Charlton in Dover and is currently Chaplain/lecturer at the North East Surrey College of Technology. Mr. Linzey was a Council member of the R.S.P.C.A. from 1972–75 and 1976–7. His book *Animals Rights: A Christian Assessment of Man's Treatment of Animals* (S.C.M. Press, 1976) is a systematic treatment of this subject in Christian ethical terms.

David W. Macdonald, MA DPhil

Read Zoology at Oxford where he also studied for a doctorate in the Animal Behaviour Research Group on the behaviour and ecology of foxes. Has worked on a variety of carnivores, including foxes, wolves, jackals, hyaenas, cats and civets with a view to interpreting their social behaviour and reconciling this with their management and conservation. Presently a Research Fellow of Balliol College, Oxford.

David Paterson, MA, FRSH, MIBiol

Born in 1930 and educated at Ampleforth and St. John's Colleges, he graduated in Science at Downing College, Cambridge. Spent 10 years working with handicapped children, and taught Chemistry and then Biology for 12 years. Joined the R.S.P.C.A. in 1972 as Chief Education Officer; now also secretary to the R.S.P.C.A.'s Animal Experimentation Advisory Committee, Secretary of the Committee for the Reform of Animal Experimentation, Chairman of the Humane Education Council and editor of the *Humane Education Journal*.

Tom Regan

Tom Regan is Professor of Philosophy at North Carolina State University, where he has twice been named Outstanding Teacher and currently holds the title of Alumni Distinguished Professor. The author of more than half a dozen essays on animal rights, and co-editor (with Peter Singer) of *Animal Rights and Human Obligations*, Professor Regan is the editor of *Matters of Life and Death* (New York : Random House), a volume which includes an original essay by Singer on " Animals and the Value of Life ".

Jenny Remfry, BSc PhD(Lond), VetMB(Cantab), MRCVS

Assistant Director, University Federation for Animal Welfare, Potters Bar, Herts.

Peter Roberts, NDA, CDA

Born in 1924 and educated at Denstone College and King's College, London, Peter Roberts managed a 350-acre mixed farm in the Midlands with a large dairy herd, and subsequently farmed for 10 years on his own account in Hampshire. He is co-founder and trustee of Compassion in World Farming and managing director of World Foods Ltd. He was an R.S.P.C.A. Council Member from 1977–1978.

Richard D. Ryder, MA, DCP, ABPsS

A Senior Clinical Psychologist at the Warneford Hospital, Oxford. Studied animal behaviour at Cambridge and at Columbia University, New York. Author of *Speciesism* (1970) and *Victims of Science* (Davis-Poynter, 1975). Contributor to *Animals Men and Morals* (Gollancz, 1972) and Regan and Singer's *Animal Rights and Human Obligations* (Prentice-Hall, 1976). Chairman of R.S.P.C.A. Council.

D. Sperlinger, BA, PhD, DCP

Born in 1948. Member of British Psychological Society and at present Senior Clinical Psychologist at Bexley Hospital. Convened a symposium on psychology and animal experimentation at the British Psychological Society Annual Conference 1977. Chairman of the R.S.P.C.A.'s Animal Experimentation Advisory Committee and a member of the Committee for the Reform of Animal Experimentation.

Timothy Sprigge

Read English at Cambridge, then changed to Moral Sciences for his PhD, for which he wrote a dissertation on moral philosophy. Spent some years engaged on the Bentham manuscripts at University College, London, and edited volumes 1 and 2 of the *Correspondence of Jeremy Bentham* (Athlone Press, 1968). Lecturer in Philosophy at University College, London, before moving to the University of Sussex, where he is now Reader in Philosophy in the School of English and American Studies, as well as being Chairman of the University Animal Rights Group.

Dr. Sprigge spent a year in the U.S.A. (1968–9) as visiting associate professor at the University of Cincinatti. He is the author of a work on philosophy of mind and ontology, *Facts, Words and Belief* (Routledge & Kegan Paul, 1970), and is a member of the N.A.V.S. and R.S.P.C.A.

Canon Eric Turnbull, MA(Cantab)

Residentiary Canon of Worcester Cathedral. President of the Worcester Animal Protection Association (an umbrella committee that seeks to co-ordinate the work of animal welfare organisations in the county). He is also a member of the Christian Consultative Council for the Welfare of Animals.

Jon Wynne-Tyson

Born 1924. Married with two children. Publisher and writer. His last two books were *The Civilised Alternative*, a study of society's values and options, welcomed by educationalists; and *Food for a Future*, presenting the background and main arguments for vegetarianism and veganism. Through his publishing company, which he founded in 1954 after a varied career which included several years' farming, he has made available a number of contributions to humane thought, including Porphyry's *On Abstinence from Animal Food*, Catherine Roberts' *The Scientific Conscience*, Manfred Kyber's *Among Animals*, Esmé Wynne-Tyson's *The Philosophy of Compassion*, and on a more domestic level Janet Walker's *Vegetarian Cookery*.

Appendix III

NOTES ON THE MAIN COORDINATING COMMITTEES AND OTHER BODIES

Committee for the Reform of Animal Experimentation (C.R.A.E.)

A Committee drawn from both Houses of Parliament and from the field of animal welfare, science and medicine, and devoted to the reform of the law and administration of the Cruelty to Animals Act 1876, relating to the care and use of living animals in research, experiments and other laboratory purposes.

Secretariat : c/o R.S.P.C.A., Causeway, Horsham, West Sussex.

Farm Animals Welfare Co-ordinating Executive (F.A.W.C.E.)

A collection of organisations, mostly charities, interested in the welfare of farm animals.

Secretariat : c/o R.S.P.C.A., Causeway, Horsham, West Sussex.

Humane Education Council (H.E.C.)

The Humane Education Council is a co-ordinating body which aims to establish the teaching and practice of Humane Education at all levels in the community.

Secretariat : c/o R.S.P.C.A., Causeway, Horsham, West Sussex.

Joint Advisory Committee on Pets in Society (J.A.C.O.P.I.S.)

An independent study group formed in 1974 to consider the position of the dog in contemporary life.

Secretariat : Walter House, 418–422 Strand, London W.C.2.

National Joint Equine Welfare Committee (N.J.E.W.C.)

Λ collection of organisations, mostly charities, interested in the welfare of horses.

Secretariat : Mrs. E. A. Emery, Althorne, The Causeway, Potters Bar, Herts.

Appendix IV

SHORT BIBLIOGRAPHY OF KEY WORKS

Harrison, Ruth : *Animal Machines*, Vincent Stuart, 1964.
Turner, E. S. : *All Heaven in a Rage*, Michael Joseph, 1964.
Dewar, James : *The Rape of Noah's Ark*, William Kimber, 1969.
Vyvyan, John : *In Pity and in Anger*, Michael Joseph, 1969.
Hutchings & Carver : *Man's Dominion*, Rupert Hart-Davis, 1970.
Vyvyan, John : *The Dark Face of Science*, Michael Joseph, 1970.
Godlovitch & Harris (eds.) : *Animals, Men and Morals*, Gollancz, 1971.
Wynne-Tyson, Jon : *The Civilized Alternative*, Centaur Press, 1972.
Roberts, Catherine : *The Scientific Conscience*, Centaur Press, 1974.
Ryder, Richard D. : *Victims of Science*, Davis-Poynter, 1975.
Wilson, Frank : *Food Fit for Humans*, Daniel, 1975.
Wynne-Tyson, Jon : *Food for a Future*, Davis-Poynter, 1975.
Singer, Peter : *Animal Liberation*, Jonathan Cape, 1976.
Linzey, Andrew : *Animal Rights*, S.C.M. Press, 1976.
Regan & Singer (eds.) : *Animal Rights and Human Obligations*, Prentice-Hall, 1976.
Douglas & Hart : *Forest Farming*, Watkins, 1976.
Clark, Stephen R. L. : *The Moral Status of Animals*, Oxford University Press, 1977.
Montagu, Ashley : *The Nature of Human Aggression*, Oxford University Press, 1977.

For further information on current issues, application may be made to:
R.S.P.C.A., Causeway, Horsham, West Sussex RH12 1HG, England.